LIVING ABROAD IN

Italy

FIRST EDITION

John Moretti

© Monica Larner

AVALON
TRAVEL

INTRODUCTION 1

Welcome to Italy 3
Map **2**
The Lay of the Land **7**
Politics **13**
Social Climate **16**

History **19**
Early History **19**
The Renaissance and the Foreign
 Invasion **25**
Unification **27**
Modern History **28**

People and Culture 37
Class Acts and *una Bella Figura* **38**
Gender Roles **41**
Business Behavior **43**
The Arts **44**

Planning Your Fact-Finding Trip 49
Preparing to Leave **50**
Arriving in Italy **55**
Sample Itineraries **55**
Accommodations **60**

DAILY LIFE 63

Making the Move 65
Red Tape **66**
Moving with Children **71**
Moving with Pets **72**
What to Take **73**

Language and Education 75
Regional Dialects **77**
Learning the Language **80**

Health 83
Types of Insurance **84**
Pharmacies and Prescriptions **87**
Potential Hazards **89**
Environmental Factors **90**

Employment 93
Self-Employment **94**
The Job Hunt **98**

Finance 105
Cost of Living **106**
Banking **108**
Taxes **111**
Investing **113**

Communications 121
Telephone Service **122**
Email and Postal Service **124**
Media **126**

Travel and Transportation 131
Map **130**
By Air **132**
By Train **133**
By Bus **135**
By Car **136**

Housing Considerations 143
Renting **145**
Buying **149**
Household Expenses **155**

PRIME LIVING LOCATIONS

Overview 161
  Map **160**

Rome 167
  Map **166**
  Housing **170**
  Getting Around **176**

Milan and the Lakes 179
  Map **178**
  Milan **180**
  Monza and Brianza **185**
  Lake Como **188**

The Northeast: Emilia-Romagna and Veneto 193
  Map **192**
  Emilia-Romagna **194**
  Veneto **200**

The Northwest: Piedmont and Liguria 207
  Map **206**
  Piedmont **208**
  Liguria **212**

The Central Regions: Tuscany, Umbria, and Le Marche 217
  Map **216**
  Tuscany **218**
  Umbria **223**
  Le Marche **225**

The South: Naples, Puglia, and Sicily 231
  Map **230**
  Naples **232**
  Puglia **235**
  Sicily **240**

RESOURCES

Contacts 248

Glossary 253

Suggested Reading 257

Suggested Films 258

Index 259

About the Author

In 1999, at age 26, John Moretti left his job as a small-town reporter in Vermont in search of fame and fortune in Italy. Fame has thus far eluded him, and fortune may never arrive on his doorstep, but he did manage to find a job. For four years in Milan, he worked as an editor at a national newspaper in English, a joint venture between *Corriere della Sera* and the *International Herald Tribune.*

His early experiences in Italy all fade into one another: being cradled as a baby by Zio Giovanni, a monsignor in Naples, who was dressed from head to toe in black except for a red pom-pom atop his hat; chasing pigeons around St. Mark's in Venice as a toddler in awkward white leather shoes; experimenting as a teenager with copious amounts of wine and mozzarella; and backpacking through Europe as a young adult. In Milan, John grew into the role of a self-described expert on a society that continues to baffle him (and everyone else who writes authoritatively on the subject).

As a freelancer in Southern Europe, John covered everything from Lance Armstrong's fifth consecutive Tour de France victory for the *New York Sun* to the plight of African prostitutes in Turin for the London-based *Independent.* His brief television career included an interview with Giorgio Armani for A&E's *Biography* and a documentary on Italian soccer for Australian television.

Before turning to journalism, John did stints as a cattle rancher in Australia and an importer of Russian-made sporting goods in Cleveland. Business and pleasure have taken him to more than 40 countries around the world. He grew up in Norwell, Massachusetts, and is a graduate of Middlebury College.

Preface

In March 1999, I found myself approaching my second year as a reporter at a small newspaper in Vermont. The daily grind included knocking on trailer-park doors to ask questions about distempered dogs, taking photos of car accidents, and tapping out stories about the new Zamboni ice-smoother at the local skating rink. On Mondays and Wednesdays, we pasted it all up with a metal ruler and a glue machine. The *Addison County Independent* was the friendly sort of place you read about in novels about Vermont, and it offered a great introduction to newspapering. But in the spring of 1999, I was 26 and living by myself on an apple orchard. I had the impression I was missing out on excitement elsewhere in the world, and as it turned out, I was.

The whole thing was my sister's idea. She announced that she was going to Rome to find an Italian guy she met while traveling through Tunisia. She planned to stay in Italy for a few months and needed a roommate. About two weeks after I quit my job in Vermont, we were in a hotel room near Piazza Barberini. We had been to Rome several times before, and so the sensations floating through the window were familiar: Mediterranean air, the smell of pizza and cigarette smoke, the buzzing and clicking of mopeds, and the squeal of tires on cobblestones. Pigeons flapped around the marble fountains. My search for an apartment in this mesmerizing city began when my sister slammed down the hotel phone and mumbled something about Italian men. She was going home.

The Eternal City was the same exuberant place I remembered from childhood, but a lot of things in Italy were changing quickly. These were interesting times. In the prime minister's chair, occupied for decades by conservative Christian Democrats, sat Massimo D'Alema, a former communist. Seven-times prime minister Giulio Andreotti faced charges of collusion with the Mafia, while the rest of the Old Guard—Bettino Craxi, Enrico Cuccia, and Gianni Agnelli—all passed away.

Italy was struggling with mass immigration. Technology had changed the face of the economy: For a fleeting moment, a Sardinian Internet startup was larger by market value than Fiat, the carmaking Goliath. The number of cell phones surpassed the number of land lines.

Throughout all this change, however, daily life in Italy has remained unchanged at its core. Everyone may be talking on cell phones, as the cliché goes, but they're only telling Mom to put on the pasta because they're on their way home.

—John Moretti

Introduction

Welcome to Italy

There are as many reasons to come to Italy as there are people who do. To cycle through the cypress-lined hills of Siena; to study the frescoes of Giotto in the Scrovegni Chapel; to lie on the rose-colored beaches of Sardinia; to ski in the Alps; to eat porcini and drink Brunello di Montalcino in the Apennines; to wander the streets of Rome—all these beautiful experiences draw the crowds to Italy. But what keeps people coming back, perhaps for a lifetime, are the Italians themselves.

THE HUMAN TOUCH

When you step off the plane in Italy, feel the balmy breeze, and hear the conversations of people who don't seem to have a care in the world, it's as if you've returned to a more innocent time. You can see the relief on Italians' faces when they hear their own language and share a wisecrack with a perfect stranger about a baggage belt that's taking hours to get rolling. This is our country, they think, warts and all, and we wouldn't have it any other way. They may have just returned from a business meeting in London or Munich or Brussels, all very impressive places where everything goes according to schedule, but people often seem as if they're not enjoying themselves.

> *This human touch, a tolerance bordering on appreciation for the country's blissful imperfections, is what makes everyday events like grocery shopping in Italy more a recreational activity than a chore.*

Sure, there are Italians who feel exasperated with a lot of things about their country, but they'll rarely complain about it. When faced with a long line at the post office, they don't fume over it and stamp their feet, but rather occupy themselves with more important thoughts, like where to go for dinner that night, or else strike up a conversation with the person next to them.

This human touch, a tolerance bordering on appreciation for the country's blissful imperfections, is what makes everyday events like grocery shopping in Italy more a recreational activity than a chore. It's not a matter of driving to the supermarket and loading as many plastic bags into a minivan in as little time as possible. Instead, you'll walk down cobblestone alleys to markets where vendors spend the time to tell you how to prepare a certain fish, or what vegetable to choose as a side dish, even if it means that the person behind you has to wait a few more minutes.

AN AMERICAN IN ROME

Of all the patience Italians possess, they seem to reserve the most for their American visitors. Some Italians, along with other Europeans, criticize U.S. foreign policy. But on a personal level, Italians and Americans share many of the same values, and any minor American deviation from Italian cultural norms is greeted with immense tolerance.

For one thing, this is shrewd diplomacy. The millions of dollars that Americans spend in Italy every year represent a good portion of the nation's tourism income, which in turn is a significant source of total revenues. When Americans stop coming to Italy in large numbers, as happened in the months following September 11, 2001, the service industry gets very jittery.

Italians have hosted Americans and American businesses for a long time now and are used to their quirks. After World War II, U.S. soldiers patrolled the streets of Rome and Naples, followed by the American café-dwellers of the roaring 1950s. The 1954 film *An American in Rome* is about an Italian so enamored with America that he pretends to be from Kansas City. The movie takes a few good-natured jabs at the baseball hat–wearing, spaghetti-slurping crowd, but the nasal American accent of actor Alberto

Sordi is still endearing to the Italian ear. In the 1980s, McDonald's, basketball, and Coca-Cola were king, and to some extent they have endured the vicissitudes of style and the antiglobalization movement of the late 1990s. The symbols still conjure a Sordi-esque vision of a wide-eyed, youthfully energetic people.

A LAND OF PLENTY

Millions of Americans come to Italy every year, and after just a two-week stay, many of them feel so at home that they are already scheming to make the move. It's hard to leave Italy behind.

The Mediterranean climate is one of its greatest selling points. In the spring, it is warm and not too wet. In the fall, it is cool, sometimes a little damp, but not too windy. In the winter, you need just a medium-weight jacket and an umbrella. Summers are very hot, except in the mountains and at the beach, where all Italians enjoy the month of August. Then come the rains, like clockwork on September 1, and tanned faces return to the city to do it all over again.

Because of this balmy Mediterranean weather, Italy calls itself "the garden of Europe." All along the highways, in small towns, and everywhere in between, the country is teeming with azaleas, bougainvillea, roses, grapes, and palm trees. The hills are alive with olives, citrus, chestnuts, mushrooms, watermelons, cherries, pears, and apples. Corner vegetable stands overflow with locally grown bright yellow peppers, green onions, purple eggplants, many varieties of ripe tomatoes (in at least three different shapes), apricots, artichokes, green and white asparagus, and avocados. If you locked yourself in the kitchen with a full day's worth of groceries, you could prepare everything in your favorite cookbook and still have much of the bounty left over.

If it seems like Italy is all about eating, that's partly true. Daily schedules, conversations, TV shows, and just about everything else revolve around the lunch table, but in between bites, Italy has a lot more to offer. For one thing, there are thousands of ways to burn off the calories without ever going to the gym. With access to a mountainous landscape and spectacular coastline perfect for outdoor sports, Italians rarely bother with exercise machines, and instead enjoy some of the best skiing, cycling, hiking, swimming, and sailing that Europe has to offer.

Alternatively, an unparalleled wealth of art and architecture is just a short train ride away in a *città d'arte* such as Florence, Venice, Bergamo, Padua, or Rome. There are more than 3,000 museums nationwide, but really the whole country is an outdoor museum with some three millennia of history on display.

Italy affords something for every taste, and with so much diversity, the biggest decision you will face is where to live. If you enjoy sunshine, laid-back living, and couscous, you can find them in Sicily. If you prefer snow and fondue, head for Val d'Aosta, with all the cultural appeal of Milan and the littoral luxuries of the Riviera both just a short drive away. Those who imagine an Italy of frescoes, wine, and refined cuisine will gravitate towards the center, while the more stereotypical Italy of chaos and pizza is still there for the asking in Naples.

IS ITALY RIGHT FOR YOU?

If it seems as if all of these pleasures would have to come at a price, the reality is that Italy is one of the more affordable places to live in Western Europe. It is true that housing prices have skyrocketed in the last decade—they have doubled, in fact—but €800 ($1,040) per month for an apartment in Rome, or any European capital, is still a very reasonable price. Other everyday expenditures like utilities and transportation are expensive all over Europe (Italy is no exception), and the introduction of the euro caused a nasty bout of inflation. But overall, consumer prices are still well below those in, say, Switzerland or France, and things that would be considered luxuries in the United States are just staples of daily life in Italy. A good cup of espresso, a nice bottle of wine, a day of skiing, or a pair of shoes will all come at a fraction of what you would pay back home, and chances are the quality of each of them will be significantly higher.

Once you've experienced all of these things—Italy's cultural and recreational opportunities, the nice weather, the great food, the people—and realized you can afford to have it all, the question is no longer why would you want to live here, but why would anyone *not* want to live here? One of Italy's primary draws might also be its biggest drawback: the patience of the people. Italy's human touch extends to the law enforcement community as well, and while it's nice to be able to have a friendly conversation about last night's soccer game with a policeman who has just pulled you over, some people might prefer a country with less tolerance for transgression.

In short, the type of person who should consider a move to Italy is one who doesn't mind cars illegally parked on the sidewalk and can adjust quickly to a last-minute change of plans. These things may never change about Italy, and, try as you might, you'll never be able to change them yourself. Then again, even if you are an organized, law-abiding person with little appreciation for those who bend the rules, there is something about living in a land of sunshine and olive trees that brings out the patience in everyone. Italy may even change you.

The Lay of the Land

A patriotic poem written during the unification of Italy noted that the three colors of the Italian flag represent the variety of the country's geography: red, the glow of the South's volcanoes; white, the snow of the Alps; green, the Po river plain. The lyrics may come off as a little cloying, but once you set eyes on Italy, it is hard not to wax poetic. It is one of the most captivating landscapes in the world, containing every conceivable hue, altitude, temperature, and texture. In a rare instance of understatement, Italians call it simply *il bel paese* (the beautiful country).

> *Once you set eyes on Italy, it is hard not to wax poetic. It is one of the most captivating landscapes in the world.*

All this is packed into a peninsula that, at 300,000 square kilometers, is about the size of Arizona, and holds some 58 million inhabitants, or roughly one quarter of the U.S. population.

Traveling its coastline and its mountainous surface, you'll see why Italian architects and road engineers had to be so talented. There is hardly a straight line or flat surface to be seen. The country has 7,600 kilometers of jagged, mostly mountainous coastline. The only inland sections that aren't covered by mountains or foothills are the Po River plain and a few patches in the South. The country's mountainous spine runs from Liguria in the northwest to Reggio Calabria at the tip of the boot. Even the two island regions, Sicily and Sardinia, are nothing but hills and coast.

Unlike in many Western European countries, Italy is not dominated by one capital city with the rest of the countryside bowing to it. Yes, all roads lead to Rome sooner or later, but all train tracks, you might say, lead to Bologna, the busiest station in the country; and much of the air traffic to Italy is now routed through Milan. Italy is sliced up into many spheres of influence that date back centuries, when the peninsula was a collection of fractious duchies, republics, and city-states.

Italians now mentally divide their unified country into North and South. You're either a northerner, a southerner, or from the boundary in between, namely Tuscany, Umbria, and Le Marche. (Le Marche even gets its name from the Germanic term for a borderland, *marka*.) This is how the prime living chapters of this book are organized: Northwest, Northeast, Center, and South.

The North can be defined as those regions whose water flows into the Po, and, in fact, those who would like to see the industrial North separate from the rest of the country consider themselves part of a make-believe land called Padania, which takes its name from the Po river plain. There

A Look at the Regions

Abruzzo
Population: 1,275,000; 118 people per square kilometer
Provinces: Aquila (AQ), Chieti (CH), Pescara (PE), Teramo (TE)

Basilicata
Population: 610,000; 61 people per square kilomter
Provinces: Matera (MT), Potenza (PZ)

Calabria
Population: 2,071,000; 137 per square kilometer
Provinces: Catanzaro (CZ), Cosenza (CS), Crotone (KR), Reggio Calabria (RC), Vibo Valentia (VV)

Campania
Population: 5,800,000; 425 people per square kilometer
Provinces: Avellino (AV), Benevento (BN), Caserta (CE), Naples (NA), Salerno (SA)

Emilia-Romagna
Population: 3,940,000; 178 people per square kilometer
Provinces: Bologna (BO), Ferrara (FE), Forli (FO), Modena (MO), Piacenza (PC), Parma (PR), Ravenna (RA), Reggio Emilia (RE), Rimini (RN)

Friuli Venezia Giulia
Population: 1,183,000; 151 people per square kilometer
Provinces: Gorizia (GO), Pordenone (PN), Trieste (TS), Udine (UD)

Lazio
Population: 5,241,000; 305 people per square kilometer
Provinces: Frosinone (FR), Latina (LT), Rieti (RI), Rome (ROMA), Viterbo (VT)

Liguria
Population: 1,640,000; 303 people per square kilometer
Provinces: Genoa (GE), Imperia (IM), La Spezia (SP), Savona (SV)

Le Marche
Population: 1,450,000; 150 people per square kilometer
Provinces: Ancona (AN), Ascoli-Piceno (AP), Macerata (MC), Pesaro-Urbino (PS)

Lombardy
Population: 8,990,000; 376 people per square kilometer
Provinces: Brescia (BS), Bergamo (BG), Como (CO), Cremona (CR), Lecco (LC), Lodi (LO), Mantua (MN), Milan (MI), Pavia (PV), Sondrio (SO), Varese (VA)

are no common ethnic or historical ties here, just a river that connects a string of prosperous peoples.

The Po starts high in the foothills of Piedmont, where the Italian Alps brush up against the French and Swiss borders. At the confluence of those three countries is Val d'Aosta, boasting the highest elevation in Europe (Mont Blanc, *detto* Monte Bianco, at 4,748 meters on the Italian side) and the lowest population of all Italian regions (about 120,000 inhabitants.) From there, the melting snow makes its way downhill to Turin and weaves just south of the vineyards that produce some of Italy's most impressive wines. At the Lombardy border, it is joined by the Ticino,

Molise
Population: 330,000; 75 people per square kilometer
Provinces: Campobasso (CB), Isernia (IS)

Piedmont
Population: 4,391,000; 169 people per square kilometer
Provinces: Alessandria (AL), Asti (AT), Biella (BI), Cuneo (CN), Novara (NO), Turin (TO), Verbana (VB), Vercelli (VC)

Puglia
Population: 4,090,000; 210 people per square kilometer
Provinces: Bari (BA), Brindisi (BR), Foggia (FG), Lecce (LE), Taranto (TA)

Sardinia
Population: 1,662,000; 69 people per square kilometer
Provinces: Cagliari (CA), Nuoro (NU), Oristano (OR), Sassari (SS)

Sicily
Population: 5,108,000; 199 people per square kilometer
Provinces: Agrigento (AG), Caltanissetta (CL), Catania (CT), Enna (EN), Messina (ME), Palermo

(PA), Ragusa (RG), Siracusa (SR), Trapani (TP)

Tuscany
Population: 3,527,000; 153 people per square kilometer
Provinces: Arezzo (AR), Florence (FI), Grosetto (GR), Livorno (LI), Lucca (LU), Massa-Carrara (MS), Pisa (PI), Pistoia (PT), Prato (PO), Siena (SI)

Trentino-Alto Adige
Population: 924,000; 75 people per square kilometer
Provinces: Bolzano (BZ), Trento (TN)

Umbria
Population: 831,000; 98 people per square kilometer
Provinces: Perugia (PG), Terni (TR)

Val d'Aosta
Population: 119,000; 36 people per square kilometer
Province: Aosta (AO)

Veneto
Population: 4,469,000; 243 people per square kilometer
Provinces: Belluno (BL), Padua (PD), Rovigo (RO), Treviso (TV), Venice (VE), Verona (VR), Viterbo (VI)

which brings frigid water down from the lakes region near the Swiss canton that gives the river its name. More powerful now, the Po rolls by small but historically significant cities: Pavia, the site of a very old university and one of the most important monasteries in Italy; Cremona, home of the Stradivarius violin; and Ferrara, which claims to have invented the modern theater. From there, the Po flows out into the Adriatic.

North of the river is a string of powerful cities that runs along the base of the Lombard Alps and the Dolomites of South Tyrol, historically part of Austria. These cities still carry the flavor of their Austrian and Venetian conquerors, as well as their Lombard settlers. Milan is Italy's financial capital and ground zero for fashion and design. Bergamo, a jewel of a walled city, produced artistic greats such as Caravaggio. Verona, fictional home of Romeo and Juliet, is set in the vineyards along the southern rim of Lake Garda, which reaches into the Teutonic-flavored region of Trentino-Alto Adige. Padua's university produced Galileo and others. Venice, the best known, perhaps needs no introduction at all.

North of Venice is a once impoverished hinterland better known now for its family enterprises, operating in sectors ranging from furniture to liquor to shoes and clothing. A few of these small business have gone on to international success. (The Benetton family, for example, from Treviso, started off with a small sweater-making business.) Further north lies Friuli Venezia Giulia, the forests and vineyards that eventually give way to the Julian Alps in the north, and to the east, the limestone karst around Trieste. The landscape appears as foreign as the largely Slovenian-speaking population that inhabits it. The entire northern Adriatic coast, which swapped hands in a brutal manner through two world wars, seems to have more in common with parts of the Austro-Hungarian empire than with Italy.

The Italian peninsula starts south of the Po, extending from Liguria, at the western end of the mountainous Italian Riviera, and sloping down into the plains of Emilia-Romagna, the breadbasket of Italy and also its wealthiest region. Emilia's cities—Parma, Modena, Bologna, and Reggio Emilia—are known as places where you're guaranteed to eat and live well. Per-capita income here is pegged at about $900 a month, which may not sound like a high number to a New Yorker, but it's more than twice the average found in the southern regions of Calabria and Basilicata and the island region of Sardinia. Romagna, along the coast, is best known for the teeming beach resort of Rimini and the ancient mosaics at Ravenna.

Tucked into the hills of Romagna, on the border with Le Marche, is the Republic of San Marino, a tax haven that doubles as an excuse for Italy to hold an extra Formula One Grand Prix every year, just outside San Marino's make-believe borders, in Imola. (It's not a novel idea. France does the same with Monaco.) In relation to the rest of Italy, San Marino is a small consideration, both culturally and geographically. If you swatted a fly on a map of Italy, it would cover more ground than this tiny republic.

South of Bologna, the Apennines spread out their hilly fingers from coast to coast. They define the northern border of Central Italy, once the cradle of the Renaissance and now a hotspot for tourists and foreign home-owners. The attractions include not only the artistic treasures of Florence, but also the vineyards in the Tuscan countryside and the coast of Versilia in the summertime. Those crowded Mediterranean beaches stretch from the Gulf of Poets, in Liguria, to the port of Livorno. They pass by the inland cities of Pisa, with its famous tower, and Lucca, a classic medieval city that never fails to charm. On the other side of the peninsula, the regions of Umbria and Le Marche host fewer blockbuster attractions, but have started to see new legions of house-shoppers drawn by the area's ideal climate and calming pastoral beauty.

Tuscany rolls downhill past the cape that juts toward the isle of Elba. The region passes through the scrub brush of the Maremma, the cowboy country of Northern Lazio, until it meets the civilization of Rome. On the Adriatic side, the highlands of Le Marche heave up to the snowcapped peaks of Abruzzo, inhabited by bears, wolves, chamois, and bighorns. Maybe because of its untamed wilderness, Abruzzo is considered part of the South, though it lies on the exact latitude of Lazio, which is thought of as the Center. More likely, Abruzzo is classified as southern because the rough-and-tumble people aren't as wealthy as their neighbors.

Here begins the Mezzogiorno (Midday), a poetic euphemism for the poorer South. What it lacks in money, it more than makes up for in warm hospitality, ancient history, good food, and pristine beaches. The waters on either side of the boot's ankle compete for the title of Most Spectacular Coastline: the Gargano Promontory's breathtaking and sparsely inhabited cliffs; and the stunning Amalfi Coast, with its jubilant flower gardens and capricious summertime fun. The land becomes more mysterious as you move south into Calabria, Basilicata, and southern Puglia. The dome-shaped *trulli* (stone houses) and tarantella of Puglia still mystify guests with their Eastern flavor, while the mountain valleys of Basilicata and Calabria retain the same sun-drenched silence they enjoyed in the days of the Greeks. Some ancient settlements still keep their secrets, buried for millennia under silt, and only now are beginning to see the light of day.

COUNTRY DIVISIONS

Each of Italy's 20 regions is divided into provinces, something like counties in the United States, in that they are based on population and share a *tribunale* (courthouse). A lot of national bureaucracy is administered at this level, such as car registration; every license plate carries the province's initials (see the sidebar "A Look at the Regions" for a full list). The province is also a point of reference when talking about very small towns. For example, instead of naming the little village in Campania where a fire broke out, a newscaster will usually say *nel Casertano* (near Caserta). Any time you pick up a brochure for a hotel or restaurant in a small town, the name of the town will be accompanied by the province's initials, to give you some indication of where it is.

Each province is divided into *comuni* (towns), the lowest level of local government. The *comune*'s jurisdiction encompasses not only the village, but also outlying settlements known as *frazioni*. As a foreigner, you'll likely make several trips to the town's offices to register for a tax ID number; and as a homeowner, you'll need to spend time at the offices to clear up permits for building, renovations, etc.

The most powerful local authority remains the region, which administers such state-run systems as education and health care. Each region has its own assembly and president, and hand-picked by the president is an entourage of *assessori,* often translated into English as "inspectors." (Those who have seen Roberto Begnini's *Life Is Beautiful* might remember his charade as an *assessore* of education, visiting a grade school with the tricolor sash awkwardly tangled between his legs, but commanding the full attention of the schoolteachers nonetheless.) Regional authorities can wield considerable influence. For example, the long-standing president of Lombardy, Roberto Formigoni, is at the time of this writing the head of a very wealthy region of more than eight million people, and therefore considers certain powers otherwise granted only to Rome, such as foreign relations, part of his own brief.

The regions may soon become even more powerful as they are granted more autonomy. Already the country has its autonomous and semi-autonomous regions, designated as such because of their cultural distance from Rome, e.g., Trentino Alto-Adige, Val d'Aosta, and Friuli Venezia Giulia. But the recent push for *federalismo*, a federal structure loosely based on the example of the United States, has less to do with culture than economics. The driving force behind federalism is the diverse character of regional balance sheets. Many northerners, especially from Piedmont, Lombardy, and the Veneto, believe that they contribute more than they benefit from national spending. Currently, regions have no tax-collecting authority, but rather rely on the distribution of national revenues, which is supposed to be proportionate. Federalists wish it were more so.

Southern politicians find themselves in a tough spot here because the South has little to gain from the movement. The former mayor of Catania, Enzo Bianco, who went on to become the Minister of the Interior in the late 1990s, tried to explain regionalization to a group of local students like this: People have different needs and customs in the North than they do in the South and decision-making powers should reflect that. Store hours are a good example. A shopkeeper in Milan may want to stay open during the traditional lunch break to attract more business, but it's too hot in the Sicilian city of Siracusa to be working at midday.

The real reason, of course, that Northerners push so hard for a federal structure is that they prefer to spend money closer to where it is earned. They have found kindred spirits in the conservatives, which is only logical, considering the center-right coalition includes the formerly separatist Northern League (though, ironically, the fervently pro-unity National Alliance is also part of the coalition).

Politics

Italian coalitions are accustomed to such strange bedfellows as these, but these precarious alliances have resulted in the collapse of more than one government. Italy has in fact gone through 59 postwar governments, at last count, causing much grumbling abroad about the country's political instability. There are dozens of major parties (and hundreds of minor ones that rarely win any parliamentary seats), so no party has a very good chance of establishing a majority on its own. Coalitions are therefore composed of a half dozen parties, some of whom share close ideologies, some of whom do not.

In the conservative camp these days are Forza Italia, the National Alliance, the Northern League, and two descendants of the once-unflappable Christian Democrats: the CCD and the CDU. The center-left includes the Democrats of the Left, the Greens, the Socialists and the Italian Communist Party. There are a number of other small groups that flesh out the coalitions, but the two king-makers, the fringe parties that have made or broken governments in the past, are the Northern League and the Refounded Communists. No mainstream party truly wants these outspoken groups in their coalition, but they rarely have much of a choice.

A technical note about Italian elections: They are slightly more complicated than in the United States. Some seats are filled by a direct, first-past-the-post vote, and some by regional proportional representation, in which the parties in general are assigned seats depending on how well they did in the elections overall. In the Senate, 83 of the 315 seats are assigned by proportionate representation, as are 155 of the 630 seats in the lower house.

The other big players on the political scene are the lobbies. The most significant of these are the labor unions—especially the left-wing CGIL and the more centrist CISL and UIL—weighing in on the side of the liberals; the industrialists' group Confindustria, on the side of the conservatives; and the Catholic Church, which applies whatever pressure it can on either side of the spectrum, depending on the issue. Clearly, the Vatican is more at ease with the conservatives' social agenda, but more recently, it has shared common ground with the liberals on matters of foreign affairs.

The Church, and the Pope in particular, commonly speak out to promote pacifism whenever Italy is indirectly involved in an international conflict. And Italy is almost always indirectly involved in any international conflict, sandwiched between the formerly Communist world and the West, and hosting a handful of crucial NATO bases. In the great tradition of Italian diplomacy, prime ministers have always walked a tightrope between offending their neighbors and commercial interests in the Middle East, and appeasing the powerful victors of the Cold War. But Italian leaders will never offer their country's soldiers or weapons in direct combat, because they are expressly forbidden from doing so in their 1948 Constitution.

The constitution also has a few quirks reserved for other branches of government. There is not one but two Supreme Courts, one for reviewing the constitutionality of laws, the Constitutional Court, and another that acts as the nation's highest appeals court, the *Cassazione*. Appeals are considered entirely new trials, and cases commonly go through two or three appeals. In fact, only after an appeal can you be considered guilty, which is fortunate considering all charges are granted a trial, without preliminary judicial review to see if the plaintiff even has a case. Another unique trait of the Italian judiciary: lawyers follow one of two possible career paths. They either become state prosecutors, which may eventually lead to a job as a judge, or else they work as defense attorneys, which will not. This system may soon be reformed. The legal troubles that media tycoon Silvio Berlusconi faced as prime minister led to his ordering an overhaul of the system, which many decried as outrageous. Others defend the separation of prosecutors and defense attorneys, arguing that any system that groups together prosecutors and judges in the same career path does not exactly reassure defendants that they are innocent until proven guilty.

A final constitutional trait that mystifies some Americans, who are accustomed to a strong executive, is the Italian presidency. The *Presidente della Repubblica* (the head of state) is not elected by the people, but rather by an assembly of representatives, and it is little more than a figurehead role. Aside from calling elections and receiving foreign heads of state (though just to shake their hands) the steward of the presidency does little more than expound on the virtues of patriotism and lay wreaths on

© Monica Larner

Nuns on Piazza Garibaldi, Rome

soldiers' tombs. The architects of Italy's Constitution had experienced problems with powerful heads of state in the past.

"THE DUTY OF THE REPUBLIC"

As for the rest of the Constitution, it guarantees essentially the same individual rights that the American one does, such as freedom of religion, freedom of association, freedom of the press, etc. (though the right to bear arms is not one of them). Then it goes a step further. "It is the duty of the republic," the Italian Constitution states, "to remove all economic and social obstacles that, by limiting freedom and equality of all citizens, prevent full individual development and the participation of all workers in the political, economic, and social organization of the country."

These are more than just nice-sounding words. Italy really does go the extra mile in providing its citizens with education, health care, and other state-sponsored provisions that can cost Americans a substantial percentage of their income. This might stir some debate as to whether it is better to follow the European example and pay higher taxes to get the social services for free, or the American example and pay lower taxes and budget for these expenses on one's own. The strange part is that Italy spends only about eight percent of its GDP on health care and about five percent on education, figures that are not much higher than in the United States. In fact, by some calculations they are lower.

There may also be some debate about the quality of the final product. Italians will be the first to admit that public universities have their shortcomings, such as never being able to find your professor, and that public health care has its flaws as well. On the other hand, public universities are much more selective and better regarded than private ones, and public hospitals have more prestige than private clinics. Best of all, they're both free, and no Italians complain about that.

Social Climate

ITALY AND FOREIGNERS

They may not always agree with U.S. foreign policy, and may point out domestic problems in the U.S. and other eyebrow-raising idiosyncrasies of American behavior, but on the whole, most Italians are willing to listen to American points of view with a certain deference. They reserve some respect for the people who helped them defeat Fascism and accommodated many of their own families during the mass migration at the turn of the 20th century. It's safe to say that, of all the nationalities that have relocated to Italy in the past decade, Americans enjoy a place of honor.

Others don't get the same warm welcome. Italy has only recently experienced the sort of immigration that has already changed the face of Germany, France, and the United Kingdom, and its response has been predictable. Italy considers itself a very tolerant country. At the same time, it is also one of the most Catholic nations in Western Europe, and the construction of mosques in the shadow of St. Peter's gets under the skin of a good portion of the electorate. The number of immigrants to Italy has risen dramatically over the last two decades, and some Italians immediately equate this with a perceived rise in the crime rate. Every time a Balkan immigrant got into trouble—burglary, kidnapping, etc.—the papers led with the story. This got the media into trouble when, after a mother and child were found dead in their bathroom in southeastern Piedmont, the headlines read: "Albanians on the Run." Turns out, it was actually the mother who killed the child and then herself. The mea culpa that followed was short-lived.

Such xenophobes have found an outlet in the Northern League. Once a separatist party fueled by small northern businesses irritated by national aid for the South, the group now has found an easier target in immigration. The Northern League makes a lot of headlines abroad and tends to paint Italy as a country of racists, but the party has lately garnered well under 10 percent of the national vote. Its power is mostly concentrated in small pockets of Veneto and Lombardy, two of the more prosperous regions where immigrants are lured to low-paying jobs.

History

E very day in Italy is a walk through history. Latin expressions are tossed around ad hoc, medieval rivalries persist, ancient dialects are still spoken, post-Fascists and Communists remain in government, and streets bear the names of historical figures. The country's past is very much a part of its present, reexamined and reinterpreted in daily conversations. Anyone who moves here should at least brush up on the basics. What follows is a brief sketch of 2,500 years of complicated history.

Early History

THE RISE AND FALL OF ROME

Passing over the peninsula's prehistoric inhabitants and the mysterious Etruscans of the Bronze Age, a good jumping-off point into Italy's history

> *What the Romans lacked in culture, they more than made up for in government, engineering, and military prowess.*

is the founding of the Roman Republic in 510 B.C. After the citizens of this small shepherding town overthrew their Etruscan overlords, they slowly grew an empire by forming alliances with other tribes in Latium, now known as Lazio. They built military roads and established colonies up and down the peninsula, offering Roman citizenship to the conquered inhabitants.

What the Romans lacked in culture, they more than made up for in government, engineering, and military prowess. In theory, political power in the republic lay with the people, who voted as centuries or tribes. In practice, though, government was entrusted to the Senate, made up of aristocratic families. This arrangement caused tension between the patricians (the nobility) and the plebeians (the populace), and led to the Social Wars in 91 B.C. With the city in chaos, a military commander named Sulla staged a bloody coup and brought his armies within the city walls, long considered a religious taboo. His cohort, Pompey the Great, then took control of the city. The republic was passed down to Pompey's lieutenant and rival in the triumvirate, Julius Caesar.

Caesar was an intellectual who studied under Greek masters and could boast almost no military training, and yet he proved to be one of the republic's greatest generals, conquering Gaul and extending Rome's borders to the Rhine. But the height of expansion came under his grandnephew, Octavian, who renamed himself Caesar Augustus. The reign of Augustus (27 B.C. to A.D. 14) gave birth to a Pax Romana, when Rome's military dominance brought an end to major battles in Western Europe for close to two centuries. It also marked the decline of democratic institutions.

Augustus claimed to hold dear the values of the republic, all the while stripping the Senate of its power. He awarded himself titles and offices, and described his role as the "first citizen." (To this day in Italy, a mayor is often referred to as *il primo cittadino*.) The emperors that followed Augustus became nothing short of dictators. Some of them were enlightened leaders, others unscrupulous tyrants. The more colorful characters in the first century included Caligula, a murderous and chemically imbalanced emperor who managed to appoint his horse a lifetime member of the Senate; and Nero, whose contributions included (allegedly) burning down the city before he was driven from power. Nero committed suicide in A.D. 68, pronouncing, "What an artist I destroy."

The Flavian dynasty represented the better half of the century. The first of these emperors, Vespasian, built the Colosseum in A.D. 80. That dynasty was followed by Trajan, under whom the empire was at its height, geographically, and later by Hadrian, who oversaw the construction of Rome's most impressive engineering feat, the Pantheon. It is the largest dome ever built of concrete, a material the Romans invented.

Next came Marcus Aurelius, a Stoic philosopher and admired statesman who built the walls that now demark the boundary of downtown Rome. Their construction coincided with a shift in Rome's military strategy from one of expansion to one of defensive isolation.

Things started falling apart for the empire in the third century. The era was marked by one assassination after another, and also by the threat of attack—either from the Franks in the North or from the overtaxed populace itself. By the fourth century, the emperor Diocletian had to resort to severe legislation to maintain order. He fixed prices, passed a decree that every son must follow the profession of his father, and levied stiff taxes. To implement these, he created a bureaucracy that divided the empire into eastern and western halves. The western half was headquartered at Milan, and later at Ravenna, two important commercial centers at the time.

Constantine, instead, relied on religion to keep order. Christianity was never very popular in imperial Rome—Nero liked to use Christians as human torches to illuminate his garden at night—but now, spiritualism swept across the peninsula. In these troubled times for the empire, the Christians witnessed a reversal of fortune, as the pagans were now persecuted. Sensing this growing power base, Constantine issued an edict of toleration in 313, and established the eastern empire's capital in Byzantium.

Byzantium prospered as the western emperors' hold crumbled, and the barbaric tribes north of the Alps showed more skill with the sword. The Goths, the Franks, and the Lombards had been overrunning the far reaches of the empire for a century, and were prepared to take the peninsula.

THE DARK AGES

Enter Alaric, a Visigoth. When he attacked Rome in 410, the citizens practically opened the gates for him—and then crept out themselves, fleeing to the hills. Their emperor, Honorius, had read the Vandals' writing on the wall already, and so was hiding out in Ravenna. Unlike some of the foreign occupiers to follow, Alaric wasn't too interested in ruling, mostly just in raiding, and the gold he looted from Rome is said to be buried still with his tomb under a river in Calabria.

Next came Attila the Hun, who was also not much of a statesman, though he was persuaded by Pope Leo not to sack the city. He was followed by Gaiseric the Vandal (who could not be so persuaded), Odoacer the Ostrogoth, and soon after, the rival who murdered Odoacer, Theodoric. Theodoric set up shop in Ravenna, holding off the Lombards, who had taken control of the northern plains and had moved all the way south to Tuscany. Theodoric was one in a long line of Italianized foreigners: "An able Goth wants to be like a Roman," he said. "Only a poor Roman would want to be like a Goth."

The popes had their own ideas of how Italy should be run. They had taken the reigns of an embattled Eternal City and stressed the notion that the Church was not just a spiritual power, but also a temporal one. Pope Gregory II cut Rome's ties with Constantinople in 731 and started looking for military allies. He was most concerned with thwarting the advance of the Lombards, as well as Byzantium's legions of—imagine the irony—Roman troops. In 800, the pope named the king of the Franks, Charlemagne, as the new Roman emperor.

The 8th and 9th centuries embodied the depths of the Dark Ages for Italy. Rome was nearly abandoned, save the popes, leaving the imperial buildings to decay while the clergy built hundreds of churches and cloisters. Most of the rest of the peninsula was overrun by barbarians, offering scant political or cultural contributions.

One place that did prosper was Venice. Over the next few hundred years, it rose to power with the other maritime republics—Amalfi, Pisa, and Genoa—whose four symbols now grace the flag of the Italian Navy. (Pisa was once on the sea.)

The end of the Dark Ages in Italy is usually defined as the birth of the Holy Roman Empire, commenced in 962 by Charlemagne's successor, Otto the Great. It saw a reorganization of power into fiefdoms, and the peninsula divided itself into a jigsaw puzzle of duchies, city-states, and republics. The fractiousness that resulted lasted until at least the unification of Italy in 1861. Many would argue it still exists today.

MEDIEVAL ITALY

When the Turks conquered the Holy Land in 1065, the popes found themselves in an enviable position. As the de facto organizing force behind the Crusades, the papacy attracted a lot of money to Italy. Indeed, it allowed for the first banking system in Europe. The title of the world's oldest institutional lender is generally credited to Monte Paschi di Siena, born in the part of Italy that prospered the most from the foreign inflow of Christian capital, Tuscany. Some of the coffers went toward the cathedral and baptistry of Pisa.

The picture of a fallen and abandoned Rome is bleak enough, but the cities it spawned across the peninsula survived. Their aqueducts may not have worked as well as they did centuries before, but the municipalities functioned much as they did under Roman rule. This was especially true

Timeline

600 B.C.: Etruscans make Rome their capital.

510 B.C.: Founding of Roman Republic.

49 B.C.: Rome, under Julius Caesar, rules the Mediteranean.

44 B.C.: Caesar is dead, long live Caesar Augustus.

A.D. 80: Colosseum is completed.

117 to 138: Hadrian builds his Mausoleum, Wall, and Villa.

249 to 250: First empirewide persecution of Christians.

395: Constantine establishes second Rome at Byzantium, Goths pour into the North.

410: Rome is sacked by Alaric, falls to other invaders in 475.

800: Charlemagne is crowned Holy Roman Emperor.

1065: Crusades begin.

1091: Normans take control of Sicily from Arabs.

1182: Holy Roman Emperor Frederick Barbarossa recognizes autonomy of the Lombard League.

1150 to 1300: clashes between Guelfs and Ghibellines.

1222: University of Padua is founded.

1303: Popes vacate for Avignon; Giotto starts work on the Scrovegni Chapel.

1499: Leonardo da Vinci completes *The Last Supper.*

1508: Michelangelo starts the ceiling of the Sistine Chapel.

1513: Machiavelli publishes *The Prince.*

1641: Galileo applies the pendulum to clocks, a year before he dies.

1796: Napoleon invades.

1853: First performance of Giuseppe Verdi's *La Traviata.*

1861: Birth of the Kingdom of Italy.

1915: Italy enters World War I on the side of Britain and France.

1934: Italy wins its first soccer World Cup (won again in 1938 and 1982).

1940: Mussolini drags Italy into World War II on Germany's side.

1943: Italy signs an armistice with the Allies; Mussolini is killed by partisans.

1961: Federico Fellini directs *La Dolce Vita.*

1969: A bomb in Milan's Piazza Fontana kills 16 and kicks off a decade of terrorism.

1978: Prime Minister Aldo Moro is kidnapped and then murdered.

1993: Prime Minister Bettino Craxi resigns on corruption charges.

1994: Silvio Berlusconi's Forza Italia party wins elections, coalition later collapses.

2001: Berlusconi is back in power after a brief, historic rule by the center-left.

in the North. In the South, Amalfi was an exception. It did a roaring trade with the same Arab pirates who were looting Amalfi's neighbors, such as the Salerno. Unfortunately for Amalfi, it had no other source of income, and so the end of this Southern dream came in 1135, when the Pisans leveled its cliff-hanging shores. Today, it is little more than a tourist attraction. (Then again, the same can be said about modern-day Pisa. Genoa definitively rid itself of Pisa's pesky fleet in 1284.)

Venice was another trade-heavy republic. It considers itself the longest-standing republic in history. The Serenissima enjoyed profitable ties with Byzantium, becoming Europe's window on the East and giving birth to such Asiatic explorers as Marco Polo. (Actually, he was born on an island in modern-day Croatia, then under the Venetian flag.) The spice trade was lucrative, and the Italians also seemed to make good use of the noodles that the Polo family is said to have brought back from the Orient.

But Venice really made hay by handling the passage of earnest knights traveling from Northern Europe to the Holy Land. So did Genoa, another seafaring giant and the hometown of a well-known explorer some three centuries later: Christopher Columbus. (Columbus came back from the New World with some interesting items himself. Where would Italy be today without the tomato?) The two cities competed to attract the Crusaders and their gold, not unlike the jockeying today to host the Olympic Games.

This kind of toll-booth income gave rise not only to the maritime cities, but also to the inland states of Cremona, Florence, Milan, Mantua, Piacenza, and Padua. Milan, for example, controlled the Alpine passes. In terms of military power, though, the northern city-states had a little outside help.

The Popes encouraged the autonomy of such *communi* because they weakened the hold of the Holy Roman Empire, which by then had gotten a little too powerful for the Vatican's tastes. The feud exploded into a war that lasted some 150 years between the Guelfs—representing the papacy, the freedom of city-states, the middle-class merchants, and, of course, religious domination—and the Ghibellines on the side of the emperor, the nobility, and the freedom of religion. It was oddly similar to the politics of late-20th-century Italy, in which the mercantile middle class supported conservative leaders on the side of the Church, while the modern aristocracy espoused more secular ideals.

It's also interesting to note that the emperor met the toughest resistance in the North, where commercial interests were, and still are, the strongest. At the start of the Guelf-Ghibelline wars, in 1161, city-states around Milan bound together in the Lombard League, which stopped the emperor, Frederick Barbarossa, in Legnano.

Northern populists are still very proud of this feat. If you buy a Legnano-brand bicycle, for example, on the fork will be the Lombard League's symbol, a soldier holding a sword high in the air. It's the same symbol borrowed by the formerly separatist and anti-immigrant Northern League party.

The signs of that medieval era are everywhere, especially in Central Italy, where the fighting was at its fiercest. Cruising around the Tuscan countryside today, you can see which castles were loyal to which side. The ones with square turrets were Guelf; with swallow-tailed turrets, Ghibelline.

The Renaissance and the Foreign Invasion

All the banking and commerce that drove the rise of the *communi* also fueled the wealth of their principal families. These families demonstrated their wealth by commissioning art. The Sforza and Visconti families in Milan, the della Scala family of Verona, the d'Este family in Ferrara, the Medici in Florence—all were gearing up for the titles of duke and duchess. They required paintings and sculptures to dress up their power, and perhaps impart a few convenient social lessons in the process. The richest families—the Barberini, the Borgia, and the Medici—were awarded an even better feudal title, the pontificate, and the popes worked just as hard in that age to outdo each other with decorative contributions.

There are hundreds of artists associated with the Renaissance, but the top families generally drew from the same pool of standouts, especially Giotto, Michelangelo, and Leonardo da Vinci. Their masterpieces now dot the Italian landscape between Lombardy and Lazio and require little introduction. These, along with the architecture of Brunelleschi and the literary works of Tuscan writers Dante and Petrarch, are what most people think of when they imagine the Renaissance. The 15th century indeed saw a flowering of creativity and opulence in Italy, much as the 13th century did, but by no means did it mark the end of the hostilities between feuding states and families. Leonardo's genius was more often put to work to create war machines and irrigation devices than to paint pretty pictures. One of the era's more pragmatic luminaries, Machiavelli, spent his time describing the sort of cutthroat competition that characterized Renaissance Italy and would ultimately lead to its invasion by foreigners.

The relative stability under the Holy Roman Empire disappeared when the emperor, who then had his court in Palermo, was defeated in 1266. The pope had invited Charles of Anjou, brother of the French king, to come down and rid the country of Manfred (no longer considered the Emperor, but simply the King of Sicily), which he did, and France was awarded Sicily for its efforts.

But the papacy and the French king didn't always see eye-to-eye. Pope Boniface VIII cooked up a plan about taxing the clergy that resulted in his arrest warrant, signed by the king. In 1303, the popes decided it would be a good idea to let things cool down with the French by moving to Avignon, where they could enjoy better relations with the king, mostly by doing exactly what he said. They stayed there for 70 years before returning to a still-turbulent Rome.

From its Renaissance right up to its unification in 1861, "Italy" continued to be a collection of Papal States, foreign-ruled kingdoms, and the odd republic. One historian pointed out that there were more independent states in Italy in the 14th century than there were in the entire world in 1934. This helped breed the phenomenon of *campanilismo* (the idea that Italians are loyal only to their local *campanile,* or bell tower). There was very little trade between the small states, contributing to a weak economy and consequently a slim chance of overthrowing their wealthy conquerors. Instead, they preferred to go to war with each other.

While fractious, each of them was more or less dominated by either the popes, Venice, Milan, Florence, or the Kingdom of Naples, which in turn had been ruled by a merry-go-round of foreigners since the Dark Ages. Only the republics of Venice, Siena, and Florence managed to keep some degree of independence. For example, in just 400 years, Naples passed through the hands of the Normans, the Spanish (specifically, the Aragonese), the French, back to the Spanish, and then was ceded to the Austrians after the War of Spanish Succession. The Austrians then transferred Naples to the Bourbon kings before it landed in the hands of Napoleon in 1796. But Naples was just one illustration of the way Italy was humiliated by foreign powers after the Renaissance, just as Machiavelli had predicted. Throughout the 17th and 18th centuries, the city-states' industries were beaten out by foreign competition and French and Austrian military might, while the port towns suffered with the rise of Dutch, Spanish, and English maritime prowess.

At one point, Spain was in control of the entire peninsula, except for Venice. In 1519, Charles V purchased the crown of Holy Roman Emperor and set his sights on Northern Italy. He already ruled the South, and held just about everything north of the Alps, all the way to Holland. Milan and the other French-held territories on the Po River plain were an inconvenient gap in his communications network, a sector that Charles V knew well. He spoke all of the languages, he said: Spanish to God, Italian to women, French to men, and German to his horse.

After he defeated the French at Pavia and stormed Rome two years later in 1527, he had done the impossible: unified Italy, albeit without Venice and for only a short period of time. Peasant revolts in Naples and elsewhere loosened Charles's grip, and the War of Spanish Succession would spin off many of those holdings to Austria. Napoleon was on the rise, and so was another new player on the geopolitical stage—the King of Piedmont. Under his flag, Giuseppe Garibaldi and his men would unify Italy again, this time for good.

Unification

The Italians have such a long history of infighting and divergent cultures that you can easily understand why patriotism is such a hard sell. Even today, the President of the Republic has to plead with his citizens to hoist the tricolor flag and sing the national anthem on holidays—an especially difficult task, considering few Italians actually know the words. This becomes obvious when you see members of the national soccer team either unwilling or unable to mouth them at the World Cup.

Even after the country was unified, the royals who brought the warring factions together were unpopular in most of the peninsula, with the possible exceptions of Lombardy and Piedmont itself. Just like the Roman emperors and foreign kings before them, the Savoys were seen as another tax-collecting entity, a force to be subverted. There was, and always has been, some concept of "Italy" as a unit going back to the Romans, but as the historian Christopher Duggan argues in *A Concise History of Italy,* it was mostly relegated to the realm of philosophers and poets.

Dante Aligheri, who witnessed his share of poverty and factionalism living in the trenches between the Guelfs and the Ghibellines during the 14th century, lamented the lack of a strong leader to conquer the warring sides: "O servile Italy, breeding ground of misery, ship without a pilot in a mighty tempest," he wrote.

These same thoughts were shared by northern liberals in the Enlightenment of the 18th century, who wanted to see Italy united—except not by an outside emperor, as Dante had hoped, but by an Italian—and rid of its foreign-influenced nobility. In the early 19th century, the most prominent of these liberal thinkers were from the wealthy and independent kingdom of Piedmont, particularly Count Camillio Benso di Cavour, Giuseppe Mazzini, and his student, Giuseppe Garibaldi.

Cavour, at the time prime minister of Piedmont, was the first to plot to overthrow the Austrians. He struck a deal with Napoleon that if the

French would march east toward Venice, Piedmont would cede him Nice and Savoy. The deal fell apart when Napoleon found out that Cavour was conspiring to annex the Papal States, and so halted his troops after they took Lombardy. Cavour was shamed, and he resigned. The war with Austria did provoke more popular uprisings, however, and when the Sicilians began getting restless under Spanish taxation, the next man to the fore was Garibaldi.

Born in Nice, he had been exiled from Piedmont on several occasions—once doing a stint as a candlemaker on Staten Island—but was perhaps the greatest patriot among the Northern liberals. He would take on his mission with fervor: to bring a ragtag army of 1,000 men armed with bayonets to Sicily and liberate it. He did, and then triumphantly crossed the Straits of Messina to march on Naples in 1860.

The Kingdom of Italy was thus born, ruled by Victor Emmanuel II of the House of Savoy, King of Piedmont and Sardinia. The Papal States having been annexed, it stretched from the Alps to Sicily, with the important exceptions of Rome and Venice.

Rome was then guarded by French soldiers, and when Napoleon had to withdraw them for use in a battle against Prussia, Italian soldiers marched in with relative ease in 1870. That same year, Italy took control of the Veneto when the Prussians defeated the Austrians.

Modern History

THE RISE AND FALL OF FASCISM

> *Italians always loved a good entertainer who could stir their emotions and divert them from themselves. . . . They were always delighted by a talented painter, musician, sculptor, architect, actor, dancer, as long as he did not engage their higher faculties. They respected and admired great scientists, especially if their discoveries were abstract and incomprehensible. They endured and feared a forceful leader, but they always thoroughly enjoyed his fall. . . . It is true that in other countries, great men have also occasionally been persecuted and put to death. Nowhere else, however, has this happened with the same discrimination, regularity, and determination.*
>
> Luigi Barzini, The Italians *(1964)*

Luigi Barzini was no apologist for Benito Mussolini. He would later go on to humiliate the Fascist dictator in his book. But what he wrote, ringing as true today as then, encapsulates the mentality of a people who would accept a figure such as Mussolini and later leave him hanging upside down in Milan's Piazzale Loreto.

Mussolini was born to a blacksmith's family in a small town near Forli, Emilia-Romagna. The region is known for its left-leaning tendencies today, and Mussolini fit the bill; he was a revolutionary, going unwashed and unshaven for weeks, and at one point living under a bridge in a cardboard box. He read rabble-rousing revolutionary literature voraciously, and, like any good charismatic leader, skipped off to Switzerland to avoid the draft. Then he returned to Italy to become the editor of a Socialist newspaper, *Avanti! (Let's Go!)*.

It's worth noting that the newspaper's name bears tremendous resemblance to that of the party invented by Silvio Berlusconi, called *Forza Italia! (Go, Italy!)*. Both were designed to appeal to popular instinct, and Mussolini's paper—filled (as were most newspapers at the time, and a few today) with inciteful propaganda—did have an impressive circulation of around 200,000 copies.

The era that set the stage for Fascism was the turn-of-the-century industrial boom in the North. The carmaker Fiat, still Italy's largest private employer, was founded in Turin. The agricultural South was mostly unaffected, and millions of southerners took off in this period for the United States, Northern Europe, and later Australia. The rise of industrialization was accompanied by restlessness on the part of laborers. Mussolini appealed to that crowd in his Communist propaganda, a genre that also typically denounces warmongers. "Who drives us to war betrays us," read one of his headlines.

But in 1914, he realized that he could gather more readers if he supported the war. He did, and was thrown out of the party, but had chosen the winning side. The popularity of such Futurist poets as Gabriele D'Annunzio and Filippo Tommaso Marinetti showed that Mussolini's young audience was eager to be rid of unscrupulous Socialist leaders, such as Giovanni Giolitti, and their cozy relationships with the enlightened industrialist families of the left: the Agnellis, Olivettis, and Pirellis. The kids wanted lightning-quick modernization, and they wanted danger. They wanted raw, unbridled power.

This they got in full—or at least the part about danger and unbridled power. In 1915, Italy entered the war on the side of Britain and France. The fiercest fighting was along the border of modern-day Slovenia, then part of the Austro-Hungarian empire, where 600,000 Italian soldiers are now buried. It was a giant disaster in that respect, but a much bigger success for the war supporters in another. Italy had technically won, and had grown its industrial base exponentially in those years, thanks to the demand for planes, guns, and strong state controls on production. The values of war, militancy, and ruling with an iron fist would carry Mussolini and his Fascist blackshirts into Rome in a risky, but ultimately successful, march. (Actually, Mussolini stayed well behind in Milan and arrived by train once the dust had settled.)

He took command in October 1922, and after a stirring speech to parliament in 1925, he ruled as a modern-day Augustus until things went awry in July 1943. Taking a battlefield mentality to the economy, he drained marshes, produced mountains of grain, built bridges and hospitals, set up what were essentially sweatshops, and emerged from it all with budget surpluses. Crime, obviously, was said to be at an all-time low, construction boomed, sporting events were massive and hyped, the state broadcaster RAI was born, and most famously, "the trains ran on time." The grandmothers of today, who made shoes in northern factories for minimum wage under Fascist banners, can't remember a better time, they'll tell you. If Italian unity and patriotism ever had its day, this was it.

But for all the Fascist talk about resolving the "Southern question," agriculture in the South hadn't improved much since the days of the Bourbons. Carlo Levi's *Christ Stopped at Eboli,* about a wealthy Piedmont doctor who gets a taste of the primitive living conditions in Basilicata in the 1930s, paints quite a different picture. This poverty produced a sort of criminality that wasn't talked about very much in the censored press.

In the late '30s, Italy fought alongside Germany in the Spanish Civil War, and a Fascist friendship grew. This became increasingly important when Hitler annexed Austria in 1938. The next year, Mussolini annexed Albania, which was already Italian in practice. In such matters, he avoided risk wherever he could—his contribution to colonialism was moving into Ethiopia—and once Hitler had conquered most of Europe by 1940, Mussolini thought there would be little risk in attacking Greece and joining the war on Germany's side.

After he lost battles in Africa (saved only by the Germans time after time) and faced strikes and food riots at home, revolts by the domestic Slavs, and a generally disenchanted Italian public, Fascism crumbled in July 1943. The king had Mussolini arrested and appointed Marshal Badoglio as prime minister. Badoglio pretended that he would continue to fight with the Germans while he arranged for an armistice with the Allies. The Germans rescued Mussolini from his prison in Abruzzo, eventually setting him up in a puppet state on Lake Garda.

The American-led Allies had started moving up into the peninsula, closing in on the German-held North. Fighting alongside the partisans, the

Allies bombed Rome and eventually ousted the Nazis. Badoglio and the King deserted Rome for Bari and signed an armistice in September 1943.

Meanwhile, Mussolini had tried to flee to Switzerland, carrying a forged Spanish passport, along the western shore of Lake Como. He was captured by the partisans near the town of Dongo, held as a prisoner, and ultimately shot there. His corpse was dangled upside down, along with that of his mistress, Claretta Petacci, and fellow Fascists, from the roof of a Milan gas station. Il Duce was gone, but the scars of World War II remained.

RECONSTRUCTION

After the war, Italy created a Constitution describing itself as a republic "founded on labor," opposed to military action as a way to resolve international conflicts, and free of the Savoy kings who had backed the man who dragged the country into war in the first place. No male heir to the Savoy throne was allowed to step foot on Italian soil, a ban that lasted until 2003.

Geographically and politically, Italy now sat on the front lines of a new international conflict that would last for another 40 years: the Cold War. Unrest at northern factories led to the creation of the Italian Communist Party, or PCI. It was well funded by the Soviets and would become the largest Communist Party in Western Europe. Meanwhile, the Americans who had helped liberate the country from the Germans would play an even more influential role in shaping the country's domestic politics. The U.S. threw its weight behind the Christian Democrats, or DC, who more or less kept a grip on power until the fall of the Berlin Wall.

Soon after the postwar boom in America gave birth to a sprawling middle class, much the same happened in Italy, revolutionizing the country's agricultural economy.

The DC's primary concern after taking power in the late 1940s was the rural poor. A series of agrarian reforms tried to make it easier for peasants to buy land. This gave way to the tradition of spending large amounts of state money to bail out the South, made somewhat easier by the economic fortunes of the 1950s. Soon after the postwar boom in America gave birth to a sprawling middle class, much the same happened in Italy, revolutionizing the country's agricultural economy. There followed a massive exodus out of the countryside and into the cities, mostly from the impoverished South to the industrial centers of Turin and Milan.

For the middle classes in the major cities, at least, the late 1950s were good years. They set the backdrop for Federico Fellini's ironically titled classic, *La Dolce Vita (The Sweet Life),* which described a Rome of movie stars and nouveau riche ideals, played out at outdoor cafés on the lavish Via Veneto—incidentally, the address of the American Embassy.

The U.S. would remain Italy's role model for decades, a phenomenon aided by the fact that American diplomats and intelligence services were hard at work here keeping the Communists at bay. For example, the Americans would not award military contracts to any factory led by the nation's largest labor union, CGIL. Whether related or not, CGIL's power base shrank in the 1950s and early 1960s.

More intrigue surrounded the involvement of the Central Intelligence Agency. Though it is impossible to prove, it can only be assumed that the CIA knew about most of the covert actions of the Italian intelligence agencies in the 1960s and 1970s, especially those surrounding what became known as the "strategy of tension."

THE YEARS OF LEAD

Much like in the United States, the late 1960s in Italy were years of near-revolution. Unrest at factories grew, accompanied by a rise in anarchists and leftist groups, the most famous of which became Lotta Continua (Enduring Struggle). The "hot autumn" of 1969, as it was called, came to a roaring crescendo on December 12, when a bomb ripped through a bank in Milan's Piazza Fontana, killing 16 people. Prosecutors were quick to blame the leftists and round them up for questioning. One of them, Giuseppe Pinelli, fell from the fourth floor office of police headquarters during an interrogation. The official report said that he committed suicide.

It turned out, though, that the leftists were not at all responsible for the bomb, but rather a far-right group from the Veneto was to blame. Further investigative journalism revealed that a member of Italy's secret service, and indeed the government at large, were part of the plot. The series of explosions that the state had in mind was referred to as the "strategy of tension"—that is, framing leftists for state-driven terrorism, and hoping that the electorate would call for a strong conservative government.

There was indeed a shift to the far right in the next elections, but the country was splitting to extremes. This tension between the Communists, the Socialists, and the Christian Democrats prompted the Communists' secretary, Enrico Berlinguer, to draft what he termed a "historic compromise" between the parties in 1972 in order to increase stability and further economic growth. Though ultimately unrealized, it did bring a moderated Communism back into mainstream politics, and historians argue that it held back the reemergence of unrestrained authority and safeguarded democracy.

Still, the workers strikes continued, and revolutionary groups grew.

The early 1970s saw the appearance of the Red Brigades, who would terrorize Italy throughout the later part of the decade, known as the Years of Lead. In their early existence, they beat up managers and set their cars on fire. Later, they moved to "the heart of the state," killing political figures, kidnapping judges and, in March 1978, the Prime Minister, Aldo Moro. The assailants ambushed his car on his way to Parliament, killed his entourage, and held him prisoner for 54 days. They killed him on May 9, and stuffed his body into the trunk of a car. There are a number of mysteries that still surround the government's handling of the Moro crisis, just as there were doubts about the real motives behind Piazza Fontana.

The decade's final tragedy took place on August 2, 1980, when a bomb in Bologna's train station killed 85 people, including some Americans. It was blamed on right-wing terrorists, and there has always been suspicion about the state's involvement. In fact, just a year after the bombing, the Italian public found out about a secretive Masonic lodge, P2, made up of the nation's most significant politicians and business leaders, whose mission was to rid the government of Communists. On the 20th anniversary of that bombing, leaders admitted that the whole truth about Bologna had still not yet been revealed.

For foreign observers, the conspiracies, disasters, and cover-ups seem to play themselves out like the investigation of the assassination of John F. Kennedy dozens of times over. It is no less difficult for Italians themselves to fully comprehend, because official explanations of a historic event are colored by a political leaning. Even the special commission meant to sort out the cover-ups, the Slaughter Commission, is highly politicized, as described by British journalist Tobias Jones in his recent book, *The Dark Heart of Italy*. Jones arrived in Parma in 1999 and spent the next four years researching the more famous debates:

> *It was as if a large number of Italian journalists, academics, and judges were still trying to solve whodunits from many years ago. The list of mysteries was endless, as were the theories they spawned. . . . It all sounds like an acute case of paranoia, especially when people try and link up the mysteries and end up with something cobbled together from the* The X-Files. *Yet, when you start reading newspaper cuttings and books on the mysteries, you realize that there really is something very unusual going on.*

CLEAN HANDS AND SILVIO BERLUSCONI

The 1980s in Italy will forever be remembered for the excesses and underhanded dealings of the Socialist government, thanks to the immense backlash against bribery in the 1990s. This scandal, dubbed Tangentopoli (Bribesville), was nothing particularly new to Italian politics, nor would it be to most any country for that matter, but prosecutors in the 1990s decided to do something about it. Much in the same spirit of the anti-Mafia investigations and trials of the same era, lead prosecutor Antonio Di Pietro took on an establishment previously regarded as untouchable.

The Mani Puliti (Clean Hands) investigation overturned an entire political class, with some Socialist leaders so shamed by the accusations of bribery that they committed suicide, while others landed in jail. The prime minister, Bettino Craxi, was run out of the country and spent the rest of his days in exile, at a vacation home in Tunisia.

One of the Milanese businessmen who enjoyed particularly friendly relations with Craxi was a real-estate developer named Silvio Berlusconi. After a short stint as a cruise-ship crooner, he made his real money developing a residential area known as Milano 2. With the proceeds, he took on the task of creating a rival broadcaster to the state-run RAI. The largest hurdle was that it was illegal to operate a private national television network. But he and Craxi worked things out, and Berlusconi the builder was on his way to becoming a media tycoon, Italy's richest man and, in 1994, its prime minister.

His holding company, Fininvest, extended into such sectors as insurance, films, food distribution, and even a soccer team, A.C. Milan, which played no small part in launching Berlusconi onto the political stage. He formed a conservative party, called Forza Italia, and swept to victory in the 1994 elections, along with the formerly Fascist National Alliance of Gianfranco Fini, and the populist and separatist Northern League of Umberto Bossi. Lingering charges against Berlusconi in the Clean Hands investigation, including the creation of a slush fund to avoid taxes and bribe judges and politicians, helped bring about his quick demise. The coup de grâce, however, was the withdrawal of the Northern League from the coalition, bringing an end to Berlusconi's first reign in December the same year.

After a year of Lamberto Dini's caretaker government, the left won the elections for the first time in its postwar history, led by "The Professor," Romano Prodi. His government lasted 28 months, a long haul by Italian standards. But in 1998, his reign suffered the same fate as Berlusconi's when its partners, the Refounded Communists, refused to sign his budget, pulling out of the coalition and forcing Prodi's resignation. The Communists were pushing for greater social spending at a time when Prodi had just brought the deficit under control, qualifying it to take part in Europe's single currency.

The next leader to the fore was Massimo D'Alema, a former Communist who went to summer camp in the Soviet Union. His tenure would be marked by a steep rise in immigration, and consequently a palpable rise in anti-immigrant sentiments. D'Alema's government lasted until elections in the spring of 2001, when Berlusconi, a.k.a. "The Knight," came galloping back with a surge of popular support, winning around 60 percent of the vote. Bossi's Northern League, no longer separatist and now running on a mostly anti-immigrant platform, was still in the coalition, but his slimmed-down power base no longer presented a threat of blackmail to Berlusconi.

Anti-immigrant fears paved the way for the Bossi-Fini laws that made it particularly hard for foreigners to live in Italy illegally or without a job. Meanwhile, the more substantiated danger of domestic terrorism was still alive and well. Two separate murders of government aides marked something of a rebirth of the Red Brigades, embodying the left's anger over labor reforms and accompanied by movements against such other perceived American ills as globalization and the sale of genetically modified foods. Still, the pro-American, pro-capitalist center-right enjoyed unwavering support. If there was any threat at all to Berlusconi's government in 2003, they were the lingering charges of tax fraud and bribery. Some of these had already been thrown out, thanks to a statute of limitations, while others were approaching a verdict.

Throughout, Berlusconi claimed that judges were politically biased against him, and introduced legislation that would not only reform the judiciary, but also make high-profile politicians immune from such charges. This battle between the self-styled entrepreneur and liberal judges painted Berlusconi either as an outright dictator or as a martyr to a conspiracy. As of the writing of this book, there was still some question as to which side would prevail as Berlusconi stepped in and out of courtrooms. But as Luigi Barzini wrote, the only thing greater than the Italians' respect for strong leaders is their pleasure in watching those leaders fall.

© Monica Larner

People and Culture

or all its sleek new trains and state-of-the-art cell phones, Italy is still an old country, not just in terms of buildings and art, but in more ways than meet the eye. The sewers of Rome use the same channels the ancients used to flush out the city's waste. Silversmiths and violinmakers use techniques developed in the Middle Ages. Family companies go back several hundred years. Mostly, though, Italy is an old place in terms of people's manners.

Italians abide by a time-tested decorum that governs every social gathering, every business deal, and every romantic interlude—the sorts of rules that, if they ever existed in America, were thoroughly wiped out over the last century.

Certainly, some of these unwritten rules have changed in Italy, too. Young people don't speak to their elders as formally as they once did, for example. People don't go to church as often as they used to. That shift away from piety and ceremony has opened the gates for a number of changes, such as the cohabitation of unmarried couples, one of many social norms that were unheard of in Italy 50 years ago. But beware: Not every stratum of Italian society abides by the same rules. Values in Italy change from family to family. How you act and the things you should say in front of certain people also depend on things such as political affiliation, geography—the South tends to be more traditional than the North—and, above all, a person's upbringing.

Class Acts and *una Bella Figura*

Everyone sees what you appear to be, few touch what you are.

Machiavelli, The Prince

You may not be able to prevent yourself from saying something you probably shouldn't to someone who belongs to a certain class, because, really, how can you be expected to know what sort of family is behind a perfect stranger? To an outsider, the line between Italian classes can be difficult to distinguish, because everyone seems so effortlessly well dressed and well mannered. Most city-dwellers at least feign an interest in the arts, and all the other erstwhile hallmarks of the aristocracy have since been usurped by even the man on the street. Italians, however, are acutely aware and perceptive about a person's background, and, more importantly, what people think about their own. They go to great lengths to make themselves appear as well bred as possible.

Attitudes toward money are giveaways to class anywhere in the world, but the verdict is a little trickier with Italians. They represent one of those rare nationalities with a reputation for being generous. The poorer a family is, generally, the wealthier it will appear. Gifts are lavish, beyond the giver's means, and when it comes to hosting a party or a dinner, Italians spare no expense. Maybe it is culturally assumed that this is the way that the aristocracy would behave under similar circumstances. Ironically, the only outwardly frugal people in Italy are, in fact, the aristocrats themselves. Like something from the pages of Chekhov's *The Cherry Orchard,* noble families who don't have to work are often the most worried about squandering their dwindling capital.

Then there are more subtle clues into someone's upbringing that don't go unnoticed in Italian society: the manicure of someone's fingernails, their political leanings, and the way they speak—all things that don't require money, but indicate how someone was raised. Manners, not material wealth, are enough to convince people of your upbringing in an era

A Healthy Attitude

The common stereotype about the cheese-eating and cigarette-smoking continentals is that they live life to the fullest and damn the consequences. It is true that diet soft drinks have little place in Europe and gyms are only slowly catching on, but Italians seem to live to a ripe old age nonetheless. This is especially true in the region of Liguria, where locals routinely set Guinness World Records for elderliness and attribute their success to one glass of red wine per day. Maybe the toast *salute!* (to your health!) has some meaning after all.

Italians may smoke more than they should (though not more than the average European, according to EU surveys) and give off the impression that the present is more important than the future, but the reality is that they are adamant about keeping in shape and do a pretty good job of it.

Whether it's the way they choose their food, how they dress for the cold, or what they put on their skin, they subscribe to the doctrine of preemptive health: It's better to keep the doctor away than run to the hospital for every ache and pain.

Popular wisdom about maintaining good health can be dubious, or even downright superstitious, at times. The most common threat to one's health is apparently the *colpo d'aria* (draft). Air-conditioning is widely believed to bring on a cold. Few public buildings use anything other than a fan, even in the dead of summer. Similarly, no one leaves the house with wet hair, regardless of the temperature outside. Grandmothers still scold young women for sitting on cold benches, as it allegedly renders them infertile. Do not be surprised to see these same women wearing fur coats in April.

when anyone with some luck in the stock market can buy a castle at a public auction, or a noble title from the back pages of *The Economist.*

In the past, one of the more entertaining litmus tests for class was soccer-team affiliation. For example, in cities with two Serie A teams, e.g., Rome, Milan, Turin, and (sometimes) Genoa, fan bases traditionally were split between the middle class on one side and the working class and aristocracy on the other. Take the example of Milan. Inter, a team owned for generations by an oil-refining family, was long seen as the bastion of the bourgeoisie, while A.C. Milan was the team of the working class—their fans were nicknamed "the screwdrivers"—and their political leanings were as red as the stripes on A.C.'s shirt. In Rome, the rabble-rousing proletariat rejoiced, in the most vulgar of terms, at every shortcoming suffered by S.S. Lazio, a favorite of the neatly dressed middle class. These days, even those lines have blurred, as ownership of clubs has swapped hands and technology has brought the games to anyone with a TV.

Anyway, who cares about class in this day and age? On the face of it, Italians seem so egalitarian and unassuming that you wouldn't think it matters a lick. But it does matter, and nowhere is pedigree more important than in

Carnival revelers, Venice

Duomo, Florence

the workplace, where nepotism is the name of the game. Admittedly, the old boy network is alive and well in the United States in certain industries, but in Italy, all good jobs are relatively scarce. There just isn't the same selection there is in the United States, where new companies are born and grow every day. In Italy, the few new businesses that do grow very large tend to be family-run. The CEOs often have the same name as the company itself. Rarely do you hear of a tycoon who started from scratch. With a few notable exceptions, those who land the choicest jobs in the business world are *raccomandati,* that is, protégés of a well-connected clan.

In the workplace, everyone knows their part and plays it well. The boss is addressed as "*direttore*" (literally, "director"). Such democratic inventions as "flat" companies and glass doors between the management and the staff are laughable concepts in Italy, where firms are run like fiefdoms—the power is almighty, but so is the protection, namely, job security. For reasons discussed later, you wouldn't think of job-hunting if you already have a job.

For those in positions of authority, a business suit is obligatory, and you'll never really feel out of place in Italy if you're dressed to impress. If you walk into a store and are well dressed, you'll be addressed as *signore* or *signora*. The same people who wear jeans and T-shirts into the store can expect to be referred to as *il ragazzo* or *la ragazza*. (It's a very rejuvenating feeling to be a 30-year-old man and still be referred to as "that boy over there who wants a coffee.") In Italy, it is not success, but merely the appearance of success, that counts.

Every Italian has a talent for keeping up impressions, and the charade is so widely practiced that there is a strict code of conduct governing every daily act. Making *una bella figura* (a good impression) requires some practice. It is an air of confidence, patience, intelligence, and respect for other people, all delivered with a dazzling smile. It can also include more material representations of success, such as showing up in the right sort of car and wearing the right clothes. It's hard to put your finger on what exactly constitutes *una bella figura* in any given situation, but it will be painfully obvious when you've made a bad one. A few examples of making *una brutta* (ugly) *figura* would be showing up to a dinner without a bottle of wine, or with a clearly cheap one when the occasion calls for something nice; tripping and falling; confusing someone's name, or forgetting it altogether; letting out a closely guarded secret; drinking too much; forgetting someone's birthday—basically the same sort of buffoonery that gets you into trouble anywhere else in the world.

Birthday parties, incidentally, have their own peculiar nuances. You, as the person celebrating your birthday, host the party, or maybe even buy the dinner at a restaurant. Gifts are almost always presented in public. As an American, you might consider it a little gauche if someone opens each of the presents in front of the invitees, but in Italy, this is standard operating procedure.

Outside of those sorts of celebrations, don't feel obliged to pick up the check at dinner if it was your idea. It's always a nice gesture, but Italians—young people, especially—will often decide to pay *alla romana* (the Roman way), which is to say everyone pays for themselves. Who knew the Romans were such cheapskates? In English jargon, it's usually the Dutch who are treated to this stereotype. (Guys, don't take this as an invitation to go *alla romana* on a date. You're usually expected to pick up the tab.)

Gender Roles

The divide between the sexes is still very deep in Italy. Men and women are different, and neither seems very disappointed in their role. Men are asked to be virile, confident, and aggressive in courting women, and women are expected to parry with coquettish nonchalance, inventing themselves as objects of impossible desire and undertaking all the burdens and privileges pertaining thereto.

Take the Miss Italia pageant, for example. Every September, it draws tens of millions of television viewers—the majority of them women, apparently, judging from the shampoo and skin-cream commercials. It attracts more viewers than almost any other televised event. In 2002, a contestant rose up against the establishment for the first time. She said that women were not objects to be judged, and that the inane questions asked of them were well beneath their intelligence. Silence. No one knew quite what to make of this irreverence, though the next day, a few observers applauded her for her pageant-ending performance. The next day, the judging resumed as usual, not a word more was spoken about it, and Miss Italia continues to be a teenage dream.

Italian women all over the peninsula are pushed to look stunning on a daily basis. The subways are filled with ads for diet programs that promise pounds lost by the week, skin creams that allegedly eliminate decades of aging, etc. Still, you will find very few women who would trade in their makeup for a flannel shirt and a pair of baggy pants. Sex appeal is an integral part of Italian culture on both sides of the gender divide. You won't find too many men with flannel shirts and baggy trousers either.

If you're single, be prepared for old-school courtship. You'll find flower vendors at every corner. Men use them frequently. They always hold doors open for women, call them on the phone regularly—though not too regularly, as the tightrope between interest and desperation is just as carefully walked in Italy as anywhere else in the world—and, on the whole, consider themselves to be pretty romantic guys. Apparently, they invented the term.

Italian women are not so easily convinced. They've been dealing with Italian men for a long time now, and they know every trick in the book. They are as savvy as they come. In turn, men have become even more crafty. Which means women have to be even quicker. Which came first, the wayward rooster or the pecking hen? Who knows? All that's certain is that the woman's hesitance and the man's devious strategies to overcome it create a vicious circle leading to a deep but intriguing distrust between the sexes. It may go some way toward explaining why Italian couples get married much later in life these days, usually well into their 30s. It most certainly explains why Italian men have such an affinity for foreigners.

The art of picking up, or *rimorchiare* (literally, "to tow," as in a car), an out-of-towner is as carefully studied as the deliberate strokes of Giotto's brush. The infamous stories about sweet-talking Romans on the Spanish Steps waiting for an innocent Northern European or American blonde to walk by are not at all apocryphal. They ring just as true today as they did back in the '50s, an era that spawned the "*rimorchio* generation," as one Italian-Scottish friend likes to refer to his parents.

Sometimes, though, the role-playing is no fun at all and borders on plain sexism. The grumbles about the half-naked TV hostesses of prime-time quiz shows—think a dozen or so teenaged Vanna Whites minus most of their clothing—reached a pitched roar in 2002, brought on by an incredulous foreign press and pushed over the edge by one particular show that actually kept the young woman in a glass cage under the contestants' table, with airholes cut out for her to breathe. The producers protested that the setup was meant to be ironic, poking fun at the sexism in other shows, but the damage was already done. The glass cage has since disappeared. The bikini-clad hostesses remain.

> *They say that the straightest line between two dots in Italy is a labyrinth. . . . In the end, though, you can't help but be pleased with the results. Good things are always worth waiting for.*

There was nothing ironic, however, in a court decision in the late 1990s that ruled a woman cannot claim to have been raped if she was wearing denim at the time, because jeans are so tight-fitting that getting them off requires the consent of the wearer. Women parliamentarians, led by Alessandra Mussolini (yes, *that* Mussolini; she's his granddaughter) protested en masse and brought international attention to the whole ugly affair. Yet, at the same time, it highlighted the fact that Italy does have quite a few influential women in politics—not representative of the number of Italian women, perhaps, but still a relatively high number, many of whom hold key ministerial posts. One post that is almost always held by a woman is head of the ministry for equal opportunity, a brief partly designed to increase women's role in public affairs. In the private sector, women are not nearly on equal footing with men, but the country does have its share of companies run by women, especially those who inherited large family firms.

Business Behavior

Making *una bella figura* is just as important in the business world as it is in dating. In fact, romance and business have a lot in common in Italy.

Both are full of countless phone calls and dinners, complicated strategies, and lofty promises that are hard to keep. Business deals are intimate affairs in Italy, built on a strong relationship. Potential partners need to get to know each other well in the lead-up to any agreement, just as an employer will want to know everything possible about an employee whom the company may be taking on for life, given the particularly tight labor laws that make firing someone nearly impossible.

On your first date, it would be rather unusual behavior to run down a list of things you expect out of your potential partner, talk through all the ins and outs of the relationship, and set a timetable for things to move forward. It's the same thing in Italian business. Don't expect to talk about any business at all in a restaurant or bar. There's enough work in the office, and anything that smacks of labor is best discussed there.

In fact, there's going to be a lot of work you never planned on, especially the endless faxes that accompany any simple request. Any seemingly straightforward transaction can drag on for months, because the rules of any deal in Italy are often made up as the parties go along. What was said on Wednesday may not be valid on Friday. People change their minds. It's not particularly efficient or reassuring, but it's human.

There will always be differences of opinion between two cultures on how best to get things done. You'll find that in any transaction, from a request for documents to larger projects like buying a house, there will be a million little details to be sorted out, and you'll throw up your hands and wonder why Italians just don't make life simpler for themselves. Think of it from their point of view. If they came to America on business, they'd laugh at how simple everything is, and wonder how anything gets done without the proper paperwork or in-depth discussion.

They say that the straightest line between two dots in Italy is a labyrinth. No issue is cut-and-dried, black and white. Italians are highly educated, artistic, and independent-minded people, which means that any decision given short shrift in other parts of the world—such as where to hang a painting—is going to take a very circuitous route in Italy. In the end, though, you can't help but be pleased with the results. Good things are always worth waiting for.

The Arts

Italians are crazy about cinema—movie theaters are just about the only place in the country where everyone shows up on time. The masters of the silver screen found an eager public that didn't seem to exist for fiction writers, at least not in the same numbers, in linguistically divided Italy. Though the country has its share of literati, there never seemed to be the same popular passion for theater and literature as is in, say, France or Russia.

That said, there are some very well known Italian authors. Much of the world has at least heard of the Renaissance authors Dante, Petrarch, and Boccaccio, and possibly have read works by Alessandro Manzoni, Italo Calvino, Primo Levi, Gabriele D'Anunzio, or Leonardo Sciascia, to name a handful. Contemporary Italian writers like Umberto Eco and Oriana Fellaci regularly make the *New York Times* best-seller lists. But the cultural treasures of Italy known far and wide are not its books, but its music, art, and architecture. Italians have contributed more to these fields than perhaps any other people throughout history.

> *The cultural treasures of Italy known far and wide are not its books, but its music, art, and architecture. Italians have contributed more to these fields than perhaps any other people throughout history.*

The first hint of Italy's influence on music is in the terminology: It's all in Italian. From the musicians' guilds of Rome to the composers of religious madrigals of the Middle Ages, and onward to the inventors of opera in the 17th century, Italians steered music's evolution for centuries and gave name to their innovations. Indeed, one of the perks of living in places like Venice, Padua, Milan, Parma, Bologna, and Rome is the opportunity to hear the works of composers like Verdi, Rossini, and Vivaldi in the very cities that inspired the music—and perhaps even played on Stradivarius violins, still proudly crafted in Cremona.

The Italians' flair for creativity manifests itself everywhere. In architecture, the Romans borrowed much from the Greeks, but made some very far-reaching improvements. For instance, they introduced a circular dimension to classic Greek colonnades, giving the world the arch—and, by extension, the vault and the dome. These became essential elements in the buildings of Christianity. Dating from the early Middle Ages, examples of this Romanesque style can be found in abundance in Ferrara, Florence, Lucca, Milan, Modena, Pisa, Pavia, and Venice, and, of course, in Rome itself. Some of the deepest impressions on the history of architecture, however, were made during Italy's Renaissance. Brunelleschi's dome in Florence, the ducal palace in Urbino by Luciano Laurana and Francesco di Giorgio, the ducal piazza of Vigevano by Donato Bramante—every Italian city, great and small, boasts at least one example of period architecture that is now closely studied around the world. The Baroque architecture of later generations—St. Peter's Square is the most obvious example—is also unequaled anywhere else.

© Monica Larner

Puppet in Taormina, Sicily

As an unpatriotic people, though, Italians have little need to propagandize these innovations as "inventions." They rightly point out that visionaries in every field, such as Galileo, Leonardo da Vinci, and Michelangelo, all drew on the work of predecessors in order to create their own works of genius. Even Giotto had something to start with, having closely studied the paintings of Cimabue and Pietro Cavallini. Still, most experts on the subject divide the history of painting into what came before Giotto and his frescoes in the Scrovegni Chapel in Padua, and what came afterward. Following in the 14th-century master's footsteps were legions of Italian painters who continued to define the Renaissance: Masaccio, Sandro Botticelli, Piero di Cosimo, Piero della Francesca, and the sculptors Donatello and Luca Della Robbia. That period of rediscovery yielded to the High Renaissance of the 15th century, which gave the world Leonardo's *Mona Lisa* and *Last Supper,* Michelangelo's *David* and *The Last Judgement,* Raphael's *The Alba Madonna* and *The School of Athens,* and the works of Titian and Tintoretto. They were followed by Caravaggio in the Baroque period of the early 17th century and Canaletto's Rococo style of the 18th century.

If, when bombarded by such terms in Italy, you ever find yourself confused by the styles or can't remember who came when, all you need to do is open an Italian newspaper or magazine or turn on TV at prime time, all of which carry nonstop art coverage. The fact that a famous art critic has his own show on television in Italy, and that people actually watch it—or that there exists such a thing as a famous art critic at all—should give you some indication of just how seriously Italians take their painting, sculpture, and architecture.

If everything in America sooner or later boils down to business, everything in Italy is an art. The shape of a coffee pot, the line of a car, the taste of a simple pasta, the finish of a wine, the way a waiter scoops up the bill, and the flair of a soccer player tapping a pass into the net are all flourishes appreciated and practiced by everyday Botticellis. In Italy, more than anywhere else, style and image are everything.

Planning Your Fact-Finding Trip

Unless you know Italy very well already, you'll need to visit the areas where you might be interested in living. More than one trip will be necessary. The country is only the size of Arizona, but as varied as the entire United States. There is an Italy that speaks German and eats speck and sauerkraut in the foothills of the Dolomites, and one that uses Arabic fishing methods in the southern Mediterranean. There are farming plains, vineyards, fishing communities on rocky coasts, villages clinging to volcanoes, and Alpine fields and valleys. Italy even claims its own "Wild West," with rodeos and lots of beef, in the Maremma area of Tuscany.

Centuries of foreign occupations have left a mosaic of cultures with different values and priorities. You feel like you've just traveled to another country when you leave your office in Turin or Milan for a weekend in Bari or Palermo. The differences between the North and South are profound, and you'll only know which lifestyle suits you better after you've spend some time in each.

Reading English-language media about Italian current events and culture is one way to take the pulse of the country you're about to call home.

Mostly, though, the decision on where to live in Italy will be narrowed down by what sort of work you do, if you work at all, and how much you can afford to spend. If you're a career person, chances are you'll need to make your home in or near one of the major cities. If you plan to open a bed-and-breakfast, you'll likely look for more bucolic settings where tourism flourishes. Entrepreneurs often feel more comfortable with the North, where the work ethic is assumed to be higher. If you're a student, you'll be confined to cities with a university program—for foreigners, this often means Padua, Bologna, Siena, Perugia, and above all, Florence.

If you're retired, well, you've earned the right to live just about anywhere you please, though it is a smart idea for homeowners of all walks of life to live somewhere near basic services, such as schools, hospitals, train stations, and airports. The dream of a country retreat can turn into a nightmare if the house is more than an hour from the nearest supermarket.

An initial fact-finding trip is a good time to check out the price of homes or apartments, meet professional contacts and potential employers (or examine the market for your business idea), and, hopefully, brush up on your language skills.

Reading English-language media about Italian current events and culture is one way to take the pulse of the country you're about to call home. Before arriving, scour maps, cookbooks, and guidebooks and read as much as possible on the art and history of the place—you won't know what you're looking at in Italy unless you know the past. (See Chapter 2, History, for a brief overview; and see the Resources section at the back of the book for additional suggested reading.)

Preparing to Leave

Traveling to Italy in this day and age couldn't be much easier. There are several direct flights per week from the U.S. to Rome and Milan and lots of connecting services to other cities. Plus, there is an ever-broadening field of new low-fare airlines that fly from several European cities to small Italian airports.

For European Union countries that adhere to the Schengen agreement, such as Italy, there are essentially no visa requirements for Americans staying fewer than 90 days (see Chapter 5, Making the Move). The only health issue is making sure your insurance covers you overseas—Medicare will not (see Chapter 7, Health). Customs regulations are no stricter than they are in the

United States—in fact, they are more lenient in many respects. After about a dozen flights to Italy, I've never actually had my suitcase checked by customs, and one time in Rome, I don't think they even checked my passport after a flight from Boston. One might assume that this has changed in a post–September 11 world, but for better or worse, it hasn't changed much in Italy. Just remember not to bring in perishable food items or huge stacks of currency.

CURRENCY

Everyone has their own theory on the best way to bring money abroad, ranging from traveler's checks to stacks of greenbacks, but if you're the type of person that likes to rely on credit cards and ATMs, rest assured there are loads of bank machines in Italy, even in the smallest towns.

A few warnings, however. Many ATMs go offline at midnight, and often the international line falls for a few hours. It's not a foolproof system. It's a good idea to get a fresh card before any long trip overseas, in case the old one is almost demagnetized.

Check with your bank to make sure that the card can be used abroad. New ones have to be activated at your own bank first, and some personal identification numbers (PINs) won't work overseas. (By the way, don't rely on letters on the keyboard to remember your PIN; some European ATMs have only numbers on the keys.)

Still, the ATM and credit card combination is arguably the best strategy. Traveler's checks are not common outside the major tourist destinations—and you will likely be looking off the beaten path for some of the best that Italy has to offer—and moving around any country with piles of dollars is never a sound plan. Stealing tourists' valuables is still a booming industry in many cities, especially Rome and Naples. The name of the game is avoiding commissions, which are high at currency exchange booths. These booths don't offer very good exchange rates, anyway. It is true that using ATMs means paying the standard fee every time you withdraw, but €1 ($1.30) or €2 ($2.60) out of a €250 ($325) withdrawal is still better than the exchangers' commissions, and you'll be getting a much better rate with your card. Throughout this book, prices are calculated at the press-time exchange rate of $1.30 per €1. For a more complete look at banking in Italy, see Banking in the Finance chapter.

WHAT TO PACK

You will need plug adapters for all of your American electronics. For any large appliance, such as a printer or a blender, you should have a 110- to 240-volt transformer. Your laptop and other commonly portable devices should already come with one.

Remember that video cassettes and DVDs are on different systems in Europe. VCRs in Europe run on PAL, or Phase Alternating Line, not the American-style NTSC, or National Television System Committee. (Italian camera operators, who swear that PAL offers more consistent quality, joke that NTSC should stand for Never Twice the Same Color.) Media companies have also set up separate DVD codes in Europe to prevent sneak previews of movies not yet released overseas. If your computer has a DVD player, be warned that you will be able to switch back and forth between European and American systems only a few times, and then the computer will experience problems.

By all means, buy any accessories for your computer or digital camera before you leave; not only are they more expensive in Italy, but many brands are not as common here, and stores may not have what you're looking for. Also, pick up any American software before you leave, unless you want the Italian-language version.

Other items that you should bring along for any extended stay include: tax documents, if you're traveling in the filing season (though the U.S. Embassy and Consulates have all the necessary forms); a résumé and any letters of recommendation; and be sure to tuck a photocopy of your passport in a separate suitcase in case the original is lost or stolen. It's hard to get a replacement without the copy.

Packing a load of aspirin is a good idea, since it can only be bought at pharmacies, as well as any prescription medication you may need. Other than that, the toiletry aisle of an Italian supermarket looks almost identical to one in the States.

Dressing for the Weather

Depending on the time of year, packing clothes for Italy can be simple or very tricky. There are dozens of different climates that have their own weather patterns in different seasons. The only constants are that the Alps are very cold in the winter, and everywhere else is torrid in the summer. Especially in the North, the humidity can be suffocating. Rains there come like clockwork in early September and mid-November, and you can count on a snowstorm or two just after Christmas.

In the center and the South, you can usually get away with just a lightweight jacket in the spring and fall, and make sure to bring very light clothes for the summer. Except maybe during the week in early August, when the heat is absolutely dizzying, Italian men never wear shorts in the city. If you think it's important to fit in, bring along some light linen pants and a few dress shirts that breathe.

WHEN TO GO

Any experienced Italophile will tell you that late spring is the best time to visit. For Naples, Rome, Florence, Venice, and Milan, this is probably true. All of those places can be rainy in the fall, and summer, in my opinion, is out of the question.

But the harsh reality is that most people can only take time off in July and August, and if it's their first time here, they want to see the major attractions. The trouble is that not only is every other American, Japanese, Australian, and German tourist here in the summer, but all of the Italians are on vacation, too, and many of the shops and cafés are closed. If you must come in the summer, it's best to avoid the cities and head straight to the sea or the mountains. And book your hotels months in advance.

You will get much more out of your first stay in Italy if you come during the off-season. Every region has its own identity that expresses itself best in a particular time of year.

Early fall: Piedmont and Tuscany. These are the major winemaking regions, and if you want to taste Nobile di Montepulciano and Barolo, it's always nice to visit the vineyards when the grapes are still on the vine. Conveniently, it's also truffle- and mushroom-hunting season in these regions, and a time to gather chestnuts.

Late fall: Milan and Emilia-Romagna. This is when the *piadine* (roll-up) sandwiches and salads yield to the hearty, trademark dishes of the Po River plain: prosciutto and *culatello* (a prosciutto delicacy), followed by tortellini and ravioli with red Lambrusco wine. Universities are in session, which means a lively atmosphere. Emilia, Bologna especially, is said to have the highest standard of living in Italy, and also tops the charts for the percentage of people that leave in the summer, when it is a ghost town.

Most importantly, business is in full swing in the fall. To understand the glamorous reputation of Milan, you should see it when people return tanned and relaxed from summer vacation, the fashion models start

National Holidays

January 1: New Year's Day	August 15: Feast of the Assumption
January 6: Epiphany	November 1: All Saints' Day
March/April: Easter Monday	December 8: Feast of the
April 25: Liberation Day	Immaculate Conception
May 1: Labor Day	December 25: Christmas Day
June 2: Anniversary of the	December 26: St. Steven's Day
Founding of the Republic	

to arrive, and the beautiful people put on parties. You might want to check out the calendar on the trade fair's website, www.fieramilano.it, to see when the fashion and design shows are. (Usually, the Salone del Mobile design fair begins in April, while the women's fashion shows are in late September and late February.) Conversely, you should stay away during those dates if you haven't yet booked a hotel. The best restaurants also fill up quickly.

Winter: Turin, Veneto, and Alto-Adige. The Dolomites need to be seen in the snow. If Easter should be done in Rome, Christmas should be done in Trento, in a frosty town with Alpine scenery and heavy meals. Plus, the skiing at Madonna del Campiglio and Cortina d'Ampezzo is some of the best in Italy.

Spring: Everywhere else. Rome, Florence, and Naples are fine to visit in the fall, but are at their peak in the spring. So are the Cinque Terre area of Liguria and the lakes region of Lombardy, both of which are in full bloom and enjoy perfect weather. The same is true for almost any pastoral area, especially Abruzzo and Umbria, which holds its cherry festival just after the winter.

Every region hosts hundreds of festivals and events throughout the year (a good database of them is at www.hosteler.net). Many are held in the summer—most notably, Spoleto's music festival in June, and the Umbria Jazz Festival and the Palio of Siena in July—either for historical reasons or to dovetail with the tourist influx. Others, such as the Venice Film Festival in late August or early September, are timed to let the tourists get out first.

If, on your first trip, you've chosen a region and are reasonably sure this is where you'd like to live, it's always best to come a second time in a different season. You may have fallen in love with the Puglia or the Italian Riviera during your stay in July, but do you realize how lonely it can get there in the winter? Like all resorts, the Italian lakes and coastlines are buzzing with festivals and activities in the summer, but it's all downhill from there.

Northern cities like Milan may seem an ideal choice for urbanites, with their swank shops, cafés, and cosmopolitan population, but most of this disappears in July and August, when the humidity and mosquitoes descend. Similarly, Venice—a.k.a. "la Serenissima"—is indeed the most serene and romantic city in the world in the off-season, but feels more like Disneyland when the tourists start arriving in May.

A city or region that was off-putting on your first trip might take on redeeming qualities if you come back in a different season. You should try short-term rentals in a few places in various months before starting an earnest search for a house.

Again, keep in mind that you won't be able to get much real estate business done in the summer. In other seasons, a three-day weekend in Italy can magically turn into a week, so don't plan to reach agents or even homeowners in the periods around Christmas, New Year's Day, and Easter.

Arriving in Italy

PUBLIC TRANSPORTATION

It would be nice if we could take Europe's network of public transportation and make it work in the United States, but the distances between cities usually make it more convenient to fly. Distances in Italy are small by comparison. It sometimes makes more sense to board a train in Rome's city center and get off in the center of Milan four and a half hours later than it does to get to Rome's airport 45 minutes out of town, board a plane 30 minutes later, take an hour's flight to Milan's Malpensa airport, and end up in the city center maybe an hour after that.

If you plan to visit cities and medium-sized towns on your initial trip, you should plan to take the train. The railways go nearly everywhere and are relatively cheap. There is also always a reliable, though not always timely, network of buses.

Getting to the countryside to visit farmhouses is another story. For that, you'll need a car. Renting one in Italy is just as easy as in the United States, but if you're coming during tourist season, reserve well in advance. Agencies can sell out quickly, especially on the Ferragosto weekend starting August 15. If you're traveling in the winter, be sure to reserve chains also. There seems to be a short supply of these at rental companies, but chains are essential on wintry mountain roads. Actually, they are required by law.

Planes, trains, and automobiles are discussed in more detail in the Travel and Transportation chapter.

Sample Itineraries

To get some feel for an area of Italy and squeeze it all into a two-week stay, you will need to concentrate on either the North, the Center, or the South. Two weeks may be all the vacation time you have, but it is time well spent, considering that you hope to move here one day. The following sample itineraries for the North and Central regions are meant to illustrate just how much you would need to pack into a 14-day stay.

You will be spending a lot of time in the car, but if you hope to see enough countryside to get a feel for what the homes are like, there is really not much of an alternative. The best solution would be to double the time of your stay, and spend an extra day in each town or city. The goal of such a fact-finding trip is to see enough of the country to pinpoint a location where you can eventually plan a short-term rental.

THE NORTH
Suggested seasons: Early fall or late spring

Arrive in Milan via Malpensa Airport
Milan is a tourist's gateway to Northern Italy and a place to make money and spend it. Shopping will top the list of things to do, though there are a few must-see attractions: Leonardo's *The Last Supper* (which requires a reservation, so book ahead of time); the Pinacoteca di Brera, the city's best-known art museum; the Castello Sforzesco, the 15th-century castle; and, of course, the 14th-century Duomo, the third-largest cathedral in the world. The Palazzo Reale next door often has great art exhibits, and nearby is La Scala, Italy's premier opera house. If you're here during design week, you should stop by the Triennale contemporary art museum; or if it's fashion week, blend into the glamour on Via della Spiga and Via Monte Napoleone.

Lago di Como (Lake Como)
Just an hour's drive from Milan, this is where the Milanese come to unwind. The deepest lake in Europe, and maybe its most scenic, it flaunts opulent villas around Cernobbio, Bellagio, Menaggio, and Tremezzo, and tempers its materialism with nature trails leading to the Swiss border.

Lago Maggiore (Lake Maggiore)
The western shore and the island of Stresa are the hottest spots.

Turin
As an industrial powerhouse and home of the carmaker Fiat, Turin has a gritty reputation, but remember that it was once home to the king of Italy, and the historic center is still just as regal as it was in the 19th century. Aside from the royal palace, Turin's most famous attraction is the shroud, a relic that is said to bear the imprint of Christ's face, and the film museum under the unmistakable spire of the Mole is an up-and-coming destination.

Asti, Alba, and Le Langhe
Heard of Asti Spumanti? This is the part of Piedmont where some of

Italy's most celebrated wines are made, especially in Asti, Barolo, and Barbaresco, in the hills just southeast of Turin. The Barbera, Dolcetto, and Nebbiolo grapes have their origins here. Take a break from sightseeing to wine and dine your palate.

The Riviera di Levante

The stretch of coastline between Genoa and the Tuscan border has some of Italy's most spectacular maritime surroundings. Portofino welcomes celebrities and their yachts. Nearby Camogli is a more humble fishing village but every bit as colorful. The Cinque Terre has become a mainstay on the classic American tour of Italy, thanks to panoramic hikes connecting the five tranquil villages; and Lord Byron preferred Portovenere, taking midnight swims across the Gulf of Poets to Lerici for inspiration.

Parma and Modena

These two cities make up the culinary heart of Northern Italy, known worldwide for their prosciutto and balsamic vinegar, respectively, and for the local pastamaking giant, Barilla. Opera also has deep roots here. Giuseppe Verdi was born near Parma, and Luciano Pavarotti hails from Modena.

Bologna

If you missed dinner in Parma, you won't be disappointed in Bologna, with its tortellini, green ravioli, truffles, and more. This is known as the wealthiest city in Italy, and the most progressive—it boasted the longest-standing Communist mayor—due in no small part to its university, which is among the oldest in Europe.

Ferrara

Here's a city you probably never gave much thought to, but it happens to have a wealthier history than many of its better-known neighbors, and the standard of living in the hometown of Lamborghini sports cars is second to none. Bicycle paths intertwine through the city center, past a beautiful cathedral and moated castle, and onward to the banks of the Po.

Venice

Aside from the usual stops at Rialto and St. Mark's Square, be sure to visit some of the smaller islands in the lagoon, and some of Venice's quieter *quartes*, such as the Ghetto and Cannareggio.

Padua, Verona, and Bergamo

The road from Venice back to Milan is spotted with some of Italy's most livable cities and fine works of art: the Scrovegni chapel of Padua and its recently restored frescoes by Giotto; Verona, fictional home to Romeo and Juliet and quite factually the home of Italy's second-largest coliseum. Bergamo might be one of the most overlooked artistic treasures of northern Italy, because it is so overshadowed by Milan. The province gave birth to Caravaggio (like many of his era, the artist took his name from the town where he was born), and the walled city holds what architects and art historians have described as the perfect central square.

THE CENTER
Suggested seasons: Early fall, late spring, or summer

Arrive in Rome via Fiumicino Airport

You could stay a month and not see everything here in the cradle of Western civilization.

Stroll through Piazza Navona and the Pantheon, past the Trevi Fountain, the Roman Forum, the Campus Martius, and the Colosseum. Next door to that, make reservations for the following day to visit the recently opened Domus Aurea, Nero's underground palace. Have dinner at an outdoor restaurant in Trastevere, Testaccio, or near the Campo dei' Fiori, all of which have a number of open-air cafés for a drink before getting to bed early to avoid jet lag. You could stay a month and not see everything here in the cradle of Western civilization, but at least make time to visit the Vatican Museums before you head north into the country.

Terni, Todi, and Orvieto
Here at the crossroads of Lazio, Umbria, and Tuscany, and in the heart of the Etruscan homeland, you can still find good values on a rustic farmhouse near the more fabled and haughty district of Chianti. Todi is already overpriced, but certainly worth a look around. Orvieto, nearby, is home to a pleasant white wine and boasts one of the more remarkable cathedrals in all of Italy. Terni is not as well endowed architecturally, but has a distinct identity as the birthplace of St. Valentine and is spotted with country homes just a 40-minute train ride from Rome.

Montepulciano, Siena, and Chianti
This is the Italian wine country you've dreamed about, and as clichéd as Chianti tends to be, it never ceases to amaze. If you're a cyclist, the best way to visit this area is by bike, with challenging hills and leisurely freewheeling through the grape leaves. Montepulciano as a town, with its postcard shops and torture museum, might be given a miss (unless of course,

you desperately need film or postcards) to give yourself more time to explore the vineyards. Chianti, too, is all about finding a nice place to have lunch and sip the local products. Unless you have great expectations and an even larger bank account, real-estate shopping here can be done from the car window with a heavy dose of imagination. In Siena, bring your camera—especially if you're here for the Palio in early July—and your appetite. There are some great trattorias here to sample the fruits of the Tuscan countryside. Fortunate American students often find themselves at programs here, and if they ever want to leave, it's only because the area can be very quiet after dark.

Florence

Aside from the usual stops—the Duomo, the Accademia and the Uffizi museums—be sure to take a stroll through the neighborhood of Santa Croce.

Arezzo and Cortona

Arezzo has long been known as the little sister that Florence loved to smack around during the Guelf and Ghibelline wars, and if Arezzo had won, foreign students might now be flocking there for its architecture instead. It is still an impressive city of art, with some of the finest works by Piero della Francesca. It is also the nation's best antiques market, and has enjoyed newfound fame as the backdrop for Roberto Benigni's film *Life is Beautiful.* Between Arezzo and Cortona are hills full of magical country homes, including the one Frances Mayes wrote about in her memoir *Under the Tuscan Sun.* Lose yourself in relaxing olive groves and wonder why you didn't move here earlier.

Perugia

Two things immediately come to mind when this city is mentioned—the university for foreigners, and Perugina chocolates (e.g., the Baci). Even if you miss the city's chocolate festival, you can still enjoy its looming papal fortress and works by native sons Perugino and Pinturicchio.

Jesi, Castelfidardo, Macerata

In short, Le Marche. The region advertises heavily to attract some of Tuscany's tourist dollars toward the Adriatic. Potential homeowners don't need the pitch. They've been scouring the towns around Fabriano and Jesi for some time now, and have come up with bargains. The stretch of Adriatic may offer a refreshing dip in the hotter months, but not much else: It's simply the fastest way to go south and then back inland toward Assisi.

Assisi

This town's role as an integral stop on any Christian pilgrimage is indebted entirely to St. Francis, the wandering minstrel and self-styled monk, founder of a monastic order, protector of animals, and champion of the poor for whom the Basilica di San Francesco was built. It is indeed not to be missed on any trip to Italy. Its ceiling was toppled by an earthquake in 1997, but has slowly been rebuilt. On your way back to Rome, stop off in Spoleto. If you're traveling between June and July, you are practically obliged to see the town's Festival dei Due Mondi, considered the nation's most important performing arts festival. Otherwise, it is still one of the peninsula's most spectacular medieval hilltowns, topped by a six-towered castle.

Accommodations

There are loads of interesting options for accommodation in Italy, ranging from short-term rentals to bed-and-breakfasts to *agriturismi* (see below) to five-star hotels, and there are almost as many publications that suggest the best ones. Guidebooks are a popular option, but remember that each listing usually only represents what the authors managed to scrape together in their short stay. The most complete guides, in my opinion, are ones from the Touring Club Italiano (www.touringclub.it), a nonprofit group that has been scouring the country for the finest hotels and restaurants for decades. The only hitch is that many of their publications and their website are in Italian only.

A good alternative to guidebooks is to go to the area's APT tourist board's website, which has links to just about every hotel, campground, and bed-and-breakfast in the vicinity. This is the most democratic method, but there are no filters for what may turn out to be a dive.

Once upon a time, traveling in Italy was a lot more adventurous, especially in the South, where there were no real hotels to speak of. When the state put the first highway through Campania and Calabria in the 1960s, it also sponsored the construction of Jolly Hotels, a brand found all over the peninsula today. Just about every other chain is present in Italy, as well as luxury hotel associations such as Romantik Hotels and Compagnia Grandi Alberghi, which guarantee an opulent stay in family-run resorts, not cookie-cutter chains, for a not insignificant price.

A step below the *albergo* is the *pensione,* usually similar in quality to a two-star hotel, and then there is the *affitacamera,* or room rental. These are most common in budding tourist spots with insufficient beds in the summer. Room rentals can be a risk, but usually make budget travelers very happy.

The two relatively new entries in the world of Italian accommodation are the *agriturismo,* a family-run farm that serves home-grown produce and has a few rooms for rent, and the bed-and-breakfast, a category that exploded in the runup to the 2000 Jubilee Year in Rome, when the city reached out to residents to carve out accommodation for the expected hordes. The *agriturismo* is certainly the rage these days with American travelers, and for good reason. The food will be authentic (if rustic), the rooms cozy, and the price reasonable. For more information about *agriturismi,* check with the national organization Agriturist at www.agriturist.it.

The final options are monasteries and convents. Pilgrims are often welcome to stay in them for a nominal fee, and the experience sometimes involves prayer and meditation. If you feel more religious than usual when visiting Rome, you can forget about the free accommodation. Some church-run residences around the Vatican now cost upwards of €100 ($130) per night.

Daily Life

Making the Move

When planning a move to Italy, the first thing to pack is patience. Navigating the local culture is going to take time. The good news from the bureaucratic front, however, is that recent laws have streamlined at least part of the paperwork. For example, Italian employees no longer need to have what was known as a *libretto di lavoro* (work card) to be hired. It was deemed redundant as of January 2003, and is now a thing of the past. The bad news is that those same laws, drawn up in part by the immigrant-unfriendly Northern League, have tightened restrictions on foreigners. For example, Italy now requires fingerprints for all non-EU citizens—Americans, Senegalese, Norwegians, etc.—when they sign up for a stay permit. Especially after the events of September 11, 2001, authorities have become more serious about stamping out illegals. One of the latest suggestions to hit the streets is an ID card with a magnetic strip that houses all kinds of personal information, from criminal records to residency status.

Once upon a time, lots of Americans lived in Italy for long periods of time

If you think it would be a lot more convenient just to become an Italian citizen, you are in luck if you have an Italian grandfather and you were born after 1947.

without ever announcing their presence. It's illegal, but it happens, and in all candor, Italians are much less worried about Americans overstaying their welcome then other nationals from outside the EU. Don't take this as an open-ended invitation. I have seen at least one American forcibly sent packing after her illegally procured job as a tour leader in Rome marched her past a group of policemen, who were paying unusually close attention to immigration laws that day. The penalties for overstaying your visa have become harsher, and you'd only be doing yourself a disservice by ignoring them in the long run. Once you've hacked through the bureaucracy, including multiple trips to the consulate, you will have many more freedoms and benefits than those who preferred to risk it and lived their lives in near-paranoia.

If you think it would be a lot more convenient just to become an Italian citizen, you are in luck if you have an Italian grandfather and you were born after 1947. Otherwise, you can qualify are if you are married to an Italian, have Italian parents, or have lived in Italy legally for more than 10 years.

In the end, remember that mastering Italian bureaucracy is a lifelong pursuit. (Many have even turned it into a career.) You will constantly have questions about the fine print of laws on permits, visas, and residency, and will need to keep abreast of changes. There are a number of resources that can help you. The best one I have found to date is *The Informer* website, www.informer.it.

Red Tape

VISAS

All 15 signatory countries of the Schengen agreement, which includes Italy, allow U.S. residents to circulate freely within their borders for a maximum of 90 days at a time. If your vacation fits into that category, all you need are a passport and a plane ticket. But Italy still has its own immigration laws, and even those Americans planning to stay for as little as two weeks are required, in theory, to apply for a stay visa within eight days of their arrival. Few people bother with the formalities. There are literally millions of Americans who come every year for two-week vacations in Italy with no paperwork other than a passport.

If you're planning a six-month vacation, you should consider the short-stay permit. A three-month permit can be renewed for an additional three months. But beyond six months, you are required to apply for a long-stay permit in Italy, the infamous *permesso di soggiorno.* Before you can apply for your *permesso,* you will need to have obtained the appropriate visa from the Italian Embassy or local consulate in the United States. There are weeks, perhaps months, of footwork on that front to be done at home before you leave. Some cases have been known to drag on for more than a year.

There are 12 types of visas in all, ranging from airport transit to sports-related, some easier to obtain than others. Americans looking to live, study, or work in Italy are most likely to apply for one of three types: a residency visa, a student visa, or a work visa. Different documentation is required for each, so check with your local consulate or the Italian Embassy's website (www.italyemb.org) before you make an appointment. All visas will require a passport valid for at least three months past your application date.

Student Visa

Student visas are relatively easily obtained, provided you have been accepted to an Italian or Italy-based university and can provide proof of financial independence during that stay. Many American-sponsored programs will handle your visa requirements for you.

At last count, there were more than 360 American programs in Italy, and other Italian universities meant for foreigners. The best known among the latter are the Università per Stranieri in Perugia, and the programs in Siena and Urbino.

If your program is more self-styled, you'll need to do the paperwork yourself. Be sure to bring to the embassy or consulate a letter of acceptance to an Italian university, proof of health insurance, and bank account information (it can be your parents' account) that shows you have enough money to live on once you're there.

Residency Visa

Residency visas also require proof of independent income. It is, in fact, the operating principle behind this kind of visa, which does not allow you to work in Italy. You must prove that you have enough money to support yourself through the length of your stay, independent of any salaries you may be receiving at the moment. You also need to show either ownership of a home in Italy or a rental agreement. Plus, you will be asked to provide your criminal record, or proof of lack thereof. This can be tricky if you don't have a record, which, of course, is what the authorities are hoping for in the first place—thus creating a Catch-22 with no immediate solution.

Family Visa

The family visa is for immediate family (spouse and/or children) of someone already working legally in Italy. If that person is an EU resident, the paperwork is quick: All you need is a letter from your spouse and the marriage certificate. You will also need a *nulla osta* ("no obstacle") document from the local police headquarters if your spouse is a not an EU resident but legally working there, plus any children's birth certificates if they are coming, too.

If, on the other hand, your spouse is still in the process of obtaining a work permit, you will need additional paperwork, such as proof of suitable family housing. In general, it is always easier applying for such residency once your family member has the job.

Work Visa

The work visa is the most difficult to obtain. It is divided into three sub-categories for the following types of applicants:

- performing arts work: for musicians in a planned concert series, actors in a planned film, etc.
- dependent work: for those employed and paid by an Italian company
- independent work: for freelancers, such as programmers and consultants

There are a limited number of such independent work visas afforded to Americans every year, and experience has shown that they disappear within a few hours after the quota is announced. The major challenge in landing a work visa is that you must have letters from the company saying it intends to hire you, or else bring you on as a consultant. This would be an unusual windfall for someone not already living in Italy.

In order to solve this paradox, many Americans arrange job contacts while on shorter vacations in Italy, and then fly back to the U.S. to straighten out their visas. Keep in mind that you should not overstay your three-month visit or your renewed six-month permit to be successful with this approach. For even more time, some people choose to sign up for a bona fide course in Italy, and then apply for a student visa. Many people manage to parlay the student permit into a work permit once the course is over.

Again, finding an employer who is willing to file the paperwork for an American has become more difficult recently, as there are new quotas set for foreigners allowed to fill Italian jobs. If you manage to qualify, you need to have your employer send the Labor Ministry a letter that says the company intends to hire you. When that has been approved, the Ministry will issue a *nulla osta* document to police headquarters. The company will also send you a work contract to present to the embassy or consulate, along with proof of Ministry approval, for your visa.

PERMITS

Again, only after you have the visa and are in Italy do you apply for the corresponding *permesso di soggiorno.* For student visas, you apply for the *permesso di soggiorno per studio;* the *permesso di soggiorno per dimora* is for those with a residency visa; and the *permesso di soggiorno per lavoro* is for those with a work visa.

All of the permits are obtained at the local *questura* (police headquarters). There, you will be asked to fill out an application, which includes three passport photographs plus a *marca di bollo* (a sort of administrative tax stamp available at the post office). You will also need some proof of health insurance.

If you are applying for a residency permit or student permit, the bureaucracy ends there. In the case of the work permit, upon presenting your visa, police headquarters will provide you with an interim work permit that is good for 90 days. In the meantime, acquire a *codice fiscale* (tax ID number), which you can do at the *ufficio delle imposte dirette* (local tax authority), to be found in the town's municipal buildings. It is an important card, as you will also need it for all kinds of purchases, such as a cell phone, a car, or a moped, and when opening a bank account. The documents you will need to show for the *codice fiscale* are limited to a passport and sometimes a stay permit, although many Americans are not asked for the latter, especially in small towns. The card will then be sent to you by mail.

The final step is to present your signed work contract to the local employment office, the Ispettorato Provinciale di Lavoro, for final approval of your application. (Ironically, that office represents the Labor Ministry, which issued the "no obstacle" document in the first place.) Once you have all those documents—the temporary permit, the *codice fiscale,* and the approval of the labor office—the *questura* will then award your efforts with the *permesso di lavoro,* available in two-year or five-year permits, or else the time period specified on your work contract, if any.

If you lose your job before the permit expires, you will need to find another one quickly. Recently passed legislation now gives employees just six months to land another job, or else the permit becomes void, whereas previously they could ride out its duration.

There is a legal alternative to the job hunt if you care for more time, though it's not entirely convenient. Once your work permit is up, you can apply as an independent worker for the *permesso di soggiorno per lavoro indipendente,* provided you have all the necessary skills.

Expat Profile:
The Importance of Being Hemingway

Like many American expatriates in Italy, he lives a life of anonymity, dividing his time between teaching English and doing translations. But what makes John Patrick Hemingway stand out from the crowd is his weighty surname. He is the grandson of Ernest, one of the 20th century's greatest writers.

Living in a modest apartment on Viale Monza in Milan, John does his best to stay out of the public eye. He shrugs off the coincidence that he lives in the same city where his grandfather convalesced from an injury sustained while serving as an ambulance worker in World War I.

Milan is the setting of a number of Ernest's writings, such as *In Another Country* and *A Farewell to Arms,* the latter of which describes a romance between a wounded soldier and a nurse. John scoffs at the coincidence that he is now married to a nurse. The two lives intertwine with uncanny similarities, but the last name John shares with his grandfather is no simple twist of fate. It is a constant reminder of the expectations he is asked to live up to.

Born in Miami, John is the son of Gregory Hemingway, the third son of Ernest's failed marriage to Pauline Pfeiffer. John came to Milan in 1984 after graduating from the University of California at Los Angeles. Two years later, he married his Canadian-born wife, Ornella, in Milan. In 1997, they had a son, and in 2003, a daughter.

On the side, almost clandestinely, he has penned short stories that have never seen the light of day. "It's a lottery of sorts," he says. "Certainly the name helps. With the stack of manuscripts on publisher's desks, it helps you get looked at as an author."

But for John, the surname is a bit like the marlin in *The Old Man and the Sea.* While it could land him professional fortune if he made the right moves, sometimes he thinks it would be easier to just cut this weighty inheritance free. "People are going to compare you to your grandfather, and obviously you're not going to come out looking very good in the comparison," he says. "You could be a very good writer, but it's unlikely you're going to become one of the greatest writers of the century."

Italy has provided something of a refuge from the fame and the infamy, he says. Although Italians place enormous emphasis on family ties and revere "Papa" Hemingway's works, they are more polite when approaching John about it than are people in America. Still, the subject comes up over and over again. "I try to explain this to people: I am I and he is he. You've got to concentrate on being your own person," he says. "Everyone's destiny is unique."

Moving with Children

The thought of moving to another country with children can be daunting, but thousands of foreign couples raise their families in Italy and usually have positive things to say about the experience. Public education is very good, recreational opportunities abound, and most of all, family—and children in particular—is the number-one priority for Italians. Kids will never want for attention.

SCHOOLS

Public schools are often at their best at the first two levels: the *scuola materna,* for three to five-year-olds, and elementary school, which in Italy runs from first to fifth grade. Elementary school students commonly study Greek and Latin, while recent reforms have made English and computer classes compulsory. In general, parents feel that students start to receive less attention as they progress into *scuola media* (middle school), *liceo* (high school), and beyond, culminating in a university system where professors are rarely found in class, much less available for counseling.

Private schools are not necessarily the best place to send a gifted student. Run for the most part by religious orders, they tend to cater to those with short attention spans or disciplinary problems. That said, there are a number of private schools with highly regarded curricula, where a top-flight education costs top dollar.

The third possibility is a private English-language school, which is a very popular option among expatriates and Italian families alike. There are British, American, and international schools in the major cities, some with better reputations than others. (A comprehensive listing of those schools is available in the English yellow pages at www.intoitaly.it.) One occasional lament from parents, however, is that there are so many Italian students in these academies that classes can sometimes move slowly to accommodate non-native speakers.

The most trying period for parents in Italy will usually coincide with their children's toddler years. There are almost always waiting lists to enroll your child into a public nursery school, and so candidates are assigned priority by a points system. It takes into consideration your financial status, your occupation, and whether there is a grandmother at home to watch over the kids, among other things.

For this reason, private nursery schools are also in high demand, and many middle-class or upper-middle-class families will find that a private nursery school tuition will cost the same as public one; count on about €400 ($520) per month. Naturally, the price increases the longer your child stays though the afternoon, though some mothers and fathers find that the money spent for the post-nap activities is a preferable alternative to babysitters.

DOMESTIC HELP

Many working couples and single parents rely on foreign au pairs, as a lot of them are native English-speakers themselves. Luckily for those young women, there are international standards for how much they are paid and what they are expected to do at the home. Those that live with the families can expect a monthly stipend of about €450 ($585), their working hours are limited to a half day, and they should not be asked to do any cleaning unless there is a specific agreement about such chores.

A housekeeper, on the other hand, will often charge somewhere around €750 ($975) per month. Because most of the housekeepers are also foreign women, often from the Philippines or Eastern Europe, the authorities keep a close eye on the sector for illegal immigration. Those found hiring illegal help can now face fines of up to €5,000 ($6,500). There are an estimated 100,000 immigrant women working as housekeepers in Italy, and polls show that about three percent of Italian children are raised by an immigrant nanny.

Moving with Pets

There are no visa restrictions on pets, but they will be expected to have a clean bill of health from the vet and have had a rabies shot between one month and 12 months before departure.

Cat owners will find kindred sprits in Rome, a city where felines roam free and have a fan club of so-called *gattare* looking after their needs. In fact, you might even consider adopting one of the many stray cats, making a furry friend and helping to solve a growing problem at the same time. There are also many stray dogs in Italy, but those lucky enough to have owners enjoy a pampering unlike anywhere else in the world. In the cities, they are paraded around in small jackets and occasionally hats, carted here and there on subways and to those restaurants that accept them, of which there are many. Pet owners in Rome have even founded what they call "Bow Wow Beach," where canines frolic with their ilk and splash out the dog days of summer in the Mediterranean waves.

It is paradise for those puppies lucky enough to live in the countryside, but bringing a dog to Italy may not be a wise idea for those planning to live in a city. For one thing, police have started handing out long-overdue fines to dog owners who don't clean up after Pippo on the street. More importantly, many apartment buildings have laws against keeping pets, which could restrict your options drastically in what has lately been a seller's market in Rome and Milan.

What to Take

So, what should you take to Italy? The best answer: as little as possible. Shipping large and heavy things like furniture will be very expensive. Pound for pound, it can cost about as much as an airline ticket for a human being. For example, shipping a standard UPS Worldwide Express 25-kg (55-lb.) box from Vermont to Milan runs about $200.

Many apartments for rent are fully furnished or at least equipped with the basics, like a bed, dresser, refrigerator, and often a washing machine. Unless you're planning to buy a house and absolutely must have your zebra-striped sofa, there really is no need to bring it. Between Arezzo's famous antiques and the contemporary furniture of Milan, there is a heavy temptation here to buy something local. Similarly, bringing clothes to Italy is like taking cheese steaks to Philadelphia. Even if you don't describe yourself as a fashionista, chances are you will have bought a partial wardrobe after only a few months in Italy. The quality is good and the prices are relatively low.

One thing that is less expensive in the U.S., however, is any sort of sporting goods. That includes just about everything, from fishing poles to running shoes to, believe it or not, bicycles. Bear in mind, though, that renting skis and snowboards costs much less in the Alps (as low as €20/$26 per day for the whole kit) than in the Rockies, and renting them in situ is a lot more convenient than hauling them around in a car or train.

By all means, take along any expensive electronics, such as a laptop computer, as they are also pricey in Italy. You should pack them with your carry-on luggage: If you have them sent separately, you could incur a 20-percent import duty, which is a large figure when you're talking about computers.

These days, there are scant few things that you cannot find in Italy or order via the Internet. One of them is a decent bagel. (There's one business idea.) So, the best packing advice I can offer is: When in doubt, leave it out.

Shipping Options

The English yellow pages website in Italy (www.intoitaly.it) has a comprehensive list of shipping companies with English-speaking staff. Please see the Contacts list in the Resources section of this book for a sampling.

Language
and Education

I f you were packing up to move to Northern Europe and didn't speak
any of the local languages, you might not be worried about learning
them. There aren't too Americans who can speak Swedish, Norwegian,
Danish, or Dutch quite as well as those people speak English. The Germans are also known to be good English-speakers, and even the French
understand you better than they would have you know.

The Italians, on the other hand, are often taken to task by their European peers for their lack of language skills, especially when, at European
Union meetings, the steady chain of fluent English speakers breaks down
when the Italian delegate steps up to the podium.

It's not that English is rarely heard in Italy—between the millions of
North American tourists that come each year and the American jargon that
has sneaked into the workplace, Italians are regularly bombarded with foreign words. Businesspeople are swimming in them. On an average day, *un
top manager* will be expected to *controllare l'email, scrollare, unzippare* and
perhaps even *scannerizzare* just to send something to *il suo staff* to get *il loro*

75

input. Then it's up to another department to *processare i raw data* before anyone can actually get to *la fase dell'implementation.* It's all so confusing to a non-native speaker that financial dailies have started distributing pocket-sized glossaries with the latest terms.

Anyone who works in this kind of environment, or in tourism, or else has traveled a lot (loads of young Italians have spent extended periods of time in London, and many in the United States) has a good command of English. But others know just enough to get by. Why would they spend time perfecting it, they'd argue, if they're hardly going to use it? This brings up the more pertinent question: Why don't Americans just learn to speak Italian?

Lots of North Americans who come to Italy on a one-way ticket do, and get on with their Italian lives right away. Others tend to embed themselves in a circle of fellow foreigners instead. It's only natural for immigrants to any country to band together to make the adjustment easier, but if you stay trapped in this cocoon for a while, you should ask yourself why you decided to move to Italy.

There's so much to gain by speaking the language well, and so much to lose if you don't. Every newscast you don't understand, every joke that goes over your head, and every other disappointment in life that results from poor communication will be patent reminders of how much you're missing.

After you've lived in a Italy for a few years, you'll start to forget that you're speaking a different language altogether. Walking into a fruit-and-vegetable store, you won't pause at the door to remember how to say the word "basil." Your vocabulary will expand by the day. You'll start dreaming in Italian and instinctively counting in Italian numbers. You and your American friends in Italy may even stop speaking to one another in English, and at some point, you'll feel as if you've lost your English altogether when the word *basilico* becomes firmly attached to that bundle of aromatic greens sitting next to the *peperoncino.* You know, next to the what's-it-called, the red stuff you add to a sauce to make it spicy.

Everyone plumps their own theory on the quickest and most efficient way to learn a foreign language. The throw-the-little-boy-into-the-pool-and-he'll-learn-to-swim approach may not be the best for every student, nor for every language, but it seems to work pretty well in Italy. For one thing, Italian is a relatively easy language to conquer, especially for those who speak a little French, Spanish, or any other Romance language. The grammar and lexicon are the same, and phonetically, Italian is about the easiest language there is. Every word is pronounced exactly as it is spelled. (English can be a nightmare in that regard. Just look at the word "nightmare.") On top of that, Italians are very patient with foreigners struggling with their native tongue. They're quite used to outsiders butchering Dante's language on a regular basis. For that matter, they're quite used to miscommunicating with other Italians.

If you don't speak any Italian and learning a new language is daunting for you, here's a hint: Watch as many Italian films as you can. It will help. Films clearly won't teach beginners the fundamentals, but they will give you a feel for the language. For those who studied Italian years ago but haven't spoken it in a while, watching movies is an excellent way to get back into practice. Fortunately, most of the Italian films available in the U.S. have English subtitles. In Italy, foreign films are almost always dubbed. In fact, the profession of dubbing is something of a revered art in Italy—dubbers enjoy almost the same name recognition as the actors themselves.

Regional Dialects

Italy has always been covered with a motley quilt of different languages, and thousands of dialects survive to this day. It's commonly pointed out that in the mountain valleys of the South, dialects could vary to such a degree that populations separated by as little as five kilometers couldn't understand each other.

Until the 1930s, literature was the only common linguistic thread. That is, the citizens of the newly formed nation could only communicate with each other through a Florentine dialect used by a Renaissance author, Dante Alighieri. Literary scholars estimate that 90 percent of the words in modern Italian can be found in Dante's works and those of his contemporaries. Later writers, such as Alessandro Manzoni, author of *The Betrothed,* may have thought up and written drafts in their native dialect—in Manzoni's case, the one from the lakes region—and then chosen Florentine for the finished product.

But literature was read only by a very slim minority in what was, until the mid-20th century, a mostly poor, agricultural country. Furthermore, books can only exert so much influence on how a language is actually spoken, and Italian in the 19th century was almost the Latin of its day: spoken by the educated class, used in the courts and for all other official business—but by and large ignored by the masses, who conversed in the local vernacular.

That all changed when the radio came to town. The Fascists, in their push to create a national identity in the 1930s, were very fortunate in rising to power at a time when radio audiences were swelling, and the first televisions in Italy were about to arrive. Radio brought Italian to previously impenetrable towns, and video threatened to kill off dialects altogether.

Tu and *Lei*

For English-speakers, the trickiest parts of mastering any Romance language are remembering a noun's gender and deciding whether to use the formal or informal version of the pronoun "you." The first distinction is pretty straightforward in Italian. If the word ends in an "a," it's feminine; if it ends in an "o," it's masculine; and if it begins with a consonant cluster like "sp," as in "spaghetti," it's neutral.

The second dilemma is more difficult, because there are no hard and fast rules. It's a social judgment, not a linguistic one, which means that the guidelines used in one generation may not be good for the next. For instance, in the past, it was always proper to use the formal *lei* to address your elders. That's not necessarily the case today. Many of today's "elders," especially those who grew up in the 1960s, shudder at the formality and will insist that you address them as *tu*. Some of your friends' parents, however, will have been brought up with a certain decorum at home, and will expect everyone but close friends to address them

as *lei*. The safest bet is to err on the side of formal, then switch over to the informal if you get the green light.

Then there are nuances that have little to do with age or respect. The *lei* form is a convenient way to put distance between yourself and a person with whom you don't want to be too familiar, especially in a business setting. Suppose you have a problem with something you bought, and you call customer support for assistance. An operator that genuinely wants to help you may switch to the informal right off the bat to establish a close rapport. If, on the other hand, you run into an operator that just wants to get you off the phone at all costs, expect a generous helping of polite distance. Another example: You walk into a restaurant when the kitchen is about to close. If you hear the *tu* form, there may be some room for negotiation, and the right smile and joke may get you a table. But if you hear a stern *lei* immediately, just say thank you and head for the door.

Before the 1950s, some 80 percent of the peninsula's population could not speak Italian. Now, official figures say, only about five percent of the population does not speak Italian on a regular basis.

That's not to say that only five percent of the population speaks in dialect. Millions of Italians still do, and consider themselves bilingual. Census data counts about 1.3 million people who speak Sardinian; 500,000 who speak Friulian; 300,000 who speak German in the region of Alto-Adige, and, in that same area, some 55,000 who speak an ancient language called Ladino; about 300,000 who use one of several French dialects in Piedmont and Val d'Aosta; 70,000 Slovenian-speakers in the Northeast; 18,000 Catalan-speakers in Sardinia; 2,600 Croatian-speakers in Molise; and 20,000 Ancient Greek-speakers in Calabria and Puglia, where another 100,000 have retained Albaresh, the language of their Albanian ancestors who arrived in Italy in the 14th century. These languages were officially recognized by the state as "protected" in a 1999 law, following a European Union directive that aimed to preserve some of the Continent's disappearing tongues, of which Italy probably has more than any other country in the EU.

> It's commonly pointed out that in the mountain valleys of the South, dialects could vary to such a degree that populations separated by as little as five kilometers couldn't understand each other.

Chances are, though, you won't run into a native Albaresh- or Ladino-speaker unless you go specifically to those enclaves. More often, you'll hear some of the more diffuse dialects, like Venetian, Milanese, Bergamasco, Genovese, Roman, Neapolitan, and Sicilian (to name some of the more recognizable ones), especially if you talk with older people. Remember that almost everyone in Italy over the age of 65 spoke something other than Italian at home when they were children.

Television may have brought a common language to successive generations, but many younger people still speak with their elders in dialect. The so-called protected languages are even taught at school. In Alto-Adige, for example, students have their choice between a German-speaking school and an Italian-speaking one, and more often than not, they choose the former, because job opportunities are seen as greater in the Teutonic world than in points south.

Other idioms aren't so welcome in class. In one highly publicized case not so long ago, a high school principal near Vicenza in the Veneto fined his pupils a few cents for every word spoken in dialect. It's only natural in a country where people pride themselves on their hometowns that a little good-natured provinciality always shines through. Even celebrities on television, the great linguistic equalizer, give some hint of their roots when they open their mouths, if not an overpowering accent that lends itself openly to caricature. Silvio Berlusconi's nasal Milanese and soccer star Francesco Totti's Roman drawl are just two of the easier targets. They don't try to hide it, as a matter of principle. The only exception might be Southerners who moved to Turin or Milan for jobs, and want to conceal their backgrounds for fear of being labeled a *terrone* (peasant), a form of intra-Italian racism that grew in the 1960s and still pervades the North today. On the other side of the coin, finding a fellow Sicilian in a position of power might just be an islander's ticket to the top.

In general, you'll make more friends in Italy if you speak with an honest accent and use simple words, rather than try to churn out polished verse. High school principals and other scholarly types may speak the language of Dante, but average Italians will snicker under their breath when they hear the perfect tense too many times, or suffer through a

© Monica Larner

pedantic insistence on the subjunctive clause. Both of these are so correct that they come off as awkward.

Unfortunately, this kind of populist attitude won't get you very far with an Italian professor, and for all the bravado and braggadocio about learning Italian on the fly, there really is no substitute for a language class.

Learning the Language

Italian courses are easy to find in the United States. Just about every local college offers a class at night or on the weekends, and any independent language institute will certainly feature it on its brochure. Learning the basics before you come is a smart idea. Mastering the grammar should only take a few months, and then you'll be free to improve your pronunciation and build your vocabulary by the time you arrive in Italy, rather than poring through lists of irregular verbs—something that could just as easily be done at home.

If you're a college student and are considering a move to Italy after graduation, obviously the wisest move is to take a semester abroad in Italy. You may end up speaking a lot of English with your cohorts, but at least you'll be surrounded by Italian-speakers for a few consecutive months. It's amazing how many American students fall in love with Florence or Rome on their junior year abroad and then decide to move back for good. That number is destined to grow as more American students keep flowing in: In 1985, U.S. undergraduates studying in Italy numbered around 4,000. By 2000, there were 12,930 of them studying at almost 400 U.S. programs or in a curriculum of their own design.

Two very popular self-styled options are the universities for foreigners in Siena and Perugia. Both offer beginner courses in Italian, as well more advanced programs. The beginner course in Siena (www.unistrasi.it) lasts two months; the one in Perugia (www.unistrapg.it), three months. Both cost in the vicinity of €800 ($1,040). There are dozens of other institutes spread throughout Italy. Two good examples are the Dante Alighieri Society (www.dantealighieri.com) in Siena, and Lingua Due (linguadue.com) in Milan, both of which offer three-week courses for about €500 ($650), plus myriad other options. For details, consult a list provided by the Italian Consulate in Boston (www.italianconsulateboston.org/new_folder/studiita.html).

© Monica Larner

Health

Health insurance is one of the first concerns of people who move to Italy. Your policy in the United States may not cover you abroad, and if you rely on Medicare, it certainly won't.

Travel insurance is typically good for about a six-month sojourn, and is the best way to get started. After all, you want to make sure that you and your family are covered from the moment you step foot on Italian soil. In the meantime, you can start preparing to enter into the Italian health care system, which has both public and private options.

If you have a job in Italy and therefore make regular payments to the health care system, you will automatically be provided with the same public coverage extended to those Italians who were employed at some point in their lives, plus their dependents. If you're not regularly employed, there is always the option of independently buying a plan that covers you through that same public system.

Alternatively, you can take out a private health insurance policy, which is going to be more expensive, but offers more benefits. Many Italians buy private policies in addition to the state-provided coverage. The costs and comparative advantages of each sector are described below.

Types of Insurance

PUBLIC VS. PRIVATE CARE

Health care is free to all Italian citizens, regardless of how much they contribute in income taxes. Part of every worker's salary goes to the national health service, the Servizio Sanità Nazionale (SSN), though insurance is administered at the local level. This means that (1) the quality of care can vary according to the region—in general, Northern hospitals are said to be in better shape than Southern ones—and (2) all of your questions are answered by your local health authority, or the Azienda Sanità Locale (ASL).

While Italian health care, even private, is rarely compared favorably with the American system in terms of technology and research, certain Italian clinics are way ahead of the game.

If you are regularly employed, you will receive public health insurance automatically. The only expense you are expected to pay is a nominal fee for each visit, something like the ones you would pay at an HMO in the United States. To register for this insurance, you need to go to the local ASL office and pick a primary care physician from a list. The doctor will be your reference point from then on—writing your prescriptions, referring you to specialists, and ordering your hospitalization if necessary.

The largest complaints about the public system are that the hospitals are not always the cleanest-looking places, and the lines can be long. Waiting several hours in pain is not uncommon, as long as the injury or illness is not life-threatening. In the most extreme cases, anyone whose life is in danger can go to a private institution at no extra charge if the wait for treatment is deemed excessive.

Italians have similar gripes about public universities. Though public education, which is free, has a certain level of prestige in Italy, professors—like doctors working in public hospitals—are given little incentive to make themselves available. Many Italian families choose to send their children to private universities instead. When it comes to health, those who can afford it don't take chances. They sign up for additional coverage at private clinics, where the wait is usually less tedious and the hospital rooms can even be luxurious.

While Italian health care, even private, is rarely compared favorably with the American system in terms of technology and research, certain Italian

Benessere: The Art of Feeling Good

Italians are on a perpetual crusade for both comfort and beauty. It is only fitting that a country with some of the most beautiful scenery in the world should have beautiful people as well, and that the pleasant climate should be matched by a general sense of *benessere* (well-being).

This ideal state of mind and body involves eating right, staying trim, keeping skin flake-free and well-tanned, and, above all, keeping stress at a minimum. The nation's fitness centers offer so-called relax rooms, with soothing colors and music for a post-workout calm.

Nothing in the world, however, can compare to Italy's spas, where stressed-out city slickers get massaged and soak up sulfuric waters. It is a tradition dating back to antiquity, when Roman soldiers would go to Tuscan springs for "the cure" after defeating a legion of Goths or the like. The mountainous peninsula is loaded with thermal springs, concentrated mostly in central Italy and the Alps. A weekend retreat often includes mud baths, massages, and aromatherapy. Some hotels even propose bathing in wine or hay.

The search for good health begins at the supermarket, where herbal treatments line the aisles. Food magazines regularly include recipes using such greenery as birch leaves and witch hazel to deliver softer skin and improved circulation, or to cure kidney ailments and gout.

It seems all too newfangled for Italy, a country previously associated with rotund, mustachioed pizza chefs feeding roly-poly mammas and their pudgy kids. But Italy revised its diet long ago, following the French lead of nouvelle cuisine, and these days its eating habits are among the healthiest in Europe.

Eating right, the Italian way, is an endless game with hundreds of rules. Here are the three most important to remember: pasta is eaten just once a day; salads come after the meal, not before; and, above all, cappuccino is a breakfast drink—milk goes out of style at noon.

---

clinics are way ahead of the game. On a recent trip to a private clinic in Milan, one American dermatologist who had trained in top programs in the U.S. was surprised to see a computerized scope that she had never seen back home. Don't assume, however, that doctors in private clinics will have better credentials than those in public hospitals. For one thing, many doctors work in both sectors. Also, some regions have worked out deals with the local clinics to send public-care patients there for certain procedures. Finally, the public domain is the stronghold of academia, and so the brightest lights in their fields—if they haven't already been lured away by big money in the United States or Germany—prefer the prestige of working in a state run university hospital over higher salaries in a clinic.

SELF-SERVE INSURANCE

If you don't have a job, you have a number of other health insurance options in Italy. These include paying for public care, paying for private care, or taking out traveler's health insurance at home before you leave.

The last option is the best way to get started, as well as the obvious choice for those who plan to stay only a few months. Many U.S. health insurance companies offer plans with the following services: nonemergency and emergency medical expenses, medical evacuation, and prescription drugs. (They also include repatriation of remains, given the worst-case scenario.) But travel insurance policies are usually only good for up to six consecutive months or multiple shorter trips. The other disadvantage of this approach is that you will have to pay up front for any medical expenses incurred in Italy. You could be stuck holding the debt for seven or eight months before the company pays you back.

Many people who do not have a regular job, and therefore do not contribute to the SSN, can take out an insurance policy with the public health system. Simply go to the local ASL office, present your stay permit, and pay a set fee of about €300 ($390). The catch is that you need to have some sort of proof of health insurance to qualify for the stay permit in the first place. You will not be issued one without some proof of insurance. A temporary policy from the U.S. will do the trick.

Alternatively, you can enroll in a private plan. These start at about €1,000 ($1,300), available at any major Italian insurance company. One advantage is that you have your choice of clinics, an important consideration for those who suffer from a chronic illness. But bear in mind that even the public system goes a long way. Many of my friends who have both health insurance in the United States and public coverage in Italy (through their jobs) prefer to have some operations done on the Old Continent. Laser surgery to correct your vision, for example, can be expensive in the U.S., because many insurance policies will not cover such nonvital operations. That is not necessarily the case in Italy. And although that kind of corrective surgery can be hit-or-miss, my friends, at least, had positive results—for free.

TAKING YOUR CHANCES

Of course, your last option is to take your chances and not hold any medical insurance at all. Note that Medicare will cover only a very small fraction of your hospital costs abroad, if at all. Also remember that this hands-off approach will pose a problem when you apply for your long-stay permit.

There is technically one other alternative for those without insurance: free health care for illegal immigrants. It is a shaky option at best. Italy has a reputation for being a compassionate country. This might seem undeserved praise, if one considers that there is no welfare program for those who have never had a job and therefore have never contributed to Social Security. The assumption here is that their families support those who cannot or will not work. And to a large extent, this holds true for those who have relations in Italy. But for the hundreds of thousands who don't—including the growing number of single male immigrants—the state provides nothing. De facto welfare comes in the form of Catholic charities. Numerous church-run organizations sponsor free hospitals for immigrants and the homeless. It is indeed a warm gesture, but suffice it to say that you never want to rely on free care.

As a final note, rest assured that you will receive emergency medical attention if you happen to be run over by a car or hit by a stray bullet—regardless of your insurance or residency status. Even illegal immigrants with no insurance are covered for ambulance and emergency room bills, as is generally the case in the United States. But don't expect a free ride in a Medevac helicopter after a skiing accident, for example.

Pharmacies and Prescriptions

Public health care covers most of your prescription drug costs. Once your doctor writes you a prescription, you will be ushered into the world of Italian pharmacies, where medicine is dispensed with a serious air and quaint packaging. Prepare for an adventure.

Pharmacy schedules are confusing, but there will be at least one open at any time in any given city or town. Just look for an illuminated green cross. If the sign is turned off, it's closed. Especially late at night, you may have to check several locations, as pharmacies take turns filling the night shift.

This can be frustrating, since pharmacies are the only places in town that sell aspirin. They are also among the few places that sell mosquito spray and plug-in vapor repellants—indispensable urban survival gear in the summer, especially in the North. The moral is: Don't wait until you have a headache or mosquito problem to go looking for relief. Always keep a supply of medicine on hand.

Once you find an open pharmacy, you'll notice that it isn't the sort of place with greeting cards and cigarettes for sale and a drug counter tucked in the back. Italian pharmacists take their vocation very seriously, and their customers afford them due respect. Theirs is one of the most sought-after fields of scientific study, ranking just after medicine among high school students aspiring to university. Candidates need to score rather high on entrance exams to be admitted to a pharmacy program.

Medicine, Shmedicine

Italians are turning to alternative medicine in increasing numbers. According to a survey in 2000 by the National Statistics Institute, Isat, up to three times as many people chose alternatives to traditional medicine in 1999 than in 1991; and roughly nine million Italians in all, almost one sixth of the population, preferred to go to someone other than a medical doctor to treat an ailment.

The study was based on a sample of 30,000 families. Women led the trend, especially those with a relatively high level of education who resided in the Northeast. The most typically cited cures were homeopathy, massage therapy, acupuncture, and phytotherapy (a somewhat rarer approach based on the curative power of plants).

Homeopathy—treating a disease with small doses of the same disease—has seen the greatest increase in popularity over the last decade. In 1991, 2.5 percent of the Italian population used that method; by the end of the decade, 8.2 percent did.

While northerners were described as the most eager to try new methods, one out of six people in the central regions did the same, as compared to one out of 15 in the South. More than 60 percent of those who sought alternative treatment were women.

About 40 percent of respondents said they approved of alternative medicine, and 23 percent said they did not, while the rest passed no judgement. As for those who had actually tried it at some point, 91 percent said they were pleased with the results.

Your pharmacist, invariably dressed in a white lab coat, will act as a sort of physician for minor ailments such as the flu or diarrhea. If you have a cold, a stomachache, or mild headache, spare yourself the hassle of going to the hospital and head directly to the pharmacist for a quick diagnosis and over-the-counter pills. Be warned that what might be done with a tablet or capsule back home may take a more frightening form in Italy. Italians are not hesitant to administer an injection. Seek out someone's mother for help.

If you take a particular medicine back in the States, make sure to jot down the generic name, as brand names are rarely the same in Europe. Also, because Italian food and drug regulations are different, you will have access to medicines that might be awaiting FDA approval back home.

Aside from traditional cures, Italian pharmacies always stock a wide array of "alternative" treatments, such as herbs and homeopathy. Both are very popular in Italy. Your quack detector may start beeping if a pharmacist suggests a sort of potion or oil that you've never heard of, but anything new is worth a try if nothing else seems to help (and as long as your life is not on the line). You could be pleasantly surprised by the results.

When picking up a prescription at the counter, you will normally have to pay a fee of about €2 ($2.60) along with your "ticket" for the subsidized medicine. If the prescription is for a serious illness, such as a heart condition, often there will be no fee at all. The government also subsidizes treatments for drug addicts.

Unfortunately, this system has been plagued by scandals in recent years. Courts have issued hundreds of indictments for fraud and bribery in the health industry, ranging from pharmacists who cashed in bogus "tickets" for state-subsidized prescriptions they claimed to have filled, to more subtle cases involving doctors accused of accepting what judges called "bribes" from drug companies, usually in the form of all-expenses paid vacations, in exchange for pushing their brands. The Health Ministry said it plans to clear up rules about promotional offers for doctors in the future.

Potential Hazards

The biggest health scare in Italy in recent years has been Creutzfeldt-Jacob Disease, caused by the so-called "mad cow" brain-wasting virus found in infected meat. The riskiest parts of the animal are bone marrow and especially cerebral and spinal fluids. For about a year in 2000–2001, the venerated Fiorentina T-bone steak was taken off menus in Florence as a result, and sheep brains, a delicacy in Rome, were banned.

As of the summer of 2003, Italy had diagnosed about 100 cases of mad cow disease and carried out more than a million tests over a two-year span, in compliance with EU laws. But health officials believe the outbreak is now under control, and even sheep brains have started reappearing in supermarket refrigerators.

Almost every winter, there is an influenza outbreak that makes headlines, as does the occasional meningitis scare, both of which generate an almost comical level of concern. To put things in perspective, the last meningitis scare came in January 2003, with a total of 36 cases nationwide. In that same month, the African nation of Burkina Faso registered 980 confirmed cases.

AIDS levels are about at the European average. According to figures from 2001, Italy was on par with France for the number of new cases diagnosed per year with roughly 1,500, and just below the Western European leader in that category, Spain. Spain also had the most confirmed AIDS cases overall, with some 60,000, followed by France with about 55,000, followed by Italy, which crested the 50,000 mark in 2001.

The Health Ministry runs a very active safe-sex campaign, with posters canvassing the subways and public buildings. But this is one of the areas where proximity to the Vatican makes such initiatives politically delicate.

Vatican officials repeat that the use of condoms in curbing AIDS is not "ethically admissible," and its influence on Catholic members of parliament should not be underestimated.

Incidentally, the Vatican runs one of the largest pharmacies on the peninsula, where many experimental treatments and pharmaceuticals pass under the radar of Italian drug laws. Of course, you'll have to go elsewhere for contraceptives.

Environmental Factors

One recent skirmish between the church and the government highlighted the state of environmental affairs in Italy. The Vatican transmitter towers that broadcast the church's Radio Maria channel were thought to be linked with higher-than-average rates of leukemia in the region of Lazio. For months, Italians were jittery about so-called "electrosmog." In the end, the claims were neither proven nor disproven scientifically. Accusations were thrown around, and then the whole affair just disappeared, as do most impulsive urges to make Italy a greener place—sort of like New Year's resolutions, except on a parliamentary level.

The most evident of these is smoking. Italy has officially quit smoking at least twice. In the mid-1970s, Parliament passed a wide range of decrees that banned puffing in public places, such as hospitals and post offices. Some 25 years later, it passed identical laws, again banning smoking in pubic places, including certain sections of restaurants. And this time, they really meant it, politicians insisted. Massive fines would be meted out to restaurants without proper ventilation. A single trip to Rome should give you a good idea of just how well those laws are being enforced, so be prepared for a third attempt at kicking the habit.

Moreover, don't expect the same level of courtesy smokers may show in the U.S. toward nonsmokers. Cigarettes aren't seen as the demonic vice that they are in America. Italians may casually light up in your home, even if it has been made clear that you are a nonsmoker, but don't take that to be an extremely rude gesture, just a simple misunderstanding of cultures.

Italy has also vowed to make a better effort at recycling, and it has an impressive program—in theory, at least. Every apartment building is equipped with separate bins for paper, plastic, glass, and aluminum, though recent exposés on television showed that collectors tended to throw it all in the same place anyway.

Critics of American environmental policy will make the claim that, although Italy may be slightly behind the rest of Europe in terms of conservation and protection, at least their hearts are in the right place. They will point to the Kyoto accords, which Italy happily signed along with its European neighbors to curb greenhouse gases, while America huffed and puffed. But as is the case with most such multilateral accords, Italy's dedication to Kyoto was mostly symbolic. The local environmental protection agency, APAT, pointed out in March 2003 that greenhouse gases had risen by five percent between 1990 and 2000, and that the country would not meet the levels agreed upon in Japan for 2010. After a few years of living in Europe, even the staunchest American environmentalists may be able to see some logic in the arguments put forth by many opponents to Kyoto: "If we sign on, we mean it, but Europe will agree to everything and then do nothing about it."

Most of Italy's greatest environmental villains are found in the industrial North. Biochemical plants just outside Venice are perennially plagued by dumping scandals or caught with illegal emissions. Residents of towns near the lagoon have been asked in the past to tape their windows shut, after one such refinery went up in flames. Milan and Turin have the worst air-pollution problems. The grandmother of a friend of mine recently went to the doctor with a worrying cough, and after looking at her chest X-ray, the doctor said she would do well to stop smoking two packs a day. The grandmother said she had never touched a cigarette—but had spent her entire life in Milan.

On select Sundays, when pollution levels reach a critical level, the city limits traffic to those cars with either odd- or even-numbered plates. Sometimes it bans traffic altogether. Lawmakers recognize that this, of course, is a short-term solution, so Italy is one of several European countries developing an effective hydrogen-powered car. Two such buses are already in circulation in Turin.

Like everything else in Italy, environmentalism is an area of sharp contrasts. Leaded gasoline has been definitively banned, catalytic converters are obligatory, more and more land is protected every year, and so on. And yet egregious anachronisms remain. Milan is the only major European city without a sewage treatment plant, for example, a problem which is supposed to be resolved immediately. For the moment, its waste still runs directly into the Lambro River, cuts across the width of Northern Italy, and comes to a swirling stop on the Adriatic coast among the eels and rice patties of the Po River delta.

© John Moretti

Employment

The financial disaster at Fiat and the death of its patriarch, Gianni Agnelli, in 2003 is a good introduction to the nuances of the Italian economy and the way its landscape is changing. The Turin carmaker, founded in 1899, was for many years the motor of the national economy, and therefore drove the immigration of Southerners to the North. It sold cars to the average Italian in staggering numbers in the postwar years, becoming Italy's largest private employer—a title it has not yet surrendered. This dominance in the industry gave rise to the notion that what was economically good for Fiat was economically good for the rest of the country. In the same vein, it also meant that any trouble at the carmaker meant trouble for everyone else.

The Agnellis rose to such wealth in the 1960s and 1970s that they became the overlords of Italian finance. Along with a group of other moneyed families, they formed the so-called *salotto buono* (literally, "good living room"), made up of oligarchs with the last word in almost every business deal. The Agnellis and their friends, most notably creditor banks such as Mediobanca, still control the country's major banks, newspapers, and insurance companies, along with the utilities and telecoms that were privatized in the 1990s.

But in 2002, faced with overwhelming competition from foreign cars and saddled with debt from unprofitable acquisitions, Fiat hit the breaking point. It announced plans to lay off some 8,000 workers, mainly in the South, and added fuel to the debate over selling the historic carmaker to a foreign company. This steered Fiat into a collision course with a state apparatus that had supported the manufacturer through tough times before, in the name of salvaging an Italian symbol, but whose electoral power base was largely in the South, where those jobs were at stake. The confrontation pitted Agnelli and the business establishment against Prime Minister Silvio Berlusconi, a real estate developer turned media magnate who embodied Italy's new money, snubbed by the *salotto buono* as a forebear of change.

Did this spell the end of the *salotto buono* and mark a downward slide for family capitalism? Hardly. Heading into what might be called Italy's post-Fiat era, the great majority of all Italian companies are still family-held (see the sidebar "All in the Family"), and the same faces still run the country's major board rooms—especially the Agnellis. These are deep-rooted traits in the Italian economy that may never see any change.

The good news for Americans hoping to build a business in Italy, though, is that bureaucracy and excessive state meddling are no longer accepted as tacitly as they once were. The conservatives have promised to shave away some of the obstacles to opening a business, easing up the rigid labor market especially. Berlusconi's government did, in fact, do away with a few taxes, soften laws on accounting (albeit conveniently for a prime minister under investigation for accounting fraud), and generally favor the employer over the employee. On paper, it all looks promising for efficiency-driven Americans, though no one believes that the tradition of red tape will ever disappear from Italy altogether.

Self-Employment

Despite the considerable challenges, many foreigners have chosen to *mettersi in proprio* (start their own businesses), ranging from Web design to goat farming. Lots of them cater to an American clientele in such fields as wine export, relocation services, and travel agencies. They are, for the most part, small businesses, employing only the owner and perhaps a spouse or children, a practice that can be chalked up to strict hiring laws and expensive benefits for employees. Businesses with fewer than 15 employees are immune from many restrictions.

The sorts of contracts handed out to employees are described in more detail below (see "The Job Hunt") but suffice to say that, compared to the United States, they are designed to favor employees. Put another way, salaries are much lower in Italy than in the United States because many of the benefits that Italian workers enjoy, such as long vacations and free health care, are subsidized by businesses.

A worker's salary is only one of many financial obligations a potential employer should keep in mind. Others include:

- The "thirteenth month," which is essentially a month's bonus tacked on at the end of the year. In some cases, there is a fourteenth and even a fifteenth month, depending on the kind of contract.
- Liquidation: An early termination of any contract requires a payment that amounts to roughly 10 percent of an employee's earnings over the duration spent at the business.
- Every month, there are pension payments to the social security system—called INPS—taken out of a worker's salary and matched by the employer.
- In those workplaces with a relatively high risk of injury, an employer needs to set aside what can amount to 50 percent of an employee's salary and hand it over to the state body for worker's compensation, called Inail.

The first step for anyone committed to opening a business is to get the appropriate permits and licenses from the town or city. In Italy, you don't just find a spot that you think would be ideal for an ice cream store and set up shop; the local government will make that decision for you. In theory, at least, this decision is based on the location of other ice cream stands nearby, and whether the market can support another. Every type of business is therefore registered at the local Chamber of Commerce.

After you have the local court's approval for the existence of your business, there are four offices with whom you must register: the Registro delle Imprese (Registrar of Businesses), the Registrar delle Ditte (Registrar of Companies), the Registro delle Imposte (Tax Registrar), and the Ufficio Registro (Tax Registrar's Office).

Next, you need to decide on a corporate structure. The simplest of these is declaring yourself a self-employed freelancer; for example, a Web designer, translator, or consultant. Why bother with the formalities? Because when you perform work for a company, they will ask you to file an invoice and will need a tax ID number in order to pay you. So, to become a legal freelancer, you must register for a *partita IVA* (value-added-tax number), and your clients will withhold 20 percent tax on every invoice you file.

Alternatively, you can incorporate your private business into a partnership, that is, a *società in nome collettivo* (SNC). The only real difference between this arrangement and freelancing option is that, with an SNC, the IVA number is assigned to the company, not the individual—and therefore the company will pay taxes in May and November, rather than having them withheld as an individual.

Further up the entrepreneurial food chain is the corporation. These come in two forms: *società a responsibilità limitata* (SRL), which is a limited liability corporation, and the *società per azioni* (SpA), a joint stock company. The first is a private company—therefore divided into quotas, not shares—that has initial working capital of at least €10,000 ($13,000). The second has a minimum working capital of €100,000 ($130,000), is divided into shares, and is the only type of company that can be taken public.

Again, the whole process of setting up a business will be complicated, and there is no substitute for getting some professional help. Registering your company, for example, is best done through a *notaio* (notary public). Fees for registering a corporation will amount to a few thousand dollars. Accounting is also a very delicate operation in Italy and is best left to a *commercialista* (accountant). These may be the only people in Italy who fully understand how the tax system works.

All in the Family

The old adage in Italy is that the first generation founds a company, the second generation grows it, and the third one runs it into the ground. But for every family business that fails, another one crops up to take its place. As a result, when compared to the rest of Europe and the United States, Italy remains a land of small- and medium-sized firms.

It is estimated that 90 percent of all companies in Italy are family-held. The tradition goes back centuries. The oldest is thought to be Barolvier & Toso, a glassmaker founded in 1295. Another ancient example is Beretta, an arms-producing dynasty that has invoices going back to 1526, and whose guns were used in the American Revolution.

Today, the phenomenon exists in virtually every sector. In fashion, the dynasties include Versace, Prada, and the Delvecchio family of Luxottica eyewear. In the food sector, there is the Barilla family. The Alessi and Merloni clans dominate design and household appliances. And the biggest names in Italian finance—Agnelli, Benetton, Pirelli, and De Benedetti—refer not only to an individual, but a family.

Alberto Falck, patriarch of the industrial group Falck SpA and chairman of the Italian Association of Family Businesses, says the reason such businesses do so well is that "in

Before you even get to that stage, however, you should do some research with the Chamber of Commerce. A preferred option among foreigners is the American Chamber of Commerce in Italy (www.amcham.it). Better, a consultant from one of the big American firms can offer you some professional help, if you can afford it. Both Ernst & Young and Accenture are very active in Italy.

TYPES OF BUSINESSES

The types of businesses that foreigners own in Italy often fall into one of two categories: taking America to Italy or taking Italy to America. Just 10 years ago, you could walk around the streets of Rome and imagine a dozen kinds of shops that might have made money and now do: video rentals, one-hour photos, gyms, sushi restaurants, etc. These products of globalization are only slowly cropping up in smaller cities, representing what might be an emerging market for retail entrepreneurs.

For professionals, it seems that there is still a sizable market for American things in Italy. All sorts of U.S. technology, know-how, and the English language itself are still very marketable here, even if the gap between the two continents has closed considerably in those respects in recent decades. Indeed, in many cases, the U.S. could stand to gain from importing certain

times of crisis, they bare their claws and protect their pups." That is to say, families protect their livelihoods more vehemently than a CEO might protect a corporation. An outside manager can walk away from a crisis and take his lumps. On the other hand, protective patriarchs tend to shy away from rapid growth. "Italian family companies are cautious," says Guido Corbetta, a professor of economics at Bocconi University who specializes in dynasties. "American companies can grow much faster, but they take on more risk."

One high-profile case is Versace, which, in 2002, turned down investors looking to give the fashion house €200 million ($260 million) to buy back control of its brand from franchisees. "We're not looking for investors," Donatella Versace said in October of that year. "For three years, investors have wanted to come into our company, and we always said no."

The Milanese stock market has tried to woo large and medium-sized family companies to list their shares, but it, too, found more reservation than enthusiasm. Fiat remains the only Italian company among the world's largest multinationals, ranking 11th in total assets with €93.9 billion ($122 billion). Italy has just 15 multinational corporations methods and products developed in a country that isn't as old-fashioned as many Americans think.

Italy's classic products, such as its wine, food, fashion, cars, and bicycles, were long ago introduced to the United States, but the more you look around the world of crafts here, the more secrets you will find and may decide to bring home. The same goes for the tourist industry: There are still a few corners of Italy waiting to be discovered by Americans who would pay good money to do so.

Then again, you may decide to forgo the import/export sector altogether and compete with Italians at their own games. One American in Venice, Thomas Price, is regularly interviewed on Italian television to talk about his gondola-making business.

Another option is what you might call A2A: American to American. Some examples would be an English-speaking real estate service, a tour company for visiting Americans, an English-language newsletter, a bakery serving American specialties, etc. These ideas are not novel, by any means—there are hundreds of Americans in Italy doing this kind of thing already—but maybe you can come up with a new slant?

The Job Hunt

EMPLOYERS

While the thought of being your own boss in Italy may sound exciting, the reality is that most of the foreigners you will run into here are working for someone else. They are often found teaching English, translating, designing Web pages, working in marketing or public relations, consulting for an American multinational, teaching at a university, writing for a newspaper or magazine, or working with a governmental organization.

Fortunately for those Anglophones without an illustrious career behind them, the very act of speaking perfect English lends a certain credibility. Italians may be suspect of American foreign policy and not particularly fond of U.S. food and fashion, but they do defer to American business sense.

Also, employers admire professional habits cultivated in the U.S. When compared to European workers nursed on labor-friendly hiring laws, prospective North American employees have a leg up on the competition, as they come from a culture where efficiency is king, and are accustomed to the kind of laissez-faire capitalism where hiring and firing are quick and easy processes.

Even the most venerated institutions of traditional Italian sectors have a native English-speaker in their top brass. One of the most famous employees in that category is Tom Ford, a Texan by birth and the lead designer at Gucci. But unless you have outstanding contacts or credentials, or else were sent to Italy by your American company, chances are that you will have to start the way most expats did: translating or teaching English while scouring the Help Wanted ads for something that fits your background more closely. (Then again, many people feel that they were cut out for teaching or translating and build it into a career.)

Fortunately for those Anglophones without an illustrious career behind them, the very act of speaking perfect English lends a certain credibility.

In Rome, a good place to start looking is an expat magazine called *Wanted in Rome* (www.wantedinrome.com). It has classified ads for short-term or long-term apartment rentals and a list of jobs for native English speakers. Its counterpart in Milan is *Easy Milano* (www.easymilano.it).

Other websites with job listings include www .zoomata.it and www.informer.it. The Monster board has an Italian site at www.monster.it, focused on an international crowd, while for Italians, the most popular venue is Corriere Lavoro (www.corriere.it/lavoro.)

A second possibility for those starting off is to go to a temp agency. The two best known in Italy are Adecco (www.adecco.it) and Vedior (www.vedior.it), where candidates can upload their résumés and await a temporary assignment. This often turns into a full-time position. As lifetime contracts are on the wane in Italy, these stopgap measures have become more useful for employers. The disadvantage for foreigners, however, is that the employers are quite unlikely to undertake the hassle of getting you the necessary paperwork for what is supposed to be a short-term position.

The best bet is to spend the first few months making personal contacts while making some money on the side. Fresh off the plane, young Americans can usually expect to find immediate employment at a bar, guiding tours, or working as a nanny, while those with some experience might land a job doing public relations, marketing, or Web design for an international company.

The fashion industry is particularly fond of hiring internationals to work in showrooms, especially if they are young, attractive women: Remember that most Europeans do not see anything wrong with what Americans might deem overt sexism and ageism. In a classified ad for a receptionist, for example, it is common practice in Italy to require that the applicant be "a friendly girl between the ages of 23 and 27."

LANDING THE JOB

A résumé in Italy includes the candidate's gender, date of birth, marital

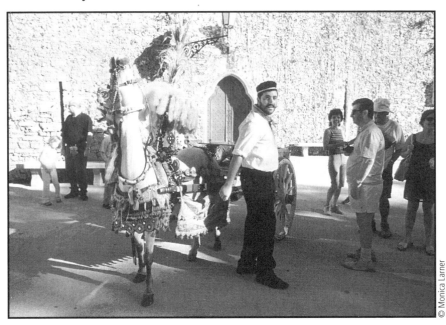

© Monica Larner

status, and almost always a photo. They are longer than the average American CV (two pages at least) and will include the type of high school attended and the score received at college graduation.

As the taste for all things American grows in Italian business, a résumé that focuses on what the candidate accomplished at various jobs and internships will be viewed more favorably. But don't expect a pure meritocracy: A personal contact will always beat an ace of a different suit.

When interviewing or sending a cover letter, be as respectful and professional as possible, as nothing turns off a prospective employer in Italy more than excessive informality. Needless to say, you should always use the *lei* form of the second person, and always address your interviewer as *dottore* or *dottoressa,* titles which assume they have graduated from college. Even for low-level and mid-level positions, the interview process will likely take a few weeks. Most of the time will be spent negotiating the salary and the type of contract that would be offered.

Because Italy is a land of small and medium-sized family firms, pockets are not as deep as they are in big American corporations. Coupled with the lower cost of living in Italy, somewhere near 80 percent of that in the United States, your salary will appear exceedingly slim at first. Pay for many professions is based on a national schedule known as the *tabelle professionali*. Entry-level workers will receive the minimum wage of that category, and unionized professionals can expect a raise every two years.

Your salary will be paid by the month and will be accompanied by a receipt that outlines how much has been taken out by taxes, social security, health benefits, and any extra days off not granted in your contract. Once you have the job and want to see how your package stacks up against similar ones, a resource you can consult is www.quantomipagano.it.

Types of contracts are becoming more varied as a business-minded government relaxes labor laws. Until the late 1990s, almost every full-time contract at firms with more than 15 employees entailed *posto fisso* (employment for life). Now, large employers are permitted to offer contracts for a fixed duration, sometimes as little as six months. However, an employee can only renew a time-limited contract once. After that, the company must offer *posto fisso*.

The relaxation of labor laws has also given rise to American-style contracts, where the hours an employee puts in are less important than the work that is actually accomplished. One fleeting example is the *collaborazione continuata e continuativa* (CoCoCo). It is a legal hybrid between freelance and full-time work, freeing the employer from certain payments, such as worker's compensation, while freeing the employee from the necessities of working fixed hours and justifying each and every sick day with a doctor's note. This particular kind of contract met with stiff resistance from labor unions, and, as of the printing of this book, looked as if it were destined to disappear. Other variations are still used in many workplaces, though, in general, the majority of contracts are full-time, complete with all the union-guaranteed benefits.

BENEFITS

For starters, you can expect 12 national holidays and at least four weeks of vacation, often five or six, depending on your contract. Many people end up taking off two weeks around Christmas and most of the month of August. Italian cities traditionally close down in August, although this is slowly changing. More companies have decided to spread out their employees' vacations to alleviate the frustration of international clients. (It also means less summer traffic on highways and fully booked resorts.) If you don't use up all four or five weeks in a year, you can theoretically carry over your vacation days into the next year, though many companies will require you to periodically go on vacation to make bookkeeping easier.

There are 12 bank holidays nationwide, and each city also gets its patron Saint's Day off. Romans, for example, celebrate Saints Peter and Paul (June 29), while workers in Milan get Saint Ambrose's day off (December 7). If a Saint's Day or national holiday falls on a Friday or Monday, workers naturally get a three-day weekend. Even better, if it falls on a Tuesday

> *Job security is so solid in Italy that it has become a major bone of contention between the unions and conservatives.*

or Thursday, it becomes a *ponte* (bridge)—a four-day weekend. For Romans, it means a fortuitous beach holiday, while Saint Ambrose marks the beginning of ski season for the Milanese.

Maternity entails five months of paid leave, spread out on either side of giving birth. Women on maternity leave receive 80 percent of their salary. Furthermore, they can request an additional six months off at 30 percent pay, and be guaranteed their jobs when they want to return to work. It is not uncommon for a woman to file for extra sick days above and beyond those nine months. Like any other sick day in Italy, it needs to be backed up by a doctor's note. A company can send a state inspector to the person's home as well, to make sure that it is not just an excuse to go shopping.

In general, employees are allowed 180 days of paid sick leave. Above and beyond that, the matter is referred to the pensions office, as the person is considered disabled. Either way, Italians don't need to worry too much about staying healthy, or even doing a very good job at the office, in order to keep their salaries.

Indeed, job security is so solid in Italy that it has become a major bone of contention between the unions and conservatives. Companies must prove a "just cause," such as breaking the law, in order to fire somebody, though even that will not necessarily result in a pink slip. Countless lawsuits—or even the threat thereof—have resulted in a fired employee's reinstatement. One such high-profile case involved baggage handlers at an airport in Milan. They were caught on videotape stealing valuables such as cash and jewels from passengers' luggage, found guilty in court, but never fired.

In fact, it is nearly impossible to terminate an employee's lifetime contract, as even the "justified motive" of downsizing has to be cleared with the unions first. Most companies just prefer to brush the worker aside by keeping up salary payments but not requiring his or her presence at work.

WORKING *IN NERO*

It is no wonder, then, that many Italian companies prefer to take the illegal route and pay their employees *in nero* (under the table). Figures from the Bank of Italy in 2001 pinned the underground economy at about 14 percent of the GDP, while contemporaneous police stings nationwide revealed that 52 percent of the companies probed were paying employees under the table. That makes Italy one of the worst offenders in Western Europe, and the real numbers are probably even higher. Large companies periodically hold "appreciation days" for local law enforcement communities, inviting them to sample the goods, ostensibly in return for lenient inspections.

The lack of an outcry against laws that engender such behavior means that things aren't likely to change soon. In 2002, Parliament decriminalized false accounting—several counts of which the head of government happened to be facing at the time. Still, Prime Minister Silvio Berlusconi, who ran on an antiestablishment platform, was only codifying a time-honored tradition: False accounting has always been seen in Italy as a necessary evil in the face of an oppressive state.

While working under the table may be a tempting offer in order to avoid the hassle of never-ending Italian paperwork, the truth is that an employee has little to gain by taking such a risk. "Freelancers," as they are euphemistically known, do not have access to the extensive health care that full-time contracts provide, nor will they receive social security payments when they retire.

It's not altogether different from the situation in the United States, with one important exception: Italians depend almost exclusively on state pensions for their retirement. The concept of the private retirement fund is only slowly catching on, and frankly, it's hard to save for your golden years when your pretax income is only $1,500 a month.

LUMACHE
5.00
KL

FACIOLINA
3.00
KL

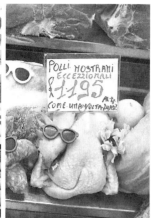

Finance

Italians have been earning and spending a pan-European currency since January 1, 2000. The euro was actually instated two years before the paper and metal made it to the banks. The lira was nothing more than the local translation in the meantime, and for every 1,936 lire pulled out of an ATM by a bank customer, one euro was deducted from that account.

After its official farewell at the stroke of midnight on January 1, 2002, the lira still hung around its old haunts. For two months, it circulated in tandem with the new, brighter-colored currency. This short grace period allowed people to empty out their pickle jars and check under their mattresses for loose lire about to expire.

Even now that the lira is long gone, it is not forgotten. When Italians refer to large amounts of money like rent and salaries, don't be surprised to hear a figure that sounds about 2,000 times larger than it should. Old habits are hard to kick, and many people still think in pre-euro terms—even price tags and receipts in many stores still have the old currency listed alongside the euro equivalent. Throughout this book, prices are calculated at the press-time exchange rate of $1.30 for every €1.

The changeover came without the Armageddon many expected, much like the Y2K computer massacre that never was. There were small hang-ups initially, such as long lines at the register as confused shoppers punched digits into calculators, and a few inconveniences still persist. On the Rome subway, for example, the cost for a ticket is now the unwieldy figure of €0.77 ($1), and the machines don't afford exact change. (See the sidebar "Put Your Two Cents In.")

The loudest complaint about the new currency, however, is that it has allowed shops to hike prices clandestinely. For months, government agencies insisted that inflation remained stable at about 2.7 percent throughout the changeover, and for the 12 months afterward. But consumers, who said that all of a sudden they saw themselves paying about two euros more for a pizza—or, in some cases, twice as much for a pair for shoes—were certain the government was lying. Some consumer groups pegged the post-euro inflation rate at more than 10 times the official rate, or 29 percent.

There was some question as to who was exaggerating more. Consumer groups paint a gloomy picture of Italian shopkeepers all the time, and the government certainly has been caught with incorrect economic data before. There is less doubt now. In its report in April 2003, the Organization for Economic Cooperation and Development (OECD) assured consumers that the changeover did produce much higher inflation in Italy than anywhere else in the euro zone. An independent survey by ACNielsen determined the cost of living was up anywhere between 10 and 20 percent. The average price of a cup of coffee had risen 17 percent, it found, while an average meal for two soared 21 percent. A report by a Swiss-based consultant firm in 2003 ranked Milan as the 17th most expensive city in the world—up from 63rd the year before. The survey's director said the euro was squarely to blame.

Cost of Living

Italians may complain about the increased cost of living, but for an American tourist fresh off the plane, Italy still seems like a bargain. Even when the euro–dollar exchange rate is working against them, New Yorkers get giddy at the cost of a cappuccino (now about €2/$2.60) or a bottle of wine (€4/$5).

When it comes to food and other daily expenditures, your money still goes a long way. A two-course meal with wine that would run about $50 in the average American city, or maybe $75 in New York, costs about $20 in Rome. And those who like shopping for high-fashion labels will feel like they're waking up on Christmas morning when they hit the back streets of Milan. Though housing costs have practically doubled in the last 10 years, rent in Italy is still affordable when compared to New York or San Francisco. In the most expensive cities, Rome and Milan, €800 ($1,040) per month should land you a fully furnished, single-bedroom apartment downtown.

Italians may complain about the increased cost of living, but for an American tourist fresh off the plane, Italy still seems like a bargain.

The longer you stay, however, the more hidden costs you will find. More often than not, they take the form of taxes. Like most European governments, Italy likes to discourage the abuse of its most precious commodity, energy. Heating a modest apartment of 70 square meters, for example, will cost at least €100 ($130) per month in the winter (and Italy is not a very cold place), thanks to high fuel taxes. For that reason, electricity is just as costly. No Italian would ever leave the house without first turning off all the lights.

Cars can almost be considered a luxury. Gasoline prices are four times what they are in the United States, and insurance doesn't come cheap either. To insure a 10-year old Volkswagen in the city, a young person will spend about €1,000 ($1,300) per year for the minimum coverage—a monthly salary for the typical Italian under 30.

How much you should budget per month depends, of course, on how much you earn and where you want to live. As a rule of thumb, the further south you go, the cheaper life becomes. To get some idea of the discrepancy, the cost of living in Naples is 79 percent of that in Milan, according to ExpatAccess, a company-relocation service. And even Naples can be out of reach for those who live in small towns in Calabria and Basilicata.

Not coincidentally, the cheapest place to live is also where there are the fewest jobs. Unemployment in Sicily is almost 30 percent. The national average is nine percent, and it would be a lot higher if not for the industrial centers of Milan and Turin. Of the 30 companies that make up the benchmark index on Italy's stock exchange, for example, 17 have their headquarters in either Milan or Turin. None have their headquarters in the South.

The smoggy North may appear to be an unpleasant place to spend your time when compared to the sunny lemon groves of Sicily, but then again, so is New Jersey when compared to the Florida Keys. Floridians can expect to be paid in "sunshine dollars." So can Sicilians.

Your compensation will depend on a lot of things: the kind of job, your skills and experience, whether the company is Italian or American, etc. But in the broadest terms, a college graduate with five years' experience who makes $50,000 per year in a major American city might expect to be paid half of that in Italy. The majority of Italian blue-collar workers and many entry-level white-collar workers earn in the vicinity of €1,000 ($1,300) per month. (Salaries are described in monthly terms in Italy, not annual.) In the end, Italy may seem like a bargain, but for those making €1,000 a month, it is just as hard as anywhere else to make ends meet.

Banking

The advent of the ATM, or Bancomat as it is known in Italy, has made banking from abroad a snap. Even foreigners who spend months at a time in Italy don't bother opening an Italian account. As long as you have an ATM or debit card, you can pull out cash on demand. Before you plan to rely on a card as your lifeline, though, check a few things:

- If the card is new, make sure you first activate the PIN in a local branch. You won't be able to activate it from abroad. Some banks also have a distinct PIN for international withdrawals.
- Don't memorize the code using letters to guide you: letters often don't exist on Bancomat keyboards.
- Your card must work with either CIRRUS or NYCE, as most do, or else be a debit card from Visa or MasterCard.

It is also a good idea to keep an extra card on hand in case one is lost, crushed, or demagnetized. Sometimes, a confused Bancomat will eat your card for no good reason, and the Italian bank will send it back to the United States for verification—no matter how much you plead that there is no problem with your account and you are who you say you are.

The downsides to this home-banking strategy are (1) there is a fee, usually €2 ($2.60), every time you withdraw on a foreign account, and (2) keeping track of the paperwork from abroad can be a hassle. Many American banks have not yet made online banking available for those living abroad, though some lenders offer a service—again, for a fee—that sends your statements to an Italian address.

For those who don't plan to settle down for the long term, opening an Italian bank account should not be a priority. If you work for an Italian company as a freelancer whose legal residence is in the United States, your payment will be sent to an American bank via wire transfer.

But if you have a regular job contract, and therefore have a registered tax ID number with the government, your employer will pay you either by

Put Your Two Cents In

After the switchover to the euro, two-cent coins took on extraordinary value in Rome, or at least at the capital's metro stops. After the price of a ticket was switched from 1,500 lire to its euro equivalent, e0.77 ($1), ticket-dispensing machines struggled to adapt. Many of them were (and still are, as of press time) incapable of producing one-cent coins in change. This means the buyer must always have a two-cent piece on hand to pay for a single ticket. Buying a ticket at the Cavour station, for example, is a several-step process. A handwritten sign on the machine outlines at least the first three: (1) "Select fare type." (2) "Provide the exact change, or deposit coins according to the schedule." The schedule outlines the arithmetic involved: One ticket (e0.77) requires one two-cent piece. Two tickets (e1.54/$2) require two two-cent coins. (3) "If you do not have correct change," it concludes, "go to the Bar/Tabacchi on Via Cavour."

It is a more confusing situation than it already sounds, because the bar on Via Cavour mentioned in the sign doesn't actually sell the tickets, and refuses to provide exact change. "They should take that sign down," the man at the bar told me.

The switchover to the euro was noted for its surprising lack of glitches, as companies and governments were lauded for coming up with solutions before any problems surfaced. Milan's transport system, for example, simply charged more for the ticket, boosting the price from 1,500 lire (€0.77) to €1 ($1.30). Rome, on the other hand, took the more democratic approach of keeping the same price. In classic Roman style, this means that lovers of democracy have to pay the price of chaos.

In the famous Boston-based folk song, "Charlie and the MTA," the hero couldn't get off the subway without a nickel. In Rome, you won't get on without a two-cent coin.

check or by a deposit in an Italian bank. Most Italian firms won't pay a full-time employee in a foreign account, as that would suggest that they and the employee are evading taxes. And a check made out in euros is worth zero in North America. In this case, opening an Italian account will become a necessity. The process is easy. The only paperwork the bank will ask for is a passport and a tax ID number. Just as in the U.S., you have your choice between savings and checking accounts, along with a number of investment options. If you want to bet on U.S. dollars over euros, for example, you can open a foreign currency account. This will allow you to deposit your dollars directly and convert them to euros only when you make a withdrawal.

Here again, there has been an uproar about price increases. The cost of operating an Italian bank account jumped about 13 percent between 2001 and 2002. One consumer group found that fees for a single account reached €400 ($520) per year. And you will be hard-pressed to find any type of savings account in Italy that actually pays you interest.

Checking accounts rarely, if ever, provide interest payments either. But the value of writing checks should not be underestimated. It is one of the easiest ways to pay. More importantly, with a checking account you'll also have access to an Italian Bancomat card, which is accepted even more frequently at stores than Visa and MasterCard.

An example: I once found myself visiting an isolated monastery off the Ligurian coast, the kind of place you can only get to by boat. My friend and I ordered sandwiches, ate them in a hurry, and then realized neither of us had any cash. There was certainly no bank machine in this town of fewer than 50 inhabitants and the nearest one was a ferry ride away. The snack bar was smack in the middle of the beach and didn't accept credit cards, but they did, miraculously, accept Bancomat cards. You will find this to be true even in urban areas.

Paradoxically, most travel agencies do not accept credit cards. The culprit is the same: merchant fees. The travel agents complain that the amount they pay to the card company totally wipes out their commissions. But then, they should ask themselves, how many foreigners are prepared to pay for a transatlantic flight with cash? For that matter, how were Italians expected to pay for a ticket without a credit card in the days before the Bancomat?

The answer, again, is cash, and lots of it. Stacks of bills in large denominations still swap hands everyday in the typical Italian store, as some customers still distrust plastic. For the storeowners, cash also means no paper trail, and therefore no real incentive to report the income. But tax police have cracked down on under-the-table transactions in recent years, sending in plainclothes officers to check whether they are offered a receipt. These days, storeowners are legally required to give every customer a receipt, and it is the customer's responsibility to have that receipt in hand when walking out the door. The storeowner will sometimes run after you if you forget to take it off the counter.

Credit cards also won't be very helpful when it comes time to pay household expenses, such as heating, electricity, and phone bills. This is done at the post office, and the only accepted forms of payment there are cash or a Bancomat card. (You cannot send in a check to the utility company itself, though you are certainly welcome to walk to their local headquarters and pay by cash if you wish.) Just bring your bill, and a lot of patience for long lines, to the nearest post office, and they will explain the procedure.

Post offices also act as a kind of alternative bank, offering accounts with post-office checks. Like banks, their hours are short: 8 A.M.–2 P.M. weekdays, though some are open on Saturdays as well. There is no fixed schedule as to which branches are open on Saturdays, but you can check the hours of individual offices at www.poste.it.

Banks are open 8:30 A.M.–1:30 P.M. and 2:45–3:45 P.M. on weekdays. Again, some are open on Saturdays.

Taxes

ITALIAN TAXES

Italy has long held a reputation as a nation of tax evaders, and having the head of government under such accusations certainly doesn't help. The parliament led by the same man, Silvio Berlusconi, voted in 2002 to forgive past tax offenders, asking them to pay a small fine instead of sending them to already crowded prisons. The Swiss francs soon flowed in. This sort of amnesty may sound shocking, but it was not a novel event in Italy. It happens every few years.

Italians will rightly point out that every country in the world has tax evasion; the difference is that the others don't wash their dirty laundry quite as publicly. Furthermore, no country has a system nearly as complex and far-reaching as the Italian one, making evasion that much more tempting and probable.

This is not to say that Italy has the highest tax levels in Europe. When measured in terms of percent of wages (for a single earner with no dependents), a 1998 report by the OECD determined that the honor belonged to Denmark, at 43 percent, followed by Germany, at 42 percent, and Italy fell into ninth place at 29 percent. What is more likely is that Italians have to contend with more individual taxes than anyone else does. Only accountants can understand them all, and self-employed people and business owners would do well to find a good *commercialista* (consultant) before opening shop. With the help of these accountants, taxpayers keep the number of tariffs they pay to a more manageable level, and in doing so, they reach a certain equilibrium: In terms of actual revenues collected per GDP, Italy's taxation rate was closer to the EU average than any other member nation.

Below is an abridged list of the taxes from which to choose. They are all known by their acronyms, sometimes even a nickname:

- IRPEF: personal income tax; essentially Italy's answer to the 1040 in the United States. As an employee, this will be deducted from your paycheck. Ranges from 12 percent to more than 60 percent.
- IVA: value-added sales tax, which you will be paying every time you buy something like a cell phone or a car. If you are self-employed in Italy, say

as a freelance writer, you must register for an IVA number as well—some people print it right on their business cards. Unlike sales tax in the United States, it is for both goods and services and not limited to retail items. It is charged every step of the way until it is ultimately passed on to the end-user. About 20 percent.

- IRPEG: the most common corporate tax. A flat rate, just below 40 percent.
- INVIM: capital gains tax.
- ILOR and IRAP: two regional taxes.

Then there is a slew of smaller taxes on such things as owning a moped, motorcycle, or car (the annual *bollo,* paid at the post office), on manufacturing, registering land, etc. Anytime you buy or register anything, be prepared to pay a tax.

The estate tax was slowly phased out in Italy until it disappeared altogether in 2002. Other taxes have been cut or simplified in the past few years, and indeed the whole landscape is usually in a state of flux. Only an accountant will be able to keep you up to date.

Tax time comes twice a year in Italy: November and July. Pay your anticipated taxes in the fall, and file for a refund in July. Employees whose taxes, social security, and health care payments have already been taken out need to file form 740. Self-employed workers fill out form 730, and corporations fill out form 760.

As e-government becomes more popular, many Italians prefer to fill out their taxes online at www.italia.gov.it. You will obviously need to be fairly proficient in Italian to do this by yourself. It is worth the money to hire an English-speaking accountant, at least to get you started.

Finally, those who plan to live off their investments should be aware that there is a 12.5 percent tax on income from foreign bonds. It is the lowest of its kind in Europe. But the best tax deal in Italy for retirees is the northern enclave of Campione d'Italia, which is actually surrounded by Switzerland. Foreigners who can claim residency there—accomplished merely by buying local property—will enjoy a special tax status.

AMERICAN TAXES

Living in Italy may exempt you from a lot of responsibilities at home, but you can never escape the IRS. Whether you earn money in Italy or not, you will have to notify them, too, of your financial situation come April.

This does not necessarily mean you will have to pay any money. If you earn less than the equivalent of $80,000 in Italy and pay Italian taxes on that income, you will not be subject to U.S. taxes on it, too. All you have to do is fill out form 2555 to file for an exclusion. But if you have retained any holdings in the U.S.—an interest-yielding savings account, stocks, bonds, money market account, etc.—you will need to file on those earnings, just as if you were living at home.

> *Living in Italy may exempt you from a lot of responsibilities at home, but you can never escape the IRS.*

The IRS has made it easier in recent years to file from abroad, and the local U.S. Embassy or Consulate will also lend a hand. All of the forms you need can be picked up at the embassy or con-

sulate. They are available for questions on your particular status, and, come tax time, usually have a consultant on hand for more complicated matters. Additional help can be found at the mission's website, www.embassy.it/irs.

The deadline for foreign filers is extended from April 15 to June 15. On the envelope, write "filing from abroad" to make sure your forms are sorted into the right pile. The envelope must be postmarked before June 15. An alternative is to pay online. The website www.irs.gov has a list of private registered companies that offer the "e-file" service, where you can pay with your credit card. It is advisable to pick up all the schedules and worksheets from the embassy beforehand. It can be hard to download certain obscure forms from those sites.

Investing

A LOOK AT THE MARKETS

In Milan's Piazza Affari stands a Fascist-era building called Palazzo Mezzanotte. For almost a century, the captains of industry and their underlings bayed for money there in the so-called Room of Shouts, where a handful of companies were publicly traded. It was a select group of people who understood the stock market in those days. Many of them lived close to the building and whispered buyout rumors in cozy restaurants nearby. The insider atmosphere remains, but the Room of Shouts is no more. It was vacated just before the market went fully electronic in 1994. Italy no longer has a trading floor, only a room full of computers fielding orders on the outskirts of Milan.

Italians have always been assiduous savers—they consistently rank second only to the Japanese in that category—but the automation of the market coincided with the first real surge of popular investing. Before the 1990s, when large state monopolies were cut up and privatized, Italians with significant savings typically kept the money in real estate or else poured it into a family business. By now, Italians have become more or less seasoned investors in securities. Many of them, despite their state-administered pensions, have taken to the markets when planning their retirements, and they've since experienced the dramatic ups and downs.

European markets burned about €1 trillion ($1.3 trillion) in the days following September 11, 2001. Italy's blue chip index, the Mib 30, lost some 25 percent, or €150 billion ($195 billion). The high-tech Nuovo Mercato index—whose total market value had inflated to around €20 billion ($26 billion) in the boom years—lost almost all of that when the speculative bubble burst. By early 2003, Italy's all-share Mibtel had a total capitalization of about €400 billion ($520 billion).

Bonds have also proved risky for the nation's investors. In 2002, a producer of canned fruit called Cirio became the first company in Italian history to default on bond payments, setting off an investigation by Consob, the Italian equivalent of the SEC.

Consob has spent the past few years trying to make the world of stocks and bonds more transparent. It has its work cut out. For starters, banks exert considerable influence on the markets. Italian lenders control some 10 percent of all publicly traded shares, and the foundations that in turn run those banks own another 5 percent. (The state owns about 10 percent.) Furthermore, the banks control many of the nation's brokerage houses that cater to small-time investors. All this leads Consob to believe that banks have a conflict of interest when advising their clients—in sum, not an entirely different reality from that in the United States.

The other bad news for investors is that minority shareholders in Italy seem to count for little. The nation's biggest players, who hold seats on multiple boards, often vote as blocks, ensuring that the companies will never be subject to a takeover. About half of Italy's public companies fall into this category. It suggests that important corporate decisions, such as the buyback price of a share involved in a merger, will always benefit the ruling class, despite the howls of the disenfranchised.

So, why does anyone invest in Italy? One reason to bet on Europe is that you can get more bang for your buck on the stock market when the dollar is relatively strong. Another thing to keep in mind is that American interest in all things Italian—and Asian, Eastern European, and South American interest, for that matter—is decidedly on the rise. Though tough times in the global economy hurt the fashion industry and weren't great for sports car sales, it's quite possible that Italian brands will continue to boom in popularity, just as they have done over the past decade. Lastly, you may notice in other chapters of this book that real estate prices in Italy are no longer cheap. That is only good news for holders of Italian stocks and bonds, who will find themselves in an enviable position once Italians start looking elsewhere to bury their savings.

HOW TO INVEST

Anyone in the United States can buy Italian stocks, as long as that person's broker is licensed to deal in European markets. Trading stocks and bonds in Italy is equally straightforward. Even nonresidents can buy and sell them through an Italian bank or broker. Most brokers work in what is called a *società d'intermediazione mobiliari* (SIM). Just as in the United States, you have your choice of trading online or doing business over the phone. Commissions generally cost about €10 ($13) per transaction.

When you open an account, first you will be asked for an identity card and some form of tax ID. Those with residency in Italy will need to show a *codice fiscale,* as they will be paying Italian taxes, while nonresident Americans, who will pay U.S. taxes, need to show a Social Security Number. They will also need to sign a document that declares them immune from Italian taxes. The U.S. is on Italy's "white list" of countries whose citizens are protected from double taxation.

Finally, brokers and banks may ask you to fill out a questionnaire, ensuring that you're a responsible investor, and ask you to sign a waiver. This is meant to weed out those who tend to overexpose themselves to risk. For those who prefer a more hands-off approach to their personal finances, there are hundreds of managed funds that deal in Italian stocks and bonds.

Brokerages

The following brokerage firms have offices in major Italian cities:

Merrill Lynch
Largo Fontanella Borghese 19
00186 Rome
tel. 800/114-330 or 06/683-931
fax 06/683-932
www.ml.com

Twice SIM
Piazza Affari 5
20123 Milan
tel. 800/279-929
www.twicesim.it (Italian language only)

Promos SIM
Via Stazio 5
80123 Naples
tel. 081/714-2222
fax 081/645-130
www.bancapromos.it

THE COMPANIES

The following (in alphabetical order) are a few of the more intriguing companies listed on the Italian exchanges. By no means does this list

Expat Profile: Jefferson Slack

The man who is supposed to make Italian soccer more profitable should be arriving any minute now at the Four Seasons hotel in Milan. There are a lot of Americans in business suits milling about with cocktails, but Jefferson Slack is recognizable as he glides past the doormen into the piano lounge. He has the sporty look and trim build of a former Ivy League athlete, with the sort of genteel corporate attire one would expect to find at the lavish headquarters of the soccer club Inter, where he works. As he orders a Beck's, starts a chat about licensing, and drops terms like "securitization," it appears that he has little in common conversationally with most of his colleagues on Milan's Via Durini.

Slack was brought in as the president of Inter-Active, a subsidiary of F.C. Internazionale created in 2001 to handle all aspects of the company's operations apart from player contracts. In short, he is responsible for making Inter more profitable without exerting any control over its single largest expenditure. That control is left to Inter president Massimo Moratti. The nitty-gritty details of how to make the money are left to the American.

Slack shows a youthful optimism, a characteristic native to his line of work. "Sports as an industry is less than 20 years old in the way it is managed," he says. "Until the 1980s, the Olympic Committee didn't have a lot of money. In 1984, Los Angeles was

represent picks from an analyst or an adviser; they are merely commonly known facts about some of the biggest names in Italian business.

Autostrade

This is Europe's largest toll road manager, controlled by the Benetton family. People in the U.S. might associate the Benettons with Italy's largest clothing company alone, but the Veneto-based clan has gone far beyond that in the past decade. Their holding group also controls Autogrill, which manages restaurants in dozens of U.S. airports and highways, including the New Jersey Turnpike. The Benettons recently sold their sporting goods lines, Nordica and Rollerblade.

Campari

The Piedmont-based maker of this famously bitter aperitif went public in 2001, but is still family-controlled. The little red bottles first appeared in 1860 and have grown steadily in popularity since. Campari also presides over the Cinzano, Grand Marinier, Glenfiddich, and Lipton Ice Tea brands.

Ducati

Ducati roared into the new millennium with resounding success in Amera watershed; the Olympics were approached as a marketing platform. . . . There is emotion in sports. It has an appeal that other products around the world would kill for."

Slack has spent his entire adult life capitalizing on that appeal. From his high school years at Roxbury Latin in Boston, well into his postgraduate studies at Johns Hopkins University in Bologna, he was a player-manager for his cycling team, signing sponsors and making deals.

After a stint as a sports marketing director in Washington, he worked as right-hand man to David Faulk, the agent who represented such breadwinners as Michael Jordan, Patrick Ewing, Alonzo Mourning, and Boomer Esiason. In 1998, he introduced American investment bank Merrill Lynch to a number of European soccer teams, starting their march toward merchandising—that is, putting team names on wristwatches, coffee mugs, etc.—something Americans know very well. It was in those years that he made important contacts with Italian clubs, and soon landed the job at Inter.

These days, Slack has just enough time to settle in comfortably at his apartment on the famed Via della Spiga, and spend free hours with his American girlfriend. The perks of his job have allowed him to take his father—the owner of one of the largest cycling stores in the Boston area—to see the Giro d'Italia from a helicopter.

ica. It sold its motorcycles to Hollywood stars and has shown positive numbers for the launch of new models abroad. Ducati, based in Bologna, is no longer Italian-owned: It was bought in 1996 by the Texas Pacific group, which also bought a part of the Vespa scooter-maker, Piaggio.

Enel

Until 1999, the nation's dominant utility was a classic state monopoly, answering neither to shareholders nor the demands of competition. That all has changed after slices of it were taken public and after the Italian energy market was opened to foreign competition (in the form of Electricité de France, which joined forces with Fiat to take the reigns of Italy's number-two energy supplier, Montedison). Enel also has a controlling stake in Wind, the mobile phone company and Internet service provider.

Fiat

Founded in 1899 and still run by the Agnelli family, this is the country's largest employer and a national symbol, though lately its carmaking division has been swamped with debt. Fiat has had to sell off some of its major assets, such as a major insurance company, in order to survive. But while Fiat cars have been selling poorly in recent years, the automaker can always rely on its host of sportier brands: Alfa Romeo, Maserati, and, of course, Ferrari.

Generali

This is Italy's largest insurer, based in Trieste. Like most insurers, there's nothing too sexy about it except its sheer size—it is the fourth-largest in Europe—and that it has become the subject of a tug of war between the nation's largest investment bank and that bank's rivals.

Juventus

The Agnelli family took its Turin-based soccer team public in 2002, making it the third Italian club to list its shares, along with S.S. Lazio and A.S. Roma. Juventus has done well at the stadium in recent seasons, and not too badly on the markets, either, in its first few years. For whatever reason, soccer shares in Italy seem to respond significantly to the final score on the field.

Luxottica

The world's largest maker of luxury eyeglass frames—founded by Milan native Leonardo Del Vecchio—has had a ticker on the NYSE since the 1980s, but Del Vecchio also listed it on Milan's Mib 30 in 2000. The company is best known for its Ray Ban and Killer Loop sunglasses, though it has a lucrative business crafting frames for Armani, Bulgari, and Valentino.

Mediobanca

The country's largest investment bank keeps itself shrouded in mystery, even after the death of its fabled chairman, Enrico Cuccia, in June 2000. (Adding to the mystique, his body was snatched from its grave eight months later.) Owned largely by other lenders, such as Unicredito and Banca di Roma, it has significant stakes in most of the nation's principal firms, many of them listed here. But under new leadership, this pinnacle of the *salotto buono* (literally, "good living room"; see Chapter 8, Employment, for an explanation) has been losing its grip on power and has missed out on major deals.

RCS

This company holds the nation's largest newspaper, *Corriere della Sera,* and a good example of shareholder pacts. The paper generates solid cash flow and wields considerable influence in public opinion, so its major shareholders have a gentlemen's agreement that it will never be subject to a takeover. Until recently, RCS (formerly known as HdP) owned some unprofitable fashion ateliers like Valentino, which also made the holding company less attractive to corporate raiders.

Telecom Italia

Telecom Italia is the number-one phone utility in the country, and also the owner of the leading cellular operator, Telecom Italia Mobile. The former state monopoly twice switched hands in dramatic fashion in the past few years. In 1999, it was the subject of a €33-billion ($43-billion) takeover by Olivetti, an erstwhile docile manufacturer of typewriters. Two years later, a group of investors, including the chairman of Pirelli cables and tires and the Benetton family, bought 23 percent of Olivetti and therefore took control of Telecom. Telecom has since merged with Olivetti, outraging minority shareholders with the price offered for the latter's shares.

Tiscali

Sardinia-based Tiscali, one of the first Internet service providers in Italy, was the darling of the new economy in the boom years, at one point posting a market capitalization larger than Fiat's. Then came the crash. Tiscali burned off €1.4 billion ($1.8 billion) in one week. It is listed on the Nuovo Mercato index.

Communications

I n the mid-1990s, when many Americans were already sending email and surfing the Internet, few adult Italians could turn on a computer. A lot has changed since then.

Internet service providers (ISPs) popped up in about 1997, and spread far and fast. Just five years after the first Italians signed up for an email address, an estimated 8.2 million of them were using the Internet—equal to roughly 100 percent of the population between 20 and 30 years old.

The communications revolution came not a moment too soon. The Internet and the explosion of mobile phones have made living here much easier for the average Italian, and especially for foreigners. For one thing, Italy's postal system was notorious. Postcards could take a few months to cross the ocean. For news from home, Americans relied on one or two English-language papers and phone calls over crackling transatlantic wires. But these days, with satellite TV, broadband Internet, and reasonable prices on even cell phone calls abroad, America is only a keystroke away.

Telephone Service

TELEFONI AND *TELEFONINI*

Italians are regularly jabbed by their European peers about their voracious appetite for cell phones. Fresh off the plane, foreigners in Rome are struck by a chorus of ring tones, chiming in where they are least expected. When I first saw a pair of nuns clicking on their *telefonini* after walking out of St. Peter's, cell phones ceased to look like a status symbol and became more of a household necessity.

At the turn of the millennium, the number of registered cell phones surpassed the number of land lines in Italy, and were poised to outnumber the population as of the printing of this book. Why would there be more cell phone numbers in Italy than people? The answer is likely that many customers have two accounts: one for work and one for personal use. To change over, all they need to do is switch the memory card behind the battery.

This tiny SIM card, just smaller than a postage stamp, is the major difference between Europe's GSM system and the one used in America. GSM offers several advantages. Say, for example, your battery dies on the train and you have to make an urgent call. You can borrow someone else's phone and plug in your own SIM card. It holds all of your personal data: your address book, text messages, and the amount of credit on your account.

GSM has another nice perk: There are no roaming charges anywhere inside Italy, and the rest of Europe is on the same system. This means you can use the same phone and number in, say, Slovenia, though you will pay more to make and receive calls—at least that is the case as of this writing. Global companies, such as the world's largest, Vodafone, are winking at the possibility that European roaming charges, too, might be scrapped in the near future.

To sign up for a cell phone number—this requires a *codice fiscale* (tax ID number)—you first need to choose a company. There are four national carriers:

- Telecom Italia Mobile (TIM), owned by the former state monopoly, Telecom Italia
- Vodafone (formerly known as Omnitel in Italy)
- Wind, popular primarily in the South
- Three, owned by Hong Kong–based Hutchinson Whampoa

The last of these companies appeared on the scene in 2002, at about the same time that a fifth one, Blu, disappeared. Blu was bought out by Telecom Italia, and its customer base was sold to Wind. Three calls itself a mobile video company because it operates exclusively on a third-generation network—that is, the kind that can transmit video images—though each of the other companies has access to a third-generation network as well. Licenses to use this system, known as UMTS, cost cell phone companies billions of euros across Europe, and many predicted at the time that UMTS would be a flop. Only time will tell if voice-only phones will be fully phased out by the time you move to Italy, though it is more than likely that the same companies will remain.

> *When I first saw a pair of nuns clicking on their* telefonini *after walking out of St. Peter's, cell phones ceased to be a status symbol and became more of a household necessity.*

You should wait until you know which company most of your friends use before declaring your own brand loyalty. This will save you money. If you are a Vodafone customer, for example, it is cheaper to call another Vodafone customer than it is to contact a TIM, Wind, or Three user.

You also need to decide between a contract and a pay-as-you-go arrangement. In the first case, you'll pay a base rate every month. As a pay-as-you-go customer, which is most common for transient types, you'll buy a scratch ticket at the local bar. It holds a secret code. Dial in the code any time you want to boost your credit. The latter is a more expensive option per minute, but offers more flexibility.

Companies offer various discount programs, so you should do some homework on the services before signing up. For example, Vodafone currently has what they call a you-and-me discount service, which you should choose if you plan to call the same person most of the time. To compare rates and services, visit www.tim.it, www.vodafone.com, www.wind.it, and www.three.com. Each site has a version in English.

LAND LINES

Italy's public phones, given a futuristic look by designer George Sowden, are inviting but largely unused. The sleek new line of Telecom Italia phones, designed by Ferrari-crafter Sergio Pininfarina, now sit like dinosaurs in the office. In general, cell phone rates are low enough that few people bother to make calls from a public phone, and some don't even bother getting a land line these days, though in both cases they're spending more than they should.

Many apartments do not come with a phone, and if you don't plan to make a lot of calls, it may not make sense for you to pay €120 ($156) to have one installed. Customers pay a base rate of about €15 ($20) per month, plus additional charges for an answering service and call waiting, and elevated rates for calling a cell phone. But for those who plan to spend a lot of time chatting, it will likely pay off to get a land line. There are two companies in the market: Telecom Italia and Infostrada. The latter is owned by Wind and rents the "last mile" of phone lines from Telecom Italia. Telecom's 2003 rates are as follows:

National Calls
Local: €.02/$.03 per minute
Within 15 km: €.06/$.08 per minute
Beyond 15 km: €.11/$.24 per minute

Calling Mobile Phones
TIM and Vodafone customers: €.22/$.29 per minute
Wind customers: €.32/$.42 per minute
Three customers: €.34/$.44 per minute

International Calls
Western Europe: €.18/$.23 per minute, €.40/$.52 for cell phones
U.S. and Canada: €.18/$.23 per minute, €.50/$.65 for cell phones
Mexico and South America: €1/$1.30 per minute, including cell phones
(There is a €.30/$.39 connection fee for all international calls.)

Some cell phone companies have discounted international rates that are routed via the Internet, provided you are calling Great Britain, the United States, or Canada. For all other countries, it makes sense to buy a Telecom Italia calling card at the local tobacco shop. There are individual cards for Greece, Estonia, Australia, and many other countries.

Email and Postal Service

INTERNET ACCESS
The strongest argument for having a land line installed in your home is to hook up to the Internet. Telecom Italia and Infostrada (Wind) both offer connections, as do a host of individual Internet service providers across the country. The best known are Libero (again, part of Wind) and Tiscali, which sell ADSL connections starting at about €15 ($20) per month. Other popular ISPs include Infinito, Dada, Tin, and Jumpy. For a complete list of the most commonly used service providers in Italy, see the Resources section.

The company E.Biscom has made huge strides with its broadband networks. The most famous of their products is FastWeb, an integrated

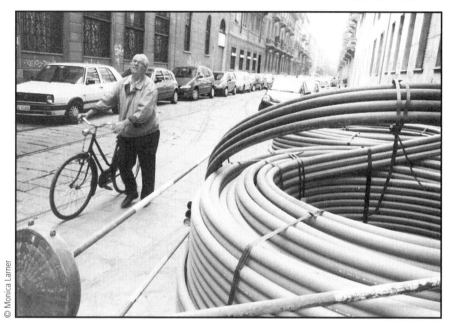

© Monica Larner

Installation of Fastweb in Milan

telephone, Internet, and digital TV network using an Internet Protocol wire. FastWeb has dug up the sidewalks of the largest Italian cities—Milan, Turin, Genoa, Bologna, Rome, and Naples—and has plans to connect the rest.

If you're only a moderate email addict, you can always rely on libraries and Internet cafés. You will find dozens of Internet cafés in every major city, a few in most medium-sized cities, and at least one or two in small towns with some kind of tourist attraction. Rates vary, but expect to pay about €5 ($6.50) per hour. You will pay a fraction of that, if anything, at a library. The catch is that libraries, especially in small towns, keep strange hours and are often closed when you desperately need them.

POST OFFICES AND COURIERS

In the end, anything is better than relying on the mail. The Italian postal system requires little introduction: It has managed to make a name for itself in America as one of the slowest in the world. These days, it is trying to improve its reputation with new management and an advertising blitz. By some measures, it has been successful. In 1993, Posta Italiana reported its first profit in 50 years, and its upgraded services have won some acclaim.

Its priority mail, which costs €0.62 ($.81) for a standard letter, really does deliver them nationally in fewer than three days—most of the time, at least. Sending a standard letter to the United States through the postal system costs €0.77 ($1), though it's still anyone's guess as to when it will arrive. Prices reach €16 ($21) for a four-pound package.

That same package will cost about €70 ($91) using DHL or €95 ($124) with Federal Express, the two most widely used international couriers in Italy, though they are certainly much quicker and more reliable than the regular mail. Both will pick up and deliver to your door. One important thing to remember when shipping packages to Italy—and declaring the value—is the 20-percent import duty. That adds up to a lot on a $2,000 computer, for example. To avoid any misunderstandings with customs, it's best to bring expensive items on the plane.

Media

NEWSPAPERS AND MAGAZINES

Italians are masters of communication in the sense that they barely need to utter a word in order to be understood. Much communication, be it in a store or on the highway, is done without a sound. This was probably very helpful in the days before television and radio created a national language, when dialects differed greatly from one valley to the next. Italians are well known for their broad vocabulary of gestures, where the slightest change of a hand's direction can alter the syntax entirely.

At the same time, Italy's political disarray suggests that, when it comes to agreeing on historical facts, communication has broken down somewhere along the way. Italy has the lowest newspaper readership in the European Union, and for those who have ever tried to make sense of an Italian article, this is hardly surprising. The point of an article is often found at the bottom, beneath thousands of words of florid description and last-name-only references that only insiders will understand.

Then there is the question of which facts are included, which are omitted, and which are given the greatest play. Academics will agree that there is no such thing as a historical truth, and if American newspapers give some hint as to why, Italian newspapers prove the point definitively.

The country has no fewer than 10 nationally distributed papers. They are as much a symbol of one's political loyalty as a source of news. Bearded intellectuals will defiantly brandish a copy of *Il Manifesto* or *L'Unità* on the subway next to the closely shaven businessman carrying a copy of *Il Giornale*—published by Silvio Berlusconi's brother, Paolo—or the more highbrow *Il Foglio,* also part of the Berlusconi universe. There are several others representing the extremes of Italy's political spectrum, though they have more of a fringe following.

> *Italians are well known for their broad vocabulary of gestures, where the slightest change of a hand's direction can alter the syntax entirely.*

The newspaper with the highest circulation, aside from sports papers, is *Corriere della Sera,* closely followed by *La Repubblica.* Based in Milan, *Corriere* is said to have represented the voice of morality during the Clean Hands investigation of the 1990s, and it is about as close as Italy comes to an objectively written, centrist paper. A major shareholder in *Corriere*'s parent company is Fiat, which also controls Turin-based *La Stampa. La Stampa,* too, is considered one of the more august journals representing the middle ground.

Rome-based *La Repubblica* began life in the 1970s as an independent voice in Italian politics, raging against the establishment. But when the conservatives lost their grip on power in the 1990s, *La Repubblica* hitched its wagon to what it must have imagined to be a rising star and now has a decidedly progressive bent.

For those who don't speak or read Italian, there is always the English-language press. Many Italians also regularly check the foreign press to see how their country is portrayed, or to get a less biased point of view.

Before the arrival of the Internet and other advances in information technology, Americans in Italy had to rely primarily on two papers for English-language news: the now-defunct *Rome Daily American* and the *International Herald Tribune.* The *Trib* started out life in 1887 as the European edition of the *New York Herald.* It was partially bought out by the *Washington Post* in the 1960s, and later merged with its major European competitor, *The New York Times.* For decades, it provided expatriates and the local elite with an all-star lineup of stories from the two papers. But in 2002, *The Times* bought it outright and helped it become *The New York Times* of the Continent. These days, the *Trib* (or whatever the new owners plan to call it in the future) faces much more competition. The number of English-language publications available in Italy has blossomed to dozens. There are the *Wall Street Journal Europe, USA Today, The Financial Times, The Guardian, The Independent,* and a wheelbarrow-full of other British papers, plus the major weeklies and monthlies: *The Economist, Time, Newsweek, BusinessWeek, The New Yorker, Wired,* and so on. They are not cheap. English-language dailies start at about €2 ($2.60), while the weeklies and monthlies can cost more than €10 ($13).

TV Trash

The bread-and-butter of prime-time programming in Italy has long been a lineup of quiz shows and 1950s-style variety shows, each with a generous helping of half-naked women and comedy bordering on slapstick. Flip the channel, and you are likely to find a B-grade American movie from the 1970s loaded with car chases and explosions.

The program with the largest market share in recent years has been *Grande Fratello,* Italy's contribution to the Big Brother genre, where 20-somethings are locked in a house for weeks while video cameras monitor their every move.

Italians have long lamented the downward spiral of programming, but it wasn't until *The New York Times* ran a particularly scathing piece in 2002 that it became an international incident. The nation's First Lady at the time, France Ciampi, had to reassure the public that she tells her grandchildren to read, and not to watch that "idiot TV."

Each of the nation's two major networks, state broadcaster RAI and Silvio Berlusconi's Mediaset, admits to being as guilty as the other of serving up trash, but they blame each other for lowering the bar each season. "The real problem with the mechanics of TV," said Franco Cardini, who was on the RAI board of directors from 1994

TELEVISION

It might be a stretch to say that satellite TV has revolutionized the way Italians watch the tube, but it has definitely changed a lot. For one, it brought English-language news to the peninsula. Customers now have their choice of the BBC, CNN, Fox, and others.

It has also changed the way Italians watch soccer. The rights to regular-season games became too expensive for free-to-air television some time ago, so now they are the domain of Rupert Murdoch's pay-TV monopoly, SkyItalia. A subscription to a team's games can cost about €60 ($78) for the season, so many Italians prefer to see them at the local bar on Sundays. That, along with rampant piracy, has made it nearly impossible for pay TV to make any profits from soccer. If satellite and broadband hookups promise to revolutionize TV in Italy in a positive way, it will be that the hundreds of channels will offer a long-awaited variety, and perhaps even some quality shows.

From the days of Mussolini until the 1980s, there was just one major broadcaster: the state-run RAI. No competition was allowed on the national level. One man, Silvio Berlusconi, managed to get around this monopoly by somewhat illegally transmitting the same programs and commercials simultaneously on local stations. The three channels of his Mediaset network—Rete4, Canale5, and Italia1—are still the RAI's only competition. (There is one other small network called La Sette that operates a single channel.)

to 1996, "is the following dilemma: If you push nonfiction and culture, your ratings go down. With game shows, dancing girls, and short films, they go up." For an American TV executive, that deduction is a no-brainer. But for a public broadcasting service that claims to have a social and moral obligation to provide educational programming, it came across as heresy.

In 2001, for example, RAI tried to clean up its act by cutting the show *Tacchi a Spillo (Stiletto Heels)*, dedicated to the subject of transvestites. At the same time, it resurrected an old program called *Babele* that showed erudite people talking about books. By dusting off *Babele*, RAI

hoped to "inform people about books without the derrières of female dancers or some little game," according to the show's host. Trouble is, nobody watched it. "TV has enough boring talk shows as it is," said one of the authors, Carlo Lucarelli, "never mind one about books."

On the bright side, Italian TV does run some outstanding documentaries—with footage rarely found in the United States—and mouthwatering shows on food and travel. The travel shows are usually aired on Sunday mornings, and the documentaries late at night, crammed between ads for horoscope readers and, again, mountains of female flesh.

RAI remains a public entity that lives off of tax revenues and a yearly viewer fee called the *canone*. It costs about €100 ($130) per year, paid via the honor system. If the police were ever to come to your house and find that you had a television but weren't paying the yearly tax, you could be fined.

This division between public and private broadcasting might suggest that RAI would offer educational and family-oriented programming, while Mediaset, which relies on commercials for revenues, has the freedom to cater to the lowest common denominator. In reality, though, both serve up their share of junk (see the sidebar "TV Trash"), because prime-time ratings matter to both. As any foreigner here will tell you, most of what you will find on Italian TV is utterly unwatchable.

Travel and Transportation

In Italy, it's often repeated that under Mussolini, at least the trains ran on time. You may hear old-timers mumbling this adage today when trains are running a few minutes late. It's an unfair assessment of a system that is, for the most part, efficient, cheaper than many of its continental counterparts, and yet close to the European average in terms of safety.

It's hard to say just how well the state railway performed under Mussolini, though it almost certainly had an occasional delay. Even the Swiss railway isn't perfect, and it serves a smaller country. What is more likely is that no one dared complain to the Fascist dictator about the train being a few minutes late, and certainly no one was getting a refund, as they do today.

Similar slander has been thrown at the state airline, Alitalia, over the years. Passengers can decide for themselves what sort of service they are getting for the money. Like any other major carrier, it has been hurt by Internet ticket sales and given a run for its money by upstart discount carriers. British airlines like Ryan Air, Go, and bmibaby have almost taken over the Italy–London route, for example. Smaller domestic rivals such as VolareWeb have also taken a slice of the pie.

> *Italy is a nation of fine race cars and speed demons, traffic laws that are considered negotiable, fiery tempers behind the wheel, and lots and lots of accidents.*

It would be hard to ignore some of the more obvious complaints, however, such as the recurring nightmare that leaves Alitalia passengers stuck at the airport due to a strike, with no airline personnel to be found. While the recently privatized carrier has made an effort to improve its image, Alitalia's customer service sometimes still feels as if it were being managed by the state.

The stereotype about Italian drivers is probably the closest to the truth. Italy is a nation of fine race cars and speed demons, traffic laws that are considered negotiable, fiery tempers behind the wheel, and lots and lots of accidents. The problem is so persistent that Pope John Paul II used to appeal to the faithful to pray for those killed on Italian highways. There are some 8,000–9,000 traffic fatalities reported in Italy every year. Old-timers can say what they will about today's trains, but annual deaths on the railways barely make it out of the single digits.

By Air

Getting to Italy from the United States is a breeze. Alitalia, for example, offers nonstop flights to Rome and Milan from Boston, New York, Newark, Miami, Chicago, and Miami. Dozens of other airlines fly nonstop routes to Italy as well.

In 2000, Alitalia opened a new European hub at Malpensa, near Milan. It is a modern-looking facility at the foot of the Alps, well connected to downtown, yet fraught with problems since its inception. In what was supposed to be its opening year, the asphalt on the runways melted. Later, arriving and departing planes blew shingles off nearby houses, causing an uproar among locals. It did not go unnoticed that the name "Malpensa" can be loosely translated as "bad idea."

Besides giving Milan a 20th-century alternative to the tiny Linate airport downtown, another reason for the new facility was to find a place less affected by the area's notorious fog. Advertisements at the airport claim that Malpensa has a gleaming record on that front, but ask anybody who has been held up for more than 24 hours there until the fog cleared, and you'll get a picture of just how meteorologically cursed northern Italy can be.

The problem is most urgent at Linate. On one foggy day in November

2001, Linate saw the worst airport accident in the nation's history when a small private plane wandered into the path of a Scandinavian Airlines taking off for Denmark, killing more than 100 people. Visibility was partly to blame.

Due to the fog, well-documented baggage thefts, and the interminable strikes by airline and airport staff, flying in and out of Milan can be a headache. Most of the time, though, it really is convenient. Malpensa has a built-in railway station with modern trains leaving for downtown every half hour. It can take as little as an hour between clearing customs and stepping off the train next to Milan's downtown castle. Linate is even better situated, just a 20-minute taxi ride from the city's epicenter, the Duomo. And since the bulk of international traffic has been redirected to Malpensa, Linate is often quite deserted. It makes Milan look more like a provincial outpost than the nation's financial capital.

Rome's airport in Fiumicino, named after Leonardo da Vinci, is also relatively convenient, if slightly outdated. The trains there are not as modern as in Milan, but only take about 40 minutes to reach downtown. Weather is rarely a problem, and except for the crowds that are common in any national capital—especially in late spring and early summer—it is no more chaotic than the city itself.

There are several minor airports in Italy that have now found a niche market in serving low-cost airlines. If you are flying from within Europe on that sort of carrier, be prepared to make one of the following cities your gateway to Italy: Ancona, Bergamo, Brescia, Pisa, Pescara, or Venice.

Just about every city in Italy has at least a small airport, but most domestic air travel in Italy is concentrated on flights to Sardinia and Sicily, or between the North and the South. The Milan–Rome shuttle is certainly the most popular for business travelers, though many people who work in the North have family in the South, and so flights between Turin and Bari, for example, often sell out over the holidays.

By Train

Considering the low price, train travel in Italy is a deal. The manageable size of the country and the obstacles to driving—high cost, persistent traffic, and highway dangers—make it the default method of transportation for many Italians and almost every foreigner.

The state railway, or Ferrovie dello Stato (FS), offers three major types of trains: the Interregionale, which stops in virtually every town along the way; the Intercity, which connects only the principal stations; and the Eurostar, the high-speed link that stops at the biggest cities.

On the Rome–Milan route, for example, most Eurostars will pick up and drop off passengers only in Florence and Bologna. It costs about €50 ($65) for a second-class seat and takes four and a half hours. An Intercity train will make about 10 stops on the same trip, taking six hours and costing about €10 ($13) less. Rome to Milan on an Interregionale would require anywhere from eight hours to an eternity, depending on the route it takes, but nobody would voluntarily subject himself or herself to a cross-country voyage on a string of local trains.

If the Italian railways have a bad reputation in Europe, it is due less to delays than to the carriages' decrepit appearance. Switching from a French regional train to an Italian one is like going back 40 years in time. The air-conditioning might very well be turned off when it is needed most—such as when the train is stopped inexplicably in the middle of nowhere for 20 minutes—and yet Italian passengers just shrug their shoulders and bear it. Summer travelers who would describe themselves as impatient people should avoid the Intercity or Interregionale at all costs.

The Eurostar is the most luxurious way to ride. It was developed as an answer to France's TGV, replacing the *pendolino* (tilting train) of the 1980s, and can reach speeds of 300 kilometers per hour. The country is investing heavily in more high-speed links in the North, starting with a Lyon to Turin track that would complete a large European network. The Eurostar does break down occasionally—eight times in one recent summer—but it is the most reliable Italian train in terms of getting there on time, mostly because cheaper trains normally give it the right of way. Official estimates say the Eurostar arrives within 15 minutes of schedule 92 percent of the time. If it is more than 25 minutes late, passengers are entitled to a partial refund.

Unlike on the Intercity and Interregionale versions, you won't find people cramming the aisles and gangways on a Eurostar. Reserved seating is required, and spots will be snatched up by Thursday night for busy Friday afternoon departures. Buying a ticket on any train requires that you pay an extra penalty, so reserving a seat beforehand is recommended. Even with a ticket in hand, you should turn up at the station at least 10 minutes before departure. Jumping onto a train at the last minute can end in disaster.

I remember beginning an Intercity train ride on a steamy summer day in Rome. As I competed for oxygen in the crowded gangway, a man in a suit leapt into the carriage as it was leaving the platform. As he muscled out the last square inch of floor space, he asked if the train was headed to Naples. As it turned out, it was headed for Florence. He was trapped for an hour going in the wrong direction. What followed was a lengthy tutorial in the fine art of Neapolitan cursing.

When planning a trip, start with the FS website (www.fs-online.com). Punch in your departure station, arrival station, and the date, and it will list all the possible trains in the following 24 hours. This is a lot quicker than running through the timetables or asking at the information office at the station, especially if you're making a series of connections. For many of the routes, you can buy your ticket directly from the website.

Anything is better than going to the ticket window at the train station. There are often huge lines, especially on the weekends, as only a fraction of the available windows are open at any given time. Aside from the website, other alternatives are to buy your ticket at any travel agency, or at the machines at the station. The people who usually end up at the ticket windows are those with lengthy questions about connections, discounts, or refunds.

There are numerous ways to save money on train fares. One is by proving you are a student or a senior citizen. Another is to buy a "green card," which is like a frequent-flyer membership that offers massive discounts on weekends.

Finally, before you board the train, remember to stamp your ticket in the little yellow machines on the platform. Otherwise, the conductor will assume you're scheming to use it again.

By Bus

In the circulatory system of Italian public transport, the trains are the arteries and veins, and the buses are the capillaries. They will be the last leg of any journey to an out-of-the way village or neighborhood. Though many small hamlets often have their own train stations, those on top of a hill or otherwise off the railroad grid can be reached only by bus. Italy has more of them than any other European country.

A bus stop is easily recognized by the orange or yellow sign, marked Fermata. Schedules for each bus and a list of stops on the route are usually posted at the stop. Unlike in most other countries, you cannot buy a ticket on board. You need to buy them beforehand at a local bar or tobacco store (marked by a black-and-white sign with the letter "T").

In cities, tickets work much as they do on a train. They need to be stamped by the little yellow or orange machine on board in order to be valid. But, unlike on a train, the tickets are almost never checked. Rome has cracked down on freeloaders in recent years, but in Milan and less-touristed

In the circulatory system of Italian public transport, the trains are the arteries and veins, and the buses are the capillaries.

towns, authorities tend to assume that no one would go through the embarrassment of being ticketless in the rare event that an official were to climb aboard.

Like anywhere else in the world, buses never come as often as you would like them to, and they are not always on time. If you plan to live in a place where a bus is the only connection to the outside world, you should carefully consider buying a car.

By Car

Much has been written about car culture in Italy, little of it flattering, and there's not much that Italians can say in their defense. Actually, they would see nothing to defend. Cars are simply driven faster, and Italians have their own code of conduct on the road.

The pace of Italian life is so relaxed that such an obsession with speed seems illogical. The streets are the only place in the country where people seem to be in a hurry. Put another way, Italians will drive very fast to get somewhere where they can walk very slowly. The same people who casually show up 20 minutes late for dinner will tailgate, pass in the face of oncoming traffic, and lean on the horn the second the light turns green. Motorcyclists routinely use the sidewalk to bypass traffic. On the highway: havoc.

Almost every Monday morning on the news, there is a body count from the autostrada. Thousands die every year, and this is likely to continue. There has even been talk in Parliament about raising the highway speed limit from 130 to 160 kilometers per hour (78 to 96 mph). Drunk driving is certainly punishable, but only after a driver is pulled over, which is rare. That said, *carabinieri* (police) have the right to flag you over to the side of the road for no reason other than to check your driver's license and registration.

Another reason to avoid the roads is that there are simply too many cars. Italy ranks third in the world for the number of vehicles per capita, after the United States and Australia. Especially on the A-1 thoroughfare that runs the length of the peninsula, traffic jams stretch for miles. Gridlock is sometimes so severe that traffic comes to a complete stop, and people get out of their cars to stretch their legs for 10 minutes, an hour, or sometimes more. Workdays provide little relief. Despite a good public transportation system, millions decide to take their vehicles onto the beltways and avenues of Rome, Florence, Milan, and other cities.

There is an endless list of other arguments against driving. Parking is

© John Moretti

Sunday cycling in Parma

nearly impossible in downtown areas. Tolls are expensive: about €10 ($13) per hour of driving in the North. Insurance policies border on highway robbery. And then there's highway robbery itself: Milan leads Western Europe in the number of cars stolen per year.

If all that weren't enough, gasoline costs four times what it does in the United States. Much of that price comes in the form of taxes. The state does what it can to make driving unappealing. Italy, like the rest of Western Europe, is far from sources of oil, and its foreign policy therefore walks a diplomatic tightrope between American allies and the alleged terrorism-sponsoring countries, such as Libya and Iran, that hold Italian investments. There are daily Alitalia flights to Tripoli and Tehran, routes you're not likely to catch from the United States.

It is unsurprising, then, that Italy is among the countries leading the push for alternative energy. Hydrogen-powered buses are already in use in Turin, and the world's first public hydrogen fuel pump is set to open near Milan. Both cities sometimes close their downtown streets to all traffic except taxis on Sundays, when smog levels are high. Other times, driving privileges are granted alternatively to cars with odd-numbered and even-numbered plates during the week.

But even Europeans are entitled to drive their cars, and the truth is

Road Rules

It is easy to be the victim of miscommunication in Italy, but nowhere is it easier, or are the consequences more severe, than on the road. Signage can be as misleading as the indications from drivers themselves.

The first thing you'll notice about city roads is that there are so many signs pointing to the highway or adjacent towns that it seems you don't even need a map. In many cases, this is true, except that the green signs pointing the way to the autostrada or the blue ones to state roads do not necessarily suggest the quickest route, but rather one that will eventually lead there. All roads lead to where you are going, sooner or later.

Italians know this, of course, and so it is common practice to stop a pedestrian to ask for directions. If your Italian is not good enough to understand the response, and you have to rely on the signs, first you need a lesson in the language of arrows. An arrow pointing left for Rome, for example, does not mean turn left for Rome. If the sign is on the right-hand side of the road and the arrow is pointing left—that is, toward the road in front of you—it means go straight ahead. A turn will be signified by a diagonal arrow pointing either up and to the left, or up and to the right. When the arrows disappear, go with the flow. You will have to take a leap of faith between signs and stay on what appears to be the major thoroughfare, even if it makes sharp turns. When there is a legitimate question at an in-

that Italians have some of the most beautiful roads on the continent. Driving your car along the country's oleander-lined thoroughfares and winding rural roads can be so pleasant that you'll feel as if you're part of a luxury car commercial (perhaps because many of those commercials are in fact filmed in Tuscany and other bucolic landscapes). You truly need a car to visit most of those country roads in the Alps, Tuscan vineyards, and far-flung towns in the South. The question then becomes: Do you need to buy one, or would you be better off renting?

RENTING, LEASING, AND BUYING A CAR

Buying a used car in Italy can be a good deal, especially if you're looking for the kind of model that would cost a fortune in the United States and would be unpractical to drive there anyway, because no one could service it.

In order to buy and drive a car, motorcycle, or moped in Italy, you will need several documents. First, you will need a *codice fiscale* (see the Making the Move chapter) before you make the purchase. The items that need to be tucked in your glove compartment are not much different from those in the United States: registration, proof of insurance, a valid driver's license, and an inspection certificate on the windshield to show that you're not polluting the environment.

tersection where it joins a large road, there will usually be another sign.

Traffic lights can also be confusing, and remember that many drivers consider a red light to be more of a guideline than a law. Also, when approaching a flashing yellow light at a four-way intersection, do not assume that there will be a flashing red in the other direction. More often than not, it, too, will be a flashing yellow.

Another of the famous *faux amis* is a car flashing its headlights at you when you are signaling to turn into its path. In North America, this usually means, "Go ahead." In Italy, it means, "Don't even think about it," and often will be accompanied by acceleration. A miscommunication could have some unpleasant consequences.

Italians also flash their headlights when there is a speed trap or traffic block ahead. The number of times they flash their lights depends on how high-ranking the authorities are. A triple flash signifies the *carabinieri,* the law enforcers with the broadest powers—and that rare stripe of official with whom you cannot smile your way out of a speeding ticket.

Finally, stay out of the left lane unless you are very serious about passing, or you will become a legitimate target for tailgaters. Some drivers are in perpetual passing mode, and will signal their intention by keeping their left blinkers on. In order to qualify for this group, you will need to maintain a speed of at least 150 kmph (90 mph).

Italian regulations on emissions became much more strict in the late 1990s. Every car must have a catalytic converter, and leaded fuel is outlawed. Those with older cars were given a grace period, but any car imported into the country must be up to standards. Still, don't be surprised to see cars or mopeds spewing black smoke. It cannot be stressed enough that, although Italy has some fine laws, few are ever enforced.

For your registration to be valid, it must have a new tax stamp stuck on it every year. The road tax is widely known as *il bollo* and is calculated on the kilowatts of power the engine puts out. For a medium-sized hatchback, it comes out to about €200 ($260). It can be paid at the post office.

Driver's licenses from any EU member country are automatically valid in Italy. For those from non-EU countries, a current license is good for one year, assuming the driver has not established residency in Italy. Residents need to transfer their licenses into Italian ones, a process that requires no exams for as long as the foreign license is valid.

Besides gas, the greatest annual expense of owning a car is insurance. The cost depends, of course, on the kind of car, the extent of the coverage, where you live, and how long you've been driving. For an eight-year-old Volkswagen Golf in Milan—one of the more expensive places to own a car—a regular policy will cost around €1,000 ($1,300) per year through

Langhe, Piedmont

the offices of a major insurance company. The biggest ones in Italy are Generali, RAS, Winterthur, and Mediolana. But cheaper policies can be found on the Internet. For example, you might want to try out Genial Lloyd, owned by RAS. Insuring the same VW Golf in Milan through their site costs about €400 ($520) per year.

The final expense, which is actually one of the first you will incur when buying a car, is an official document of sale. It needs to be signed by a notary.

Renting a car through the largest groups in Italy—Europcar, Avis, Hertz, and National—costs about €60 ($78) per day for a compact car, though most of them have a three-day weekend special for about €100 ($130). If, on the other hand, you require a car more than a month at a time, leasing will be much cheaper. At Europe By Car (www.europebycar.com), a 60-day lease has a base price of €1,200 ($1,560). The car is straight from the factory. In theory, you are buying the car and then selling it back, but they only ask for a €100 ($130) deposit, so that clearly is not the case in practice. For a little extra money, you can lease some pretty sporty numbers as well. They come with full insurance, roadside assistance, etc. Another such company is Auto Europe (www.autoeurope.com).

Although there is no legal reason to use anything other than a U.S. driver's license when renting or leasing a car for that period of time, companies will sometimes ask you to arrange an international driver's license ahead of time. All it requires is sending an Italian translation of your local driver's license, and the company should be able to handle the rest.

Here are some additional tips for renting and leasing a car in Italy: If you plan to go to the mountains in the winter, make sure to ask for chains in advance. The car won't come with snow tires, and many mountain towns require cars to have chains, and police issue fines on the spot for those that don't. Also, since Italy is so close to many non-EU countries in Eastern Europe, it is tempting to take a rental car there. Most Italian rental cars are not insured in those countries, however, and major agencies based in Rome, Milan, and other large cities will put the kibosh on those plans quickly. You can always take a train and then rent a car once you're in Eastern Europe, but another option is to call rental agents in Trieste, most of whom are less skittish about letting their cars travel eastward.

© John Moretti

Housing Considerations

Renting or buying a house is the essence of living abroad; it's what separates you from the tourist. The experience of owning a home in the Italian countryside has become almost legendary, as have the headaches that go along with it. While renting an apartment is less of a responsibility, it also presents its pitfalls.

The same can be said about owning or renting property anywhere, but Italian real estate poses unique benefits and challenges. Italy has a historical claim to some of the most admired architecture in the world. This may be the reason you decided to live here. You wanted to carry your groceries from the open-air market past Baroque palaces and medieval frescoes, and step into your Liberty-style apartment building with a wrought-iron elevator shaft and bicycles parked in the courtyard. Or you wanted to hide away in a tile-roofed villa with terra-cotta floors surrounded by vineyards, where you can lean out your window to smell basil in the garden and hear the chatter of grandmothers.

These simple pleasures of domestic living in Italy make all the complications worthwhile. By complications, I don't mean the handheld shower heads and the three-kilowatt electrical outlets. These are local touches that most people would say lend a more human touch to European living. If you were addicted to the consumer comforts of North America, such as crushed-ice dispensers and garbage disposals, you probably wouldn't have chosen to live in Italy in the first place.

Complications, rather, are the difficulties and bureaucratic underpinnings of buying and keeping up real estate here, the archaic methods of paying the bills, and the often frustrating attitude of repairmen. The good news is that these drawbacks are slowly improving.

RENTING VS. BUYING

Whether you should rent or buy in Italy depends, naturally, on your future plans, and especially on the housing market. Real estate prices skyrocketed in Italy in the late 1990s, and many economists forecast that the Europe-wide bubble has to burst soon. As a rule, Italians always buy before they rent, no matter what the cost. The nation has one of the highest home-ownership rates in Europe.

As a rule, Italians always buy before they rent, no matter what the cost. The nation has one of the highest homeownership rates in Europe.

According to a recent survey by the National Statistics Institute, Censis, 60 percent of all Italians thought buying a home was the best possible investment. This is hardly surprising when you consider that the price of homes has doubled in the past ten years, while Italians are relatively new to trading stocks (which have done poorly over the past few years, anyway). Aside from that, banks offer little or no interest on savings or checking accounts.

Add in the national obsession with saving money, and you will understand why young Italians live with their families until they are well into their 30s, at which point they are either married or simply tired of mom and dad's nagging and have enough money to buy some privacy. It may sound pathetic to an American who moved out at age 18, but skipping the rental stage is a wise financial move for those with enough patience and humility to live at home as a grown adult.

Buying is always a smarter choice, but there are a number of risks in Italy that can really burn you: buying in the wrong area, ignoring serious structural damage or shortcomings, or, worst of all, overlooking a legal morass. The advice that most property experts give is to rent first in an area where you think you might like to buy. If you feel the pressure to buy right off the bat, you should first get to know the neighborhood and the houses themselves by talking to the locals.

Renting

For reasons described above, families often own several floors of an apartment building—if not the entire *palazzo*—and rent out the parts that they don't live in. Foreigners are ideal tenants, since housing laws are so restrictive that it is very difficult to evict an Italian tenant. If Italian residents can prove that there's no other place to live in the vicinity, they can stay in that house until it is proven otherwise. Nonresidents are not protected by these laws, besides which they are sometimes willing to pay more than market price to settle disputes quickly.

Most short-term rental possibilities are well-furnished apartments in the city and private villas in tourist destinations, costing anywhere from 25 to 100 percent more than similar long-term rentals. Often located in nicer neighborhoods or resorts, short-term rentals are a comfortable solution for people fresh off the plane. It shouldn't take more than a month to find a cheaper apartment, and a month in a hotel would cost appreciably more.

These sorts of limited contracts (see the sidebar "Common Housing

Common Housing Terms

affitare: to rent

agriturismo: rural bed-and-breakfast

arredato: furnished

bollete: utility bills (gas, electric, telephone, etc.)

bombola: a tank (usually methane or propane for the home)

box: garage

camera: room

campanile: bell tower

condomino: homeowner's association, which collectively pays for such things as elevators, garbage removal, etc.

gattara: woman who adores cats

geometra: surveyor/deputy architect

inquilino: tenant

mansardo: slanted ceilings

monolocale: one-bedroom apartment (a two-bedroom is a *bilocale,* a three-bedroom is a *trilocale,* etc.)

palazzo: a building

portinaio: doorman/building superintendent

ristrutturato: renovated

soffito: top-floor apartment; not a spacious penthouse, but a small converted attic

sottodichiarazione: underdeclaring the value of a house during a sale for tax purposes (commonplace, but illegal)

spese: normally, this means "shopping"; but in terms of housing, it refers to utility costs

Terms") are an obvious choice for vacationers in, say, Tuscany or Venice. For urban professionals, yet another such alternative is a residence. These are much like hotels, with a reception desk and laundry service, except that people stay in them longer—maybe a year or two. They are charmless and short on floor space, but they are inexpensive.

Many new arrivals with low expectations and less money choose to rent a room. If you look through the classifieds or university bulletin boards, you'll run into announcements from students looking for a fourth or fifth roommate, or else a family that has a spare bedroom with some privacy, possibly even an independent entrance. In Rome and Milan, these rooms can be found for as little as €500 ($650) per month, about 60 percent of the standard rent for a one-bedroom apartment.

But in the end, there's no substitute for your own place, if you can afford it. If you're dreaming of hardwood floors, a large terrace with grape leaves overhead and a view of the city, a huge shower with stone floors, and large closets in the bedroom to fit all the clothes you plan to purchase in Italy, you're half in luck. The large closets should be easy enough to find, and you may be able to land the terrace, for a price. Almost every apartment in Italy has some sort of balcony, except a few of the oldest ones in the historic center. The hardwood floors are more difficult to find—linoleum is par for the course, tiles if you're lucky—and you can forget about the big shower. Bathrooms in Italy are much more compact than the American standard. If you have old-school taste, you may be pleasantly surprised by the gas stoves in the kitchen, and the latest kitchenware and stylish coffeemakers are just a quick shopping trip away.

The classified ads—discussed individually in Chapters 14–19, the Prime Living Locations—will tell you if it's a *monolocale* (one-bedroom) or *bilocale* (two-bedroom) apartment, the square meters of floor space, and whether it is *arredato* (furnished). There may be some mention of parking if you live outside the city.

Another consideration is the heating, which may or may not be mentioned. Central heating—which is most often regulated by month of the year, not the temperature outside—is the most common. But you may have the luck to land an independent thermostat, in which case when the heat goes on and off is not at the discretion of the *Farmer's Almanac*.

Air-conditioning? In a word, no. Aside from the extraordinary electricity cost, it's seen as a curse in Italy and the singular cause of most unexplained illnesses. Air-conditioning is therefore used mostly in workplaces when the outside temperature becomes truly unbearable. Even then, it breaks down periodically. On rare occasions, steamy weather can produce such a stress on utilities that they declare blackouts, when electricity is shut off in certain neighborhoods for hours at a time. Keep an ear out for such developments in the depths of summer. You don't want to be caught in an elevator when the power goes out.

Some conveniences, such as washing machines, are optional. Dryers are almost unheard of. Refrigerators will likely be smaller than you are used to, and in general, electric appliances are deemed unnecessary when a good old mechanical one will do the trick.

FINDING THE RIGHT PLACE

Any city-dweller knows the two secret ingredients to a comfortable apartment: lots of light and little noise. The former is relatively easy to find in Italy; the latter is nearly impossible.

It is no exaggeration of stereotypes to say that Italians are a boisterous people. There is some social value to understatement and subtlety, but for the most part, screaming over someone else's arguments is preferred. This makes for lively conversation, entertaining talk shows, and above all, noisy residential living. Try to get a feel from the outgoing tenant about the people living above and on either side of you and how much of a ruckus they make. Apartment buildings are almost always built around a central courtyard, and the late-night conversations from adjacent balconies are projected directly into your own. If there are a lot of children in the building, prepare yourself for evenings of soccer or volleyball games.

That said, most apartment complexes have condominium-style rules that forbid such things as taking your trash to the courtyard bins after a certain hour. But that won't protect you from the roaring motorcycles outside, nor the infamous local church bell. Pater nostrum, save us from the church bell. No matter how religious you may be, you should put as much real estate as possible between you and the nearest place of worship, because the bell rings out to wake the slumbering sinners every 15 minutes, starting at 7 A.M.

Conversely, if you make too much noise at night, you will soon find yourself on the wrong end of a broomstick whacking on the ceiling below. Noise seems to travel downward, especially in flimsily-built apartments, and if you have the misfortune to have light sleepers living beneath you, even the clicking of your shoes on the floor will be grounds for a cease-and-desist letter from their lawyer.

Italians therefore pay close attention to which floor an apartment is on, and it may be mentioned straight away in the classified ads. Obviously, a ground-level apartment on a busy street is going to be a nightmare, as is a sixth-story place in a building without an elevator.

RENTAL AGENTS AND CONTRACTS

Within the classifieds, many of the phone numbers will look suspiciously identical. Real estate agents hold the lion's share of what's available on the market, and that is mostly bad news for you. Agents will ask for a fee equal to one month's rent. So, if you lease the apartment for just six months, that's a 17 percent commission. It's important to remember that everything is negotiable in the universe of Italian real estate, especially the rent itself, and agents' commissions are no exception.

Even the outgoing tenants may ask for a cut—it's referred to as "key money," a fee to hand over the keys. This is illegal and has become less common in the past few years. Still, it can show up in different forms: If you take over an apartment contract from a friend, for example, you have essentially inherited that person's debts, such as lingering energy bills or any damage caused to the apartment, unless you specify your liabilities carefully—and in writing—with your landlord.

The most common contracts these days are four-year agreements, which makes it easier for landlords to free themselves of a delinquent tenant, but doesn't necessarily mean that you need to be in there for four years. You are legally required to find another tenant to take your place if you want to leave sooner, but this is rarely a problem in the big cities, where a good apartment will be snatched up quickly.

You will be asked for at least one month's deposit from the owner, and sometimes as much as three months. Most contracts will stipulate that any repairs made to the apartment, including repainting or cleaning fees, will be deducted from your deposit when you move out.

If it is a furnished apartment, the owner keeps a detailed list of every item in there, right down to the last napkin holder, and will run through the list on move-out day. It's almost impossible to avoid losing some of your deposit; the owners' grievances can be outright comical, e.g., the sheets weren't ironed neatly enough, so you should negotiate for just one month's deposit if at all possible.

It may be included in your rent payment, and therefore goes unnoticed, but every apartment owner needs to pay a contribution to the *condominio* (association of apartment owners in the building). The associations pay for the *portinaio,* a sort of hybrid between a doorman, a building administrator, and a concierge; plus cleaning services, garbage removal, lights, elevators, etc. Some associations make you pay more for the elevator if you live on the upper floors.

Finally, prepare yourself for significant utilities bills (discussed later in this chapter). They can reflect anywhere between 10 and 25 percent of your monthly rent.

Buying

There can be no better reward for a life well lived than a stone-walled farmhouse in the Italian countryside. Something with vines crawling up the sides, a wicker-covered jug of wine by the doorstep, and a garden full of cherry tomatoes and white asparagus. To complete the scene, you will need a wise old neighbor to remind you to keep your garden's mint from taking over the vegetables, and to show you how to prune your century-old olive tree correctly. With some money, some wisdom, and a lot of legal help, it can happen.

When buying their first place abroad, Americans sometimes worry about the nation's political stability. They fear that their real estate may somehow be taken away from them in the future. This is not a concern in Italy, nor anywhere else in Western Europe, for that matter. But there is another fear that is well grounded—namely, that unfamiliarity with local laws might spell disaster.

The first thing to remember when settling on a home is that buyers and sellers will very often declare a price much lower than the one actually paid, to the tune of 50 percent or more. Sellers like this arrangement because it means declaring less income. Buyers, on the other hand, may be

> *There can be no better reward for a life well lived than a stone-walled farmhouse in the Italian countryside.*

able to negotiate a lower price if they agree to do business this way (although housing prices in Italy, just as in the United States, are always negotiable). It is no different than getting a little discount in Italian restaurants for paying in cash, but on a much grander scale. This practice of recording a false sale price, known as *sottodichiarazione,* is illegal, and can present real problems for the buyer.

For example, if you buy property from a company that has recently gone belly up, creditors can reclaim the property when the company is liquidated. You will be reimbursed for the property, but at the lower declared value. *Sottodichiarazione* also creates a dilemma if you sell the property later and pay capital gains taxes. You will be taxed on an inflated figure, assuming you file the same declared value to the IRS.

The most common pitfall for Italian homeowners, and one that may be unavoidable, is the risk that the construction company goes bust after you have paid them a deposit, but before the home is finished (or even started!). You will be in court for a long time, and may never recuperate your down payment. In some cases, the deposit equals about half of the selling price.

Beware of wills. If you buy a home that is contested in a will, you could face angry co-beneficiaries who have five years to try to get the property back. Finally, for reasons described above, never buy an occupied apartment or home in the hope that the tenants will move out. They won't, and will overcome even the most devious maneuvers, such as your shutting off the water or electricity. I have seen more than one apartment with a garden hose running through the bathroom window, and it wasn't there to water the geraniums.

SELECTING A HOUSE AND SIGNING THE CONTRACT

Window-shopping for Italian homes has become much easier with the Internet. No longer do you need to rely on a real estate agent's description of a place to find out whether it is simply a pile of rocks. Several sites have downloadable photos of all of their properties, sometimes accompanied by an asking price, which means you can start the first stage of your research from the comfort of your living room.

Once you have an idea of what sort of property costs how much, you can turn to a real estate agent to show you the houses firsthand. You have your choice between an Italian agent and a foreign agency. The advantage to dealing with the Italians is their in-depth knowledge of the area and ability to answer any question you may have. And there is an endless list of questions, for example: Do the owners owe any money in taxes or

© Monica Larner

loan payments on the property? What other liabilities, such as condominium fees, does it have? Is the building structurally sound, and if not, how much will you need to spend to get it into livable condition? Is the water from a private well, and if so, are the pressure and quality acceptable? Is the property owned by a company or an individual? Do local zoning laws allow you to turn the residence into a business, such as a bed-and-breakfast or a workshop? Will you be allowed to do all the renovations and improvements you have planned, such as adding a swimming pool? If these renovations have already been done, have they been done legally, or will you have a liability on your hands? The trouble for American buyers is that many of the local agents don't speak fluent English, which is why many prospective homeowners turn to a foreigner.

There are two other professionals who will be able to answer these questions for you more thoroughly, and both play essential roles in every real estate transaction: the *geometra,* a sort of deputy architect and surveyor; and the *notaio,* a cross between a lawyer and a notary public. It is difficult to translate their titles into plain English because the professions simply don't exist in the English-speaking world. The *geometra* will survey the property, handle any subdivision issues, and, although not a professional architect, can give you a good idea of whether there are any structural faults, and how much the house will cost to renovate. In rural areas especially, the *geometra* often works in tandem with the local real estate agent, which of course raises red flags about the person's objectivity. There is always the option of finding someone from outside, though this will add to the cost, and an outsider will not know the local market and considerations as well as the agent-appointed person does.

Depending on the job, the survey will cost in the vicinity of €1,000 ($1,300). The report will be in Italian, so unless you have a very good command of the language, you should budget in some translation costs.

The major function of the *notaio* is to register the sale of the property with the state. The state land register is the basis for all tax calculations, and the *notaio,* as a public servant, is charged with assuring that you will be taxed on the property's full value. Because the *notaio's* fees are expensive (see below), because they double as a sort of tax collector, and because their services are essential for any legal maneuver, theirs is not the best-loved profession in Italy. It ranks down there with real estate agents, *carabinieri* (police), and politicians. Still, they provide all the necessary documents about the property, and any contract must be signed in their presence.

The first thing to remember about real estate contracts in Italy is that they are divided into two stages—the *compromesso* (intent-to-buy document), which is not always binding; and the *rogito* (deed of sale), which is. The intent-to-buy is something used by real estate agents and developers to initiate the sale, and they're not always bulletproof. For example, if you're buying a preexisting building, the *compromesso* may come in the form of an offer to buy, which can be reworded to make it a non-binding contract. Otherwise, it may be a full-fledged *compromesso,* which will outline all of the terms of the agreement, such as whether the property contains elements that are part of a cooperative (i.e., *condominio,* the price, the eventual date of sale, etc.).

If, on the other hand, you are buying a property that is not yet completed, the agreements will either stipulate that you buy the property as is, or else after a specified time or a certain amount of work has been done to it. The latter, based on work completed, is always preferable to an agreement that is based on time, since Italian contractors and repairmen are not known for their punctuality.

There are obviously myriad questions to be asked before signing a contract, and only a good, English-speaking attorney trained in international law will be able to make sure that all of your demands are met.

A few basics are often overlooked. For example, you should be aware of exactly what comes with the house. It is amazing what some homeowners

think is valuable when they move out, and you may find your newly purchased home void of such assumed assets as light fixtures and toilets.

PURCHASE FEES

Once you have signed the deed of sale, it's time to settle up and pay all
the assorted taxes. If you purchased the property from a company,
there is a 10 percent value-added tax to be paid, or 20 percent if the
property can be described as a "luxury." Otherwise, you will pay a 7 percent duty, a 3 percent real estate tax, and a local tax that is about one
half of 1 percent.

Last, but not least: the notary's fees. These are non-negotiable fees
fixed by law, and they vary according to the value of the property. For real
estate worth €200,000–500,000 ($260,000–650,000), the fee equals about
1 percent, and decreases as the property's value increases from there.

Financially speaking, buying a property abroad is always more complicated than buying one at home, because it presents unique considerations. The first of these (unless you plan to pay for the home in cash) is
where to get the money. One choice is whether to mortgage an existing
home in the U.S., or take out a loan for the home you are about to buy in
Italy. There are advantages and disadvantages to each.

There are currency risks involved. If you take out a mortgage for your
Italian home, the monthly payments will be in euros. And, chances are,
you're paying it off with dollars—unless you have an income source in
euros, such as renting out part of the home, which can be risky in itself.
The dollar–euro fluctuation can be damaging. In 2002 and 2003, the dollar plummeted about 15 percent against the euro, and so a couple previously paying a euro-denominated mortgage of $2,000 per month would
suddenly find themselves forking over $2,300.

The payments will likely come out of your Italian bank account. For
those not working in Italy and depending on savings in the U.S., this
means picking the right time to transfer funds. Clearly, when the dollar is
strong, you'll want to transfer as many dollars as possible into euros in your
Italian account for future payments.

Keep in mind that there are always hefty fees on wire transfers, and
there's really no way to avoid them, short of traveling with 3,500 one-hun-
dred dollar bills in a carry-on bag, which is a pretty risky affair and won't
go over well at the customs office. An alternative is to ask your bank for a
certified check—an international draft—but this process can take a long
time, the exchange rates are unfavorable at the Italian bank, and they will
also exact a fee. In the end, a wire transfer is probably the best way to get
the job done.

The other factor to consider when choosing whether to set up a mortgage in Italy or in the United States is interest rates. As of press time, they were at rock bottom in both countries, and since Italy joined the euro zone, the European Central Bank's base rates have been more or less in line with those of the Federal Reserve.

BUILDING AND RESTORING

The processes of buying and building on land in the United States and buying and building on land in Italy are different. In rural American towns with lax zoning laws, you can usually find a cheap piece of land and build whatever you want. Owning land in Italy, on the other hand, was historically the right of the aristocracy, and in some ways, it can seem that things haven't changed too much since the days of feudalism. Especially in desirable northern and central regions, acreage is expensive. Remember that there are nearly 60 million Italians (a quarter of the U.S. population) living on a peninsula about the size of Arizona, and there's not much land left for legal construction.

That said, buying a cheap, run-down farmhouse is not much different than simply buying a plot of land. You're going to have to start from scratch. The first step is making sure, ahead of signing the contract, that you will be able to get the necessary building permits. These are going to take a long time to nail down, and you should enlist the help of your architect or *geometra* for this. Keep in mind that if you buy historic property that is listed in the register of historic homes, it will be nearly impossible to touch a single windowpane, much less put in a swimming pool.

It should be pointed out that many people in Italy undertake illegal construction and wait for the government to pass an amnesty, which they do every few years, then pay a fine to clear the matter from the books. (Incidentally, illegal construction is a huge problem in the South, where companies regularly put up cement monstrosities in protected areas. These sorts of infractions aren't resolved with an amnesty. They are resolved with a bulldozer and a wrecking ball.)

The biggest mistake that foreigners make when buying an older home is underestimating the money and time it will take to make the place livable, never mind likeable. Yes, there are homes to be had—even in Tuscany—for less than €60,000 ($78,000). But they have no electricity, no water supply, and certainly no septic tank; many have dirt floors, and when the advertisement says that the roof needs work, that means it needs a new one—at a cost of perhaps €100,000 ($130,000). You can count on about €1,000 ($1,300) per square meter to renovate a house well. For medium-sized homes that sell for less than €100,000

© John Moretti

($130,000), the final cost to you, after repairs, could be more than twice the selling price.

If you make a brutally honest assessment of whether you can afford all the upkeep, and if you are prepared for it, you will truly get your money's worth. Though popular literature about buying a home in Italy describes the snail's pace of Italian craftspeople, they actually do an expert job. Careers in masonry, carpentry, and metal-working are usually handed down through the generations, and the craftspeople have a well-earned reputation throughout the world as artists who produce works of reliable quality. They know their materials, and they will come up with creative solutions to problems that might never have crossed your mind. The end result may not be the bargain you expected, but aesthetically, it will have all you dreamed about.

Household Expenses

You'll find a few surprises when you open your first household bills: The phone bill isn't itemized, for example, and you pay for your own water. Most shocking, though, will be the amount due, since energy in Europe costs a bundle. Utilities will be a significant line item in your budget,

© Monica Larner

and if you're building or renovating a house, you should study your needs well before deciding what kinds of services will be most efficient.

More and more companies are setting up online bill payments, which is a long-awaited development, since paying the bills has traditionally been a pretty complicated affair. You never pay by mail, and checks are rarely accepted. Aside from the new online services, you have three ways to pay. You can go to the company headquarters itself, with the bill and a fistful of cash. You can arrange for a direct transfer from your bank account, which makes disputing a bill more difficult, since they already have your money. Or you can pay at the post office. The last option wouldn't be so bad if post offices were open for more than a few hours a day. But for now, expect massive lines come payment time.

You can expect electricity bills to be the greatest expense, and there's not much you can do about it, short of buying a generator or running off solar power. The only way to save money is to remember to turn off the lights and appliances when you're not using them.

ENEL (Ente Nazionale per l'Energia Elettrica) is the partly privatized former monopoly that still provides most of Italy with its power. The other major provider is Edison. They outfit the average household with three kilowatts, which is about enough to run three or four appliances (and pretty wimpy ones at that) at a time. This also helps explain why there are very few clothes dryers in Italy, and why the average Italian family couldn't run an air-conditioner even if they wanted one. Even without heavy appliances, you will often overload the circuit, so when moving into a new house or apartment, find out right away where the circuit breakers are.

Like most bills, the electricity *bollete* arrives every two months and is based on expected consumption. At the end of the year, the company calculates how much you actually used, and you will either be credited or debited accordingly. Mostly, you'll be debited. Indeed, electricity costs are so high that, whenever possible, Italians rely on natural gas. Heating is generally gas-powered, as are water heaters and the stove. This also makes it easier to save money by simply shutting off the boiler, or switching off the gas line altogether, when you leave the house for a long time. (Note: In apartments, you won't be able to do this if the heating is central.)

As long as you live in the city or the center of town, your house should be on the gas network. If not, you can buy your methane in large tanks (called *bombole*) and run a line into the house. In general, it is a very cost-efficient and fairly clean energy source, but it can be dangerous. It seems that every year, there is a tragedy somewhere in Italy when a rickety old apartment building explodes due to a faulty gas line.

Next envelope, please: the water bill. Prices are laid out by local entities, and therefore vary according you where you live. Often, it is a pretty negligible expense, but could be as much as €50 ($65) a month if local prices are high and you do a lot of washing. Or worse, if your neighbors do a lot of washing, and the water bill happens to be shared by the *condominio* (owners' association).

Not everyone will get a water bill. It may be included in your electricity bill. Or, if you're a renter, your landlord may just include it into the monthly rate. For homeowners in the country, you will likely have a private well and will just pay for the electricity to pump it.

Aside from the phone bill and the television tax (see Chapter 10, Communications), your final utility expenditure is the garbage tax. This calculation is based on the amount of floor space in your home, which has long been a bone of contention for those who would just prefer to see it based on the amount of trash produced. Renters are not likely to see an individual trash bill, since it is almost always paid by the owners' association and then passed along to tenants within the rent. As in the United States, garbage collection is seen—in the south of Italy especially—as the fiefdom of underworld dons. Naples therefore has a perennial problem with its garbage collection. This is passed off as a labor strike but quite transparently is an appalling Mafia power play, especially as the trash always seems to pile up in the hottest months. In

Rome, trash bins were once removed from public places, since they were considered an eyesore. This only made things worse when individual bags started appearing in the streets.

On the surface, at least, Italian cities have comprehensive recycling programs, with household bins for plastic, paper, and compost, and communal bins for tin and glass. But frequent exposés have shown that, once the collectors haul it off, the stuff usually ends up in the trash, anyway.

Prime Living Locations

© Monica Larner

Overview

Choosing the right place to live in Italy is like surveying a dessert cart. Everything looks too good to pass up. A waiter might suggest a few specialties, but you're always going to wonder what you missed. There are no bad choices among Italy's cities and regions, though some are more practical than others. If you're a career person, for instance, remote southern locations should probably be scratched off your list. Other places, like the choicest towns in Tuscany, will be financially out of reach for the average homeowner.

The following two chapters highlight Italy's two largest cities, Rome and Milan, each of which offers greater numbers of job opportunities for foreigners. Then there are four chapters dedicated to the best of rural and small-town Italy: The northeastern-central regions of Veneto and Emilia-Romagna, the northwestern regions of Piedmont and Liguria, the center regions of Tuscany, Umbria, and Le Marche, and three regions from the South: Campania, Puglia, and Sicily.

Venice and Florence are not covered. Though they are two of the most popular places to visit in Italy—and for good reason—they are not, in my opinion, the best places to live. Tourist season itself is one major reason to steer clear. The streets in both places are so crowded with English-speakers in the warmer months that it hardly feels like you ever left home. You'll have to battle the crowds on the streets just to get a bottle of milk. (Disgruntled locals in Venice will tell you that even milk is hard to find, now that the tourist shops have overtaken the corner grocery stores). You'll have to struggle with long lines at the train station. Veneto and Tuscany have so much to offer outside of their famous capitals that you might as well take advantage of these lesser-known places and live like a local, saving the tourism in Florence and Venice for weekends in the off-season.

ROME

Rome has been a magnet for foreigners ever since the Goths sacked the city and moved in. Its featured attractions need little introduction. Millions of Americans come to this hub of Western Civilization every year, and many of them refuse to leave.

While the monuments are what initially attract foreigners to Rome, the Roman way of life is what makes it so hard to leave.

The weather in Rome is superb. Though it lies on roughly the same latitude as New York City, palm trees lazily grow out of ancient ruins, and the most you'll need to wear in winter is a lightweight jacket. That alone is reason enough to move in, but Rome's history is its greatest asset. The aura of the ancients is present in every little act of modern life in Rome, whether it is setting an appointment to meet friends in front of the Pantheon, driving to work on the Appian Way, or coming home late at night to your apartment behind the Colosseum. The eternal monuments are a constant reminder of the greatness of this city and the wisdom its people have attained through the centuries.

Indeed, while the monuments are what initially attract foreigners to Rome, the Roman way of life is what makes it so hard to leave. These people have spent millennia identifying the essential and enduring elements of life, and the answers almost never include work. On any given afternoon, well-dressed Romans will let the hours roll by at lunch, then glide off on their *motorini* to their next appointment with pleasure. Few seem bothered with such banausic preoccupations as a paycheck. This feature of daily life will be off-putting to those who demand efficiency, but for those armed with sufficient patience and seeking a relaxed lifestyle, there really is no other place to be.

MILAN AND THE LAKES

For many foreigners, Milan is defined as a fashion capital, where models rush between sleek office buildings for photo shoots and others shop frantically to catch up with the trends. This definition isn't altogether off the mark. In the late 1960s and early 1970s, Milan stole the fashion-capital title from Florence, and it is now the home of the big-name labels and all the catwalk shows that count.

Milan is also the hub of financial services and the headquarters of the country's biggest businesses. For that reason, it is known to Italians as a place to make money and a career, and that's about it. Yes, it looks a little drearier than the nearby Riviera or the Alpine scenery just to the north, but the indoors lifestyle contributes to the city's mystique. If the Milanese aren't at the office, they're hanging out in nice bars and restaurants or entertaining at home; then they escape on the weekends to Europe's renowned playgrounds, just an hour or two away.

Especially close to the city is Italy's lakes district, Lake Como in particular. This Alpine lake is so well connected to the city, in fact, that many locals enjoy the best of both worlds by residing near paradise and working downtown. The suburbs of Brianza, which stretch from the city limits to the lakeshore, are attractive in their own right.

THE NORTHEAST: EMILIA-ROMAGNA AND VENETO

The northeast corner of the country, bound on the north by the Dolomites, on the south by the Apennines, and on the east by the Adriatic Sea, has produced some of Italy's most prosperous cities, which enjoy a very high standard of living. Emilia-Romagna, traditionally the wealthiest regions in Italy, and the Veneto, once upon a time among the poorest, have little in common historically or culturally, but foreigners will find a similar style of life in these two regions today. Both are composed of comfortable, medium-sized cities boasting world-class universities and hospitals, with fertile farms and vineyards surrounding them.

Verona, for example, is small and picturesque, a fitting setting for Shakespeare's *Romeo and Juliet,* which may be a reason that many foreign couples, especially from Britain, have begun to call it home. Expatriates have also flocked to Bassano del Grappa and other northern towns, especially since the provinces of Treviso and Vicenza house important military installations. Some of the country's choicest rural living is found there, most notably in the vineyards that produce the grapes used in prosecco, Italy's answer to champagne.

Emilia-Romagna's wealth shows up in its homegrown luxuries. Ferrari, Maserati, and Lamborghini cars are from here, as are a number of their

> *Those with discerning taste and a penchant for epicurean pleasures need look no further than Emilia-Romagna.*

owners. If you choose to live in Emilia-Romagna, the greatest hardship you're likely to face is picking the city itself. Bologna, Ferrara, Modena, and Parma are all very comfortable places to live, with blossoming industry and a transportation infrastructure that is second to none. Each can lay credible claims to the finest cuisine in the country. Those with discerning taste and a penchant for epicurean pleasures need look no further than Emilia-Romagna.

THE NORTHWEST: PIEDMONT AND LIGURIA

Piedmont and Liguria contain the best that Europe has to offer, condensed into a mountainous corner. The region starts at the Alps' tallest peaks, rolls through foothills that produce truffles and Barolo, and then melts into the Italian Riviera. In late spring, you can ski snowy slopes in the morning and bask by the Mediterranean in the afternoon, stopping off for some excellent wine and cheese in between.

The two regional capitals of Turin and Piedmont don't draw many tourists, but they do produce jobs. Turin is home to the nation's largest private employer, Fiat, which has fallen on hard times in recent years as car sales have sagged, but will always hold a place in history as a driving force behind the Italian economy in the 20th century. It and the region's high-tech industry ensure that Piedmont will never be just another pretty place to visit.

It is little wonder, then, that surveys regularly name Piedmont towns as offering the best quality of life, while the region of Liguria has an equally convincing claim to fame as home to the oldest inhabitants in the world. The secret to longevity, its centenarians say, is a relaxed lifestyle and one glass of wine per day.

THE CENTRAL REGIONS: TUSCANY, UMBRIA, AND LE MARCHE

Picture this for a lifestyle change: You're driving back from the beach in a red Alfa Romeo convertible, winding your way through aromatic Tuscan vineyards at dusk. You round the corner, marked by a hilltop castle, and pass a field of sunflowers. Turning onto a dirt road, you see your house come into view: a stone-walled villa with a large garden and a vista over the hills.

Unfortunately, many others have already bought into that dream. The hills just north of Siena—playfully known as "Chiantishire" for the number of English homeowners there—has become exceedingly expensive. The same is true around Todi, in Umbria, also studded with million-dollar homes. But other areas of Umbria still offer up bargains. Terni, for example, is an oft-overlooked corner of Umbria, which is surprising when you consider that it is only 40 minutes from Rome by train. It's also not too far from Perugia, a mecca for foreigners, thanks to its university.

As Tuscany and Umbria outprice themselves, Le Marche has become the next frontier for foreign homeowners. There are loads of bargains in this mountainous region by the sea, although admittedly it is further away from international airports than its famous neighbors.

THE SOUTH: NAPLES, PUGLIA, AND SICILY

While the entire South may seem like a foreign country to the rest of Italy, there is something familiar about it for Americans. This is the Italy the rest of the world came to know when mass emigration emptied out its rural towns at the turn of the 20th century. In many cases, it seems that little has changed since then. The hospitality is still legendary; even families that don't have much money will spend a small fortune to accommodate visitors. Family values are still very strong, and old traditions like chivalry have never disappeared.

Unfortunately, things haven't improved much in terms of the economy. Campania, Puglia, and Sicily have still failed to catch up with the rest of Italy, if they care to do so at all. There has been some progress in cleaning up organized crime (without which, the national statistics bureau likes to point out, the South would be on financial par with the North). But Southerners don't seem to be in any hurry to reverse their fortunes if it means changing their pace of life. Spend just one week there, and you'll understand why.

© Monica Larner

Rome

I t's lunchtime in Rome, and you wander into a pizzeria by the Pantheon. The *pizzaiolo* cuts you a slice with zucchini and eggplant, you plunk down your €2 ($2.60) and walk back into the balmy air to find a place to sit down. Munching away, you look down to find that this round piece of stone where you have planted yourself is not exactly a bench. It is the big toe of an erstwhile colossus that loomed large above this street some 2,000 years ago.

This sort of thing happens every day in Rome. The alleyways and thoroughfares are so thickly sprinkled with the remains of ancient history that you couldn't possibly notice them all. Anywhere else, this marble appendage would have been carted off to a museum, but in the Eternal City, it's merely part of the landscape. There are buildings that fell apart centuries ago, and no one has bothered to fix them. Flowers, ivy, and graffiti crawl over the remnants and fill history's void with beauty, showing that, in Rome at least, time heals all wounds.

Dialect Box: Rome

Roman dialect, known as *romanesco,* or pejoratively as *romanaccio,* has hundreds of colorful expressions. Here are a few of the more polite ones, what they sound like they might mean, and what they really mean.

Parla come magni.
Sounds like: Talk like you eat.
Means: What are you trying to tell me?

Semo a cavallo.
Sounds like: We're on horseback.
Means: We're in good shape.

Nun stamo a venne li fiori 'n cima a la collina.
Sounds like: We're not selling flowers on the hilltop.
Means: Let's stop wasting time.

Te stai a allarga'.
Sounds like: You're extending yourself.
Means: Stick to things you know.

Stai popo a sgrava'.
Sounds like: You're giving birth.
Means: You're exaggerating.

Sta 'n campana./Stai manzo.
Sounds like: Stay by the bell./Stay beef.
Means: Stay on your toes.

Nun c'e trippa pe' gatti.
Sounds like: There's no tripe for the cats.
Means: We're broke.

Stai a guarda' er capello.
Sounds like: You're looking at the hair.
Means: You're being too picky.

Ma 'sto semafero ch'e, dipinto?
Sounds like: What, is that traffic light painted there?
Means: I really wish it would turn green.

The cradle of Western civilization is a paradise for history buffs and people who enjoy life in the slow lane. With fine weather and smiling faces everywhere you turn, it is easy to sit around and outwait any hardships that present themselves. If patience is a virtue, Rome must be the most virtuous city of all.

For everyone else, the city is a grueling test. Rome suffers from—or, some would say, enjoys—a syndrome called *menefreghismo.* This is the attitude that the present matters little, that problems like ringing telephones will eventually go away, and that nothing, ever, is urgent.

The city doesn't bat an eyelash at new ideas. It has seen them all: democracies, emperors, popes, conquering hordes, dark ages, rebirths, more conquerors, monarchists, fascists, communists, and the sunrise and sunset of the Internet millionaire. Despite this, or more likely because of it, nothing ever truly changes. The city still has its popes, fascists, communists, and Internet entrepreneurs, all of them only slightly

© Monica Larner

reformed. Even Italy's exiled royals have been allowed to return. In Rome, a scandal today is forgotten tomorrow, and you will always be forgiven.

Rome's live-and-let-live attitude has attracted admirers from all corners of the globe, and it has long had a lively English-speaking contingent, going back to the days of Byron and Shelley (now buried in the city's Protestant Cemetery). They were followed in the 1950s by the café-dwellers of Via Veneto, and later by crowds of Americans when air travel became affordable to the middle class.

Though it hosts millions of religious pilgrims and thousands of regular tourists, Rome has never been considered a cosmopolitan capital on par with the likes of Paris or London. When in Rome, outsiders were expected to eat and behave like the Romans, and they did so enthusiastically. Over the past decade, this has changed a little, thanks to the forces of globalization and growth in immigration. Where once there were modest trattorias, now there are Irish pubs. Corner stores in the historic center have become McDonald's, and even a handful of sushi and African restaurants have sprung up. For cautious Americans, this all means a gentle introduction to a foreign land.

It's also a good place for them to find a job, since a number of English-speaking institutions are headquartered here: universities, international organizations, media groups, etc. Some American companies operate out of Rome, though many prefer to locate themselves in Italy's financial and business capital, Milan. (Jealous northerners will often remind their countrymen that modern Rome—much like Washington, D.C.—would be little more than a southern backwater had it not been for its fortunate

Entire university courses are devoted to studying Rome's cityscape, which may seem chaotic at first, but in fact was a masterpiece of urban planning.

political status, and the jobs that this created.) Rome is therefore a good place for those fresh off the plane to land a short-term lease and try out their luck in the job market before planning a longer-term move.

THE LAY OF THE LAND

Entire university courses are devoted to studying Rome's cityscape, which may seem chaotic at first, but in fact was a masterpiece of urban planning, perfectly laid out to make the most of each approach to a monument. Don't expect the geography of Italy's medieval cities, where everything revolves around a central cathedral. Rome is a mosaic of ancient, medieval, Renaissance, and Baroque structures dotting either side of the Tiber river, and each neighborhood has its own particular importance.

The oldest and most orthodox way to refer to Roman geography is by its seven hills: the Aventine, Capitoline, Celium, Esquiline, Palatine, Quirinal, and Viminal. Romans still use these names to refer to an institution now located there: Il Quirinale is the President's offices, Il Viminale is the Ministry of the Interior, Il Campidoglio (Capitoline) is City Hall, and so on. Referring to the hill will usually work if you're describing a general area of the city center, but it will only get you so far when flipping through the classified ads for apartments.

Officially, the city is divided into 22 *rioni* (districts), which can be found on government maps and in erudite city guides. They were imposed upon the city about a century ago, after Rome became the capital, and they never gained the name recognition of, say, Paris's *arrondissements*. Sometimes, they can sound downright awkward. For instance, if someone were advertising an apartment on Via della Croce, they would much sooner refer to the area as "della Croce" or even "Piazza di Spagna" than use the official *rione*, "Campo Marzio." Some official *rioni* names, however, are very commonly used, especially Prati, Trastevere, Testaccio, and Monti.

Instead, classified ads and the average Roman will mention the nearest subway station, if there happens to be one nearby, or else the nearest square—such as Popolo, Navona, or Bologna—or, in some cases, an ancient road, such as Appia, Cassia, or Flaminia.

Housing

The capital has become expensive. It's still not quite at the level of New York, London, or Paris, but the explosion in prices has been drastic. As late as the mid-1990s, you could find a decent one-bedroom apartment near the center for the equivalent of €400 ($520) per month. Now it costs about twice as much. Prices vary widely depending on standard measurements such as location, size, and amenities, but also on more Rome-specific considerations, such as the presence of an ancient column or some other artistic treasure buried in the walls.

The greatest factor, of course, is location. Rent for apartments inside the city's Aurelian walls is almost always more expensive than those outside them. The following descriptions of neighborhoods give an indication of what you might expect to pay in rent per square meter, the measurement used in all classified ads. For a single-bedroom apartment, multiply by 50 or 60. For a two-bedroom place, multiply by 70 or 80.

WHERE TO LIVE

Downtown

The first on any list of Roman neighborhoods is the *centro storico* (downtown), which in Rome's case means the part that holds the major monuments and squares. This vaguely defined "historic center" is bound on the

Pantheon

Pajata: The "Insides" Story

The menu at Checchino dal 1887 is bound to raise some eyebrows. Just a stone's throw from Rome's former slaughterhouse in Testaccio, the restaurant's posted list of brains, intestines, tails, and feet looks, to the uninitiated, more like a recipe for a witch's brew than an array of local specialties.

Many a tourist and even some locals would rather not see, let alone eat, a plate of animal innards. Yet no other dish can claim to be as Roman, and what some might consider a macabre meal can be found in every quarter of the capital.

Coda alla vaccinara, il cervello, and especially a *pajata*—ox tail, sheep brains, and calf intestines, respectively—roll off the Roman tongue with such gusto that the words sound politically charged. And to some extent, they are. All of the dishes were born from poverty, made of the slaughterhouse scraps that the *vaccinari* (workers) were allowed to bring home to their families.

Pajata was for centuries the staple meat dish in Rome's historically poorer districts, like Testaccio and Trastevere. These days, at restaurants from the upscale Checchino to the more modest Ostaria da Edmondo—not far from the Olympic stadium—*pajata* is served as a fanfare for the common man.

western side by a sharp curve in the Tiber, and more or less contained on the eastern side by the Colosseum, Santa Maria Maggiore, the Baths of Diocletian, and the city's ornate park, the Villa Borghese. If you had an apartment here, you could walk to a dozen of the Western World's most photographed monuments in just a few minutes, plus most of the government buildings. The prices reflect this. If a map of downtown Rome were a Monopoly board, the Spanish Steps would be Boardwalk and the Via Veneto would be Park Place. Rents there are highest, wavering between €20 ($26) and €25 ($33) per square meter. Apartments near the Pantheon, Piazza Navona, and Piazza del Popolo will come close to that price, as will any address directly across the river in the *rioni* of Borgo and Castel Sant'Angelo. There, you can wake up in the morning and walk over the Tiber on your way to work as flocks of pigeons flap into the pink, hazy sunrise.

The southeastern limits of the downtown are marked by the *rione* of Monti, a cozy corner of alleyways between the Termini train station and the Colosseum. It is an excellent choice if you have the means. It has a more neighborly feel than the posh districts in the center, and doesn't cost quite as much; count on about €15 ($20) per square meter.

On either side of the Vatican are two of the more comfortable, upper-middle-class quarters of Rome, called Prati and Trastevere. They each attract slightly different crowds. Trastevere is a dream for students, artists, and other bookstore-browsing types who have a bit of

"*Pajata* is the most important dish at my restaurant," says Checchino owner Elio Mariani. "It is the most representative of the *quinto quarto*"—the somewhat sarcastic term for innards, the "fifth quarter" of the animal. The importance of *pajata* is a common refrain among Testaccio restaurateurs, but an odd claim for a kitchen that purports to have invented a rival Roman favorite.

Legend has it that the daughter of Checchino's founders took an ox tail and some cheek meat from the slaughterhouse across the street, and added it to a celery stew usually reserved for pricier cuts of beef. Thus, *coda alla vaccinara* was born.

Pajata, also spelled *paiata* or, less commonly, *pagliata,* is made from the upper intestines of a yearling calf. Animals that young still feed from their mothers, and it is important that their intestines contain the mother's milk. Only a fraction of the very upper section of the intestine is used, so that the bits of grass—called *paja* in dialect—the calf has grazed on are only partially digested. Any further along the digestive tract becomes something that not even the poorest of Romans could bear to stomach.

extra cash to spend on an apartment with character. It may be a stretch to call it Rome's answer to Greenwich Village, but there is a decent number of hole-in-the-wall bars and restaurants with a rustic flavor. There is even a small English-language movie theater, the Pasquino. If you're single and in your 20s or 30s, or even middle-aged with an appreciation for hip venues, this would be an ideal place to live. Depending on the sort of apartment, rent ranges from €15 ($20) to €20 ($26) per square meter. Prati is more staid and quiet, the home of the national broadcaster RAI and a number of law offices, and is generally a serene place to raise a family. There are some very good restaurants in the area and a few decent shops, but mostly it is a modern residential zone with wide, relatively uninteresting boulevards. It is just slightly cheaper than spicier Trastevere.

Across the river from Prati is a similarly conservative, family-oriented neighborhood that's even better-known for its yuppies. Parioli is so stately, in fact, that many national governments have set up their embassies here. Cafés and shops play to the whims of cautious diplomats looking to make a good impression. If you see a group of young men with neatly ironed slacks driving expensive mopeds, you may safely assume that they are *pariolini*. All snickering aside, Parioli is a very clean neighborhood with some elegant apartments, and if that's your cup of espresso, it's well worth the price: about €20 ($26) per square meter.

Outside the Center

The *centro storico,* Monti, Borgo, Prati, Parioli, and Trastevere, are about as good as it gets, geographically. If you can't walk to where you are going, it's only a short moped or bus ride away. But as real estate prices in Rome become out of reach even for moneyed foreigners, you will probably want to look a little further afield for the bargains, and Rome has a number of well-connected neighborhoods outside downtown.

Monteverde has long been a popular option for Americans looking for a nicer-priced apartment. Although it is tucked back on Janiculum Hill behind Trastevere, it might as well be downtown if you consider the convenient public transportation along Viale Trastevere. There are modern, air-conditioned trams that run from the heart of Monteverde to Largo Argentina, just steps from the Pantheon, in about 15 or 20 minutes. Monteverde Vecchio, as the name might suggest, has older and more interesting architecture than its younger brother, Monteverde Nuovo, and is therefore a tad more expensive. With the exception of the district's more luxurious buildings, both are still cheaper than downtown. You can find an apartment in Monteverde Vecchio for as little as €10 ($13) per square meter, and even slightly less in Monteverde Nuovo for something a little shabbier.

A similarly priced neighborhood can be found on the opposite side of Janiculum Hill from Monteverde, directly behind the Vatican. It takes its name from the avenue that runs through it, Gregorio VII, but it's also known as Pio XI after the square where the street ends up. (Streets and squares around here are often named after popes.) This is a modern and comfortable neighborhood, but relatively short on charm.

Another middle-of-the-road option is Testaccio, just south and across the river from Trastevere. The general area is also known as Ostiense. This is the old butchers' district (see the sidebar "*Pajata:* The 'Insides' Story"), which today holds meat markets of a different kind: discos and singles bars. There are also some excellent restaurants in the area, serving true Roman specialties. Plan on about €12–14 ($16–18) per square meter.

Further south down via Ostiense, you'll reach EUR, Mussolini's ambitious, sprawling exposition center. The architecture is Fascist, naturally, and the apartments surrounding it house mostly middle-class couples and families. For the same €1,200 ($1,560) that you could spend for a one-bedroom apartment in Piazza Spagna, you could find a three-bedroom, two-bath complex with a terrace and a garage in EUR. The price is right, but the commute can be tedious.

Closer to the center are a few other affordable areas. Two behind the Termini train station are worth noting: San Lorenzo, the stronghold of Rome's student population, at about €10 ($13) per square meter; and Piazza Vittorio, once an immigrants' neighborhood that is quickly becoming gentrified. Depending on the size and frills, apartments in this part of the Esquilino cost between €12 ($16) and €15 ($20) per square meter. Indeed, many neighborhoods just outside the historic center started off as low-income housing and are now some of the most preferred properties in the city. In the southern neighborhoods of San Saba and Garbatella, there are single-family houses with unusual architecture so appealing to families that they are very rarely up for grabs. There are some rentals on par in price with Trastevere.

The Suburbs

In relation to Milan, suburban options in Rome are not quite as appealing. For one thing, the towns immediately outside of Rome are mostly examples of urban sprawl, whereas Lombard cities like Monza and Bergamo have a history in their own right. Also, the public transportation to the outskirts of Rome leaves a little to be desired, comparatively speaking, and you will almost certainly need a car.

> *Olgiata's appeal for Americans is the proximity of the Overseas School of Rome, one of the more famous English-speaking schools in the country.*

One good suburban option, however, is Olgiata, off the Via Cassia, where many American expatriates have set up house. It is a gated community with modern villas and swimming pools, the sort of place where you might expect to see more satellite dishes and SUVs, because Olgiata is more about New World comfort than Old World charms. Its appeal for Americans is the proximity of the Overseas School of Rome, one of the more famous English-speaking schools in the country. The largest drawback is that you really need a car.

Owning a car also opens the doors to one last, and very good, alternative to urban living in Rome. The lake district has dozens of quaint villages with prices to match. South of the city are towns on Lake Albano and Lake Nemi where apartments go for as little as €6 ($8) per square meter. Similar prices can be found on Lake Bracciano, north of the city, which has already drawn a foreign crowd, thanks to ads in English-language publications like *Wanted in Rome*.

REAL ESTATE AGENTS: ROME

**Nelson International
Real Estate**
tel. 06/333-7162
cell 337/747-493
An English-speaking agency with apartments in Rome.

Rivoli Real Estate
tel. 06/483-456
An agency with a selection of furnished and unfurnished properties throughout Italy, and especially in Rome.

Wanted in Rome
www.wantedinrome.com
An English-language weekly with all sorts of information for foreigners moving to Rome, especially a comprehensive classified ads with apartments and jobs. Also available at newsstands.

World Real Estate
Via Paolo Emilio 7
00192 Rome
tel. 06/321-109-98
fax 06/321-3962
info@romepower.com
www.romepower.com
Provides all sorts of services for foreigners, particularly real estate rentals, with hundreds of options in Rome.

Getting Around

Choosing a place somewhere near where you work is important, because the city streets are crowded and public transportation is not the best in the country. This has a lot to do with Rome's ancient past; it's hard to build a subway when you bump into a buried archeological treasure every few feet. Planning the simplest tunnel or parking garage is a constant struggle against the remnants of Roman history.

The subway has just two lines. The first, the red line, starts near the Vatican, crosses the river, skirts the northern edge of the historic center, passes the Termini train station, and finishes in the southeastern outskirts. The second, the blue line, starts in the eastern suburbs, runs through Termini, the Colosseum, and Testaccio, then ends near EUR in the southwest. If you have the luck or the foresight to live and work near one of those lines, getting around won't be too hard. The subway is fairly efficient, though packed at rush hour.

The great majority of Romans live outside walking distance of a subway stop, and so public-transport commuters rely on buses and trams. Both are reliable in the sense that they exist and will come eventually (except during strikes). They are not famous for their punctuality. Bus tickets are

© Monica Larner

valid for 90 minutes, which starts the moment you punch the ticket in the on-board machines. If you don't punch the ticket, you'll get a fine in the off-chance that an inspector steps on.

No discussion of Roman buses would be complete without a brief mention of old No. 64. This route cuts through the heart of the city, from Termini to the Vatican. As you might expect, it's loaded with pilgrims, priests, tourists, and some very crafty pickpockets. If you do ride No. 64, and chances are you often will, make sure to keep an eye on your bags and pockets.

Like anywhere else in the world, it takes a certain type to enjoy riding the bus. They're particularly hot and stuffy in Rome, and every time you board and look out the window, you start dreaming about getting a scooter. The classified ads are full of used mopeds, and they come pretty cheap—as low as a few hundred euros. They are the ideal form of transportation in a city that certainly wasn't designed around the automobile, and where downtown is off-limits to most cars except taxis.

If you don't want to deal with the paperwork of getting a license plate and the other necessary permits, there are loads of agencies around that lend out mopeds by the hour or by the day. You might even be able to strike a deal where you can rent one for a month at a substantial discount.

If you prefer pedal power to motors, by all means, bring your bike along, but don't expect smooth riding in Rome. In Italy's northern cities, getting around town by bike is a way of life; in Rome, it can be a shortcut to death. And in-line skating is out of the question, except in the leafy Villa Borghese, where skates can be rented. There's no better way to spend a lazy Sunday afternoon.

Milan and the Lakes

At first blush, Milan is a bland European metropolis where the quality of life pales in comparison to other, more pleasant Italian settings. Small talk at the dinner table invariably begins by stacking up Milan against Rome. The capital always comes out looking good in the comparison.

But as the dinner progresses, some of Milan's finer points are brought to light—its proximity to popular vacation spots, its ethnic diversity and nightlife, its relative orderliness, its high profile in the worlds of design, media, and finance, and its curious subtleties—all of which Rome lacks to varying degrees. In the end, many of those around the table will confess that they now find Milan hard to leave.

The capital of Lombardy is not only the obvious choice for those interested in working hard and enjoying a cosmopolitan setting, it is also a great springboard for road trips out of the city, located about 90 minutes by car from the Riviera and less than an hour from the Alps. France, Switzerland, and Austria are all just around the corner. The surrounding cities of Como, Pavia, Cremona, and Bergamo are each national treasures in their own right. At first, you will find it tempting to head out of town every weekend. Then, as you move to the city's rhythms and turn up its hidden offerings, you may find it hard to tear yourself away.

Milan

Milan has been known as the nation's fashion capital ever since Giorgio Armani and Gianni Versace showed up on the scene in the 1980s. Now home to dozens of labels on every fashionista's shopping list, Milan is a mainstay on the circuit that runs from New York to London to Paris. Be sure to visit during the *settimana della moda* (fashion week) to get the full picture.

More broadly, Milan is a design center. We're not talking about just clothes, but rather cars, furniture, and cutting-edge household goods. The lines that define Fiat, Alfa Romeo, and the sort of kitchenware you'd like to show off were drawn by such local names as Pininfarina and Alessi. In April, the city's exposition center holds the Salone del Mobile, the world's premier design show. It attracts artists and architects from around the world, yet anyone who needs to be near the vanguard of the industry already lives here.

© John Moretti

Bergamo skyline, Lombardy

Dialect Box: Milan

Zucch e melon a la soa stagion.
Literally, "Pumpkins and melons have their seasons," this refers to middle-aged people who want to appear younger than they really are—e.g., a balding man who wears a hairpiece or an older woman with an exceedingly short skirt.

Và a Bagg a sona l'òrghen.
Literally, "He's going to Baggio to play the organ," this refers to slack-ers who like to waste their time. Baggio, now part of the downtown, was once a suburb of Milan whose parish was too poor to afford an organ, so the pastor painted one on the walls.

Taccàsù el capell.
Literally, "He's hung up his hat," this refers to a man who has married a wealthy woman and no longer has to work.

Italy's stock market is based in Milan—no actual trading floor, mind you, as it is completely electronic—and most of Italy's financial services are firmly rooted here. If you're coming to Italy on a business trip, chances are you'll be spending a few days in Lombardy.

Finally, the city holds a self-conferred title as the nation's moral capital. This is a reference to the "Clean Hands" investigations, whose prosecutors worked out of Milan's high court. Consequently, the local newspaper and Italy's leading daily, *Corriere della Sera,* became a symbol of the transparency that brought the "Bribesville" days to an end.

The journalists, lawyers, judges, bankers, and others who make up this busy city have a different social life than many of their Italian peers, but it is contemporary and cosmopolitan in a way that Rome is only now becoming. The mosaic of nationalities reveals itself in Milan's restaurants: Japanese, Turkish, Eritrean, Chinese, Moroccan, Sri Lankan, Korean. It does not yet have the selection of, say, Chicago, but you will be hard-pressed to find anything but Italian food elsewhere in the country. The city's multi-ethnic population also reveals itself in the religious community. Milan has the largest mosque in the country, several synagogues, and more churches than it will ever need.

Diversity is one reason that Milan draws parallels with American cities. On top of that, it is sprawling, busy, and bordering on stressful. If you're making the move for relaxation or an excuse to underachieve, this is not the Italy you are looking for. Milan is inhabited by professionals who dream of success in the boardroom, or else moving back to a quainter part of the country as soon as they have the money to do so.

THE LAY OF THE LAND

When Italians visit cities in the United States, they often have a hard time finding the "center" of town. That's because it doesn't exist—at least not in the way they imagine it, with a cathedral at its epicenter and major streets leading directly to it or in concentric circles around it.

Milan is a classic example of the medieval European planning that U.S. cities lack. It is a bull's-eye, with the cathedral at the center. It and the castle sit inside the city's innermost circle, the neighborhood Italians like to refer to as the *centro storico*. About a half kilometer further out along the radius is a loop road that demarcates what an American might call "downtown." Here are the proverbial city walls, each with a gate named after the destination of that road: Porta Romana, Porta Venezia, Porta Ticinese, etc. Outside that, the rent gets cheaper, the architecture generally less inspired, and all of it is encompassed by the *tangenziale* (beltway).

Some of the nicest areas to live without paying extraordinary sums are near the city walls. The most popular of these residential areas are Porta Venezia, Porta Romana, and Chinatown, which is near Porta Garbibaldi. Then there are the city's two best-known nightlife districts, Brera and the Navigli. The latter is named after the canals that run through it. (Milan used to be covered with such waterways, much like Venice, until almost all of them were paved over to fight water-borne diseases.) Prices in the Navigli can be slightly higher, because this is an attractive location for young people.

Of course, choosing an apartment for rent or sale will depend mostly on availability. There are a number of nice places in the city to live, but you will really have to shop around for yourself to see what you like and what's actually there for the taking.

Milan's rent has surged in recent years, and the city remains the most expensive place to live in Italy. If you demand a place within the loop road, expect to pay at least €700 ($910) for a small one-room apartment, and about €1,200 ($1,560) for two bedrooms. The prices go up from there. In a recent consumer-group survey, the average monthly rent for an apartment was pegged at €1,100 ($1,430), which takes into consideration every size, location, and level of luxury. A nice alternative for young people is to scour the universities for postings, which can sometimes turn up a room in a student-held apartment for about €500 ($650) per month.

WHERE TO LIVE

Chinatown has become one of the more attractive neighborhoods for its exotic flavor and wide selection of restaurants. Purchase prices for single-bedroom apartments (about 55 square meters) start at €150,000 ($195,000). Two-bedroom apartments (about 80 square meters) start at nearly €250,000 ($325,000). The neighborhood also has a high ratio of studios (each about 30 square meters) which run in the €60,000–80,000 ($78,000–$104,000) range and are usually advertised as "investments," so as not to suggest that the owners might subject themselves to living in such cramped quarters.

In the 1960s, artists moved into Brera, and it became what might be called Milan's rive gauche.

The Navigli and especially the adjacent Sant'Ambrogio neighborhood are considered two of the most posh residential areas. Many of the apartments have been restructured by budding architects and may be on split levels. Expect to pay about €200,000 ($260,000) for a small one-bedroom apartment. A place to house the whole family, although in luxurious surroundings, will cost at least €500,000 ($650,000) and will often run to €1 million ($1.3 million). Sant'Ambrogio is certainly the most convenient location in town, well-connected by all kinds of public transport, and even the cathedral is a short walk away—a good thing, because you won't find anywhere to park a car there.

Brera is a Cinderella story in the annals of real estate, an example of how a neighborhood can be gentrified in a single generation. In the early postwar years, it was home to the city's brothels. It was, coincidentally, also home to some very stately buildings just steps from the cathedral. In the 1960s, artists moved into Brera, and it became what might be called Milan's *rive gauche*. The roaring '80s—termed *"Milano da bere,"* loosely translated as "Milan in a glass"—brought a boom of more mainstream nightspots. By the 1990s, it was already among the most expensive neighborhoods in town. Expect rents to be about 20 percent higher than in the other downtown neighborhoods, though you never know what you might find.

There is a lot of cheaper stuff to be had, especially well outside the city. One extreme example is in the town of Busto Arsizio, in the outskirts near Malpensa airport. A construction company recently advertised a two-bedroom apartment there for €75,000 ($98,000) and an entire penthouse floor for €200,000 ($260,000) in a sparkling new building. (Note: When buying a house under construction, you run the risk of the company's going bankrupt before it's finished—and after you've handed over your life savings. This phenomenon is more common than you may think, and has been the subject of many investigations. See the Housing Considerations chapter for more details.)

REAL ESTATE RESOURCES AND EXPAT CONTACTS: MILAN

EasyMilano
www.easymilano.it
English-language classifieds for apartments, jobs, and just about everything else. A good introduction to expat life in the city. Published every other Thursday and distributed at hundreds of locations.

Professional Women's Association
www.pwa-milan.org
A good way for women who are new to Milan to meet those with similar interests.

TrovoCasa
www.corriere.it/trovocasa
An excellent resource for local real estate classifieds, distributed on Wednesdays with *Corriere della Sera*, along with the supplement *ViviMilano*.

ViviMilano
www.corriere.it/vivimilano
Published on Wednesdays and distributed locally in *Corriere della Sera*. The most comprehensive guide to happenings in and around Milan.

GETTING AROUND

Getting around Milan is easier than in many major European cities. Since it is much more compact than, say, London, a subway ride from one end of the line to the other takes only about 30 minutes and costs only €1 ($1.30). Milan's subway network is the largest in Italy, which is not saying much, but it takes you almost everywhere you need to go. Despite its frequent strikes, when the city is thrown into a chaotic traffic jam, the subway is reliable because the trains generally show up on time. The last ones run at 12:30 A.M.

Trams are also largely trustworthy and certainly the most characteristic of all public transport. Alas, some of the old cars have been sold off to San Francisco and replaced by pan-European-looking green units. They are air-conditioned, but lack the charm of the orange trams with their wooden benches, fin-de-siècle light fixtures, and the sound of old wheels rattling on steel.

Then there are the buses. As in any other part of the country, they almost show up on a whim. If you're going to an appointment with that rare person who appreciates punctuality, you're better off in a taxi. Bear in mind that after 9 P.M., taxis start their meters at €6 ($8)—it's not a tourist scam, just an added cost for a night on the town. Taxis also have a certain snob appeal. The Milanese always prefer driving to public transportation. Italy has the third highest rate of car ownership in the world, and it seems like every single one of them is on Milan's streets during rush hour. But driving is a luxury in which you do not need to indulge yourself, unless you live off the beaten path and beyond the reach of the buses.

Monza and Brianza

Like most Italian cities, Milan has its share of commuters. They come from neighborhoods in the east, west, and south, but at the end of the workday, most of the trains head north, toward the lakes. At 6 P.M., there is an all-out stampede for the city's northern stations, Cadorna and Garibaldi. There, the trains leave for the provinces of Lecco, Como, and Varese, all of them hosting bedroom communities (though that term in Italy suggests something more interesting than it might back home).

The highest concentration of commuters comes from a loosely defined area called Brianza. It comprises the northern quarter of the province of Milan, with Monza as its imagined capital. The suburbs are so densely populated that every year, there is some discussion about redrawing political boundaries to give Monza a provincial status of its own. It already has an enlarged train station, its own dialect, and a distinct flavor, combined with a noble beauty that makes it worth considering as a home base while working out of the big city.

As an alternative to commuting, entrepreneurial-minded expats may consider buying a small business in Brianza. The area is brimming with everything from travel agencies to boutiques to small factories that serve industrial clients. In Italy, it can be difficult to buy an existing business because most of them are privately-held family firms, where the shareholders' number-one priority is the future of the next generation. That said, there is a number of businesses for sale all the time in the outskirts of Milan, which suggests the next generation has plans of its own.

WHERE TO LIVE

Real estate prices in Brianza vary greatly depending on the town, ranging from the blue-collar Sesto San Giovanni, termed "the Stalingrad of Italy," to the haughty addresses of the rich and powerful. The most famous resident of nearby Arcore, for example, is media baron Silvio Berlusconi, the nation's wealthiest man and occasionally its prime minister.

Many foreigners choose Monza because it is well connected to the city via public transportation, and yet offers the relative peace of a

Dialect Box: Brianza

El Poo el sarav minga Poo se Ada e Tesin no ghe mettessen coo.
Literally, "The Po wouldn't be the Po if the Adda and Ticino didn't flow into it." That is, behind every great and powerful person is an army of helpers.

Chi ha danee fa danee,
chi pioeucc fa lenden.
"People with money make more money, people with lice make lice eggs." The concept is the same the world over: It takes money to make money, and poverty breeds poverty.

O gent o argent
Literally, "Either people or money." That is, in order to build a house, work the land, and so on, either you have friends to help you, or you're going to spend a lot of money.

residential town. It is known for its good public education, though many English-speakers prefer to send their children to a British academy in town or another of the myriad such schools in Milan.

Monza, now a suburb, once had a strong identity of its own. Americans may recognize the name from the old Chevrolet Monza. The inspiration for that model is thought to have come from the Ferrari Monza or the Alfa Romeo Monza, both of which reflect the city's fame as home to the Italian Grand Prix.

The racetrack sits inside the massive Parco di Monza, Europe's largest public park and originally the garden of the Villa Reale. The villa is the city's centerpiece, a neoclassical palace that served as the summer home for Italy's Turin-based royal family in the 19th century. The grand boulevard that leads to the palace is lined with the stately abodes of the royal court.

The Monzese cling dearly to the days of aristocracy. Many of the older generation will tell you how their grandparents were florists or tailors to the King and Queen, giving the city a bourgeois flavor in the historic sense of the word. The Milanese and Monzese share a term for the modern version of such wealthy burghers, *bauscia,* which can be applied to virtually anyone who drives the latest BMW and generally espouses nouveau-riche values.

The stores and restaurants in Monza are as upscale as you can expect to see just outside the big city. The real estate prices reflect this, although you can still get much more space for the money here than in Milan. A one-bedroom apartment for a couple, roughly 70 square meters, costs in the vicinity of €120,000 ($156,000). The majority of the apartments were built for families, however. A three- or four-bedroom place, with lush balconies and floor space ranging from 90 to 150 square meters, costs between €160,000 ($208,000) and €250,000 ($325,000).

Rents in Monza, which has become more and more popular among young professionals, have almost reached the levels of Milan, but not quite. For example, if €800 ($1,040) per month affords you a small one-bedroom apartment in Milan with a kitchen tucked in a corner, in Monza it can land you a full kitchen and a larger living room. In general, you won't find the same number of tiny living quarters in Monza as you will in Milan. Most of the apartments here were designed for more comfortable suburban living.

Real estate near the park or in one of the alleys near the cathedral is the most expensive. It is also the most elegant. Many three-story buildings near the park were built for friends of the royal family. Nearer the cathedral, there are classic split-beam houses with new copper tubing and an Alpine flavor. Outside that, it's the same old 1960s-era sprawl of high-rises of mediocre construction.

From Monza, Brianza extends northward through the foothills of the Alps before giving way to the towns around Lake Como. There are hilltop castles along the way, winding roads with wisteria-laced brick walls and bubbling brooks that only become polluted rivers once they've passed through Monza and Milan. Here, the real estate is a mix of apartments and villas, depending on the size of the town. Keep in mind that this is a growing suburban area, not altogether a bucolic medieval paradise like Tuscany. The beauty is the convenience of having a modern and cosmopolitan city next door, while still bordering on some of the best Alpine scenery and recreation in Italy.

One of the most scenic towns is Montevecchia, a hilltop village with such pleasant curvy roads and leafy parks that it is on the regular Sunday circuit for cyclists from Milan. Real estate there is in the middle to high range for Brianza. A two-apartment villa costs about €400,000 ($520,000). Other towns in the area—Giussano, Lissone, Carate Brianza, and Sovico, to name a few—have a more suburban feel. Space here has become tight, ever since a housing boom kicked off in Brianza in the 1970s; apartment buildings are still going up at a clip. In a past generation, you might have expected a nice country villa for cheap. Now, much of what you will find are *palazzi,* with 10 to 20 apartments for families, ranging in price from €150,000 ($195,000) to €250,000 ($325,000) each. Rents in some of the smaller towns in Brianza are slightly lower than in Monza.

Keep in mind that Brianza is just one wedge of Milan's sprawling northern suburbs. The province of Lecco to the east and the province of Varese to the west have quiet, well-connected towns with character and history. The small and picturesque village of Gorgonzola, for example—where the famous cheese was born—is on the green line of Milan's subway and only about a 40-minute ride from the center. On the western side of Brianza is Saronno, which food buffs may recognize as the home of *amaretti* (almond cookies). The modern and reliable Malpenna Airport Express makes one of its four stops in Saronno, bringing it to within 30 minutes from downtown.

Lake Como

Stendahl, D.H. Lawrence, and other writers have heaped all sorts of praise on the lake district, and on Lake Como in particular. Italy's best-known tour guide, Virgil, labeled it succinctly as "our greatest lake." At 416 meters, or about 1,200 feet, it is unquestionably the deepest. Alpine foothills tumble vertically into the water. The roads are lined with the kind of trees and flowers you might expect in the tropics, framed by snow-capped peaks in the near distance. It is a mystical garden suspended between the austerity of Switzerland and the relative hedonism of Italy below.

© Monica Larner

Varenna, Lake Como

Dialect Box: The Lakes

Cent cò, cent crap'
"One hundred heads, one hundred opinions."

Quell che fa ciapà la cioca l'e sémper l'ûltem bicér.
"The last glass is always the one that makes you drunk."

Quii de Valtulina: scarpa grossa, crapa fina.
"People from Valtellina: big shoes, sharp minds." (That is, they may be peasants from the mountains, but they're not dummies.)

Its shape is an upside-down "Y," with the southeastern leg called Lago di Lecco. The most prominent villas cling to the steep banks of the opposite leg, which stretches up from Como, continues first to Tremezzo and Menaggio, where the two legs join, and then onward to the tip of the lake and the beginning of the mountainous Valtellina valley.

Once a hilly redoubt for wandering authors and a haven for tennis-playing aristocracy, Lago di Como has become a home for Hollywood stars. They retreat here from the flashbulbs of Milan's catwalks, where they often show up to give designers that extra pinch of publicity. Giorgio Armani's poster boy, George Clooney, recently purchased a villa here, and Madonna often visits her friend Donatella Versace at the designer's lakeshore mansion.

Other villas have a bit more history behind them. The Villa d'Este, just outside of Como in Cernobbio, started life as the private residence of Tolomeo Gallio, the local cardinal. Throughout its 400-plus-year existence, it has been owned by a ballerina, a Napoleonic general, a queen, and a Russian empress. Today, it houses minor aristocracy as a luxury hotel. Italian and international business leaders hold their gala conferences in Cernobbio, which even today exudes a princely air.

The Villa Carlotta, further up the lake, was built in 1690 by a family of wealthy textile merchants. It was then bought and sold by an aristocratic family before being purchased in 1843 by Princess Marianne of the Netherlands. She gave it to her daughter Charlotte, for whom it is now named. The highlight of the villa is the exotic garden that runs along the lakeshore. The towns around those two historic properties have arguably the most beautiful real estate on the lake and, as a matter of record, the highest prices.

Around the Villa d'Este, it is difficult to find any hidden jewels for sale. They've been snatched up by very well-to-do Italians and foreigners. There are, however, still a few deals to be had near the Villa Carlotta, in the area around Menaggio and Tremezzo, the series of towns known as the Tremezzina. When people tell you they're going to visit Lake Como, this is generally where they mean. Tremezzo and Menaggio are packed with German, English, and North American tourists in the summertime, more often than not in their late 60s or 70s, enjoying lengthy meals at hotel gardens and waltzing the night away.

The best time to enjoy the lake is in the spring, before the crowds arrive. The shores explode in color, as wisteria covers the villas' iron gates and petunias hang off Roman-era walls. (The inhabitants of Lake Como, or "Lario," as the locals once called it, were Roman citizens starting in 59 B.C.) Early fall is also an excellent time to take on the hiking trails, before the cold November rain arrives. Several trails lead to mountain refuges that serve polenta and wine as a reward for the climb. Winters are deathly quiet. Rental prices in the off-season are a half or a third of what they are during June, July, and August.

WHERE TO LIVE

Realtors here will tell you it's too difficult to give a general price range of what is for sale, because the selection is so wide. Anything on the lakeshore itself, if a place even goes on the market, will be in the €3–4 million ($4–5 million) range. Further inland, there are more approachable prices, at about €300,000–600,000 ($390,000–$780,000) for a house. One item recently for sale in the town just above Menaggio was a rustic stone house with 150 square meters, a large front yard, and a lake view for €350,000 ($455,000).

For that same price, there are family-sized apartments for sale in large villas and castles. Since most of the villas have attained prices out of reach for the average homeowner looking to live on the lake, many large properties have been subdivided. Again, the range is vast, comprising everything from the somewhat modest €300,000 ($390,000) apartment to the luxurious one that runs in the millions.

A more humble option, with similarly beautiful scenery—and, more importantly, a train station within walking distance—is the eastern leg of the lake between Lecco and Varenna. The towns to watch out for in the classified ads are Lierna, Malgrate, Mandello, and Varenna itself.

It is common to find two-apartment villas for sale, or single-apartment villas in a cluster of others. Land isn't cheap in this part of the world, and to keep at least some open land along the lake, local governments have developers create what are known as *ville a scheira* (cluster-villas). A two-bedroom villa of this sort with a nice terrace, wine cellar, and lake view sells for about €200,000 ($260,000). As might be expected, a two-apartment villa sells for about twice that.

Those intent on working in Milan while living on the lake should probably consider living in Como or Lecco proper. So many people drive into Milan that it makes sense to take a train, and both cities are well connected in that regard.

In Lecco, a nice two-bedroom apartment with a balcony, garden, and garage by the lake will cost about €140,000 ($182,000). Demand there has surged in recent years, with the supply holding steady, but prices are not quite as high as in Como, where you can expect to pay slightly more for the same sort of apartment. Incidentally, Como is a popular spot for professional soccer players and coaches, as it is relatively close to the stadium but still far enough away from the pressures of being a celebrity in the big city.

Because the lake is a popular holiday destination, rental prices vary according to season. For a one-bedroom apartment in Menaggio, for example, expect to pay about €300 ($390) per month in winter, and twice that in the summer months.

REAL ESTATE AGENT: LAKE COMO

Immobiliare Menaggio
Via Como 6
22017 Menaggio
tel. 0344/301-67 or 0344/301-81
www.immobiliaremenaggio.com
A small, English-speaking agency
with a wide range of options on
the western shore.

The Northeast:
Emilia-Romagna and Veneto

I t's a little unorthodox to group Veneto and Emilia-Romagna in the
same chapter. The Veneto is described in weather reports and
history books as the Northeast, a traditionally impoverished land of bo-
real forests and goose farms whose underdog entrepreneurs only brought
prosperity to the region in the latter half of the 20th century. Emilia-
Romagna, on the other hand, described as the Center-North, prides itself on a long tradition of wealth and nobility. It is a mainstay of the so-
called Red Belt of left-leaning voters that includes Tuscany and Umbria,
while the Veneto is a power base for the formerly separatist, anti-immi-
gration Northern League, and friendly turf for conservatives. The two regions may share the Adriatic coast and have a common border on the
Po, but the river divides centuries of cultural history. The Veneto was
shaped by the Venetian Republic and the subsequent occupation by the
Austrians, while the duchies of Emilia-Romagna swore loyalty to the Pope,
temporarily hosting the capital of the Roman Empire at Ravenna.

But Emilia-Romagna and Veneto have much more in common when you start talking about a style of living. They have some of the nation's most affluent and comfortable towns, and they contain a disproportionate share of Italy's fine art and culture. Parma, Modena, Bologna, Ferrara, Verona, and Padua are all midsized cities—large enough for a top-flight soccer team, but too small for a subway. Public transportation is still very good—in Emilia-Romagna's downtowns, for example, digital readouts at bus stops tell you how many minutes you need to wait—and with a smallish number of Americans living in each of the cities, you'll never feel entirely isolated. Overall, there is a sense of community here that some may find stifling, but others will find reassuring.

For English-speakers, Bologna, Padua, Parma, and Verona are the most cosmopolitan spots, and may even feel like home, as they tend to attract the most ethnic diversity. On the flip side of the coin, non-English-speaking immigrants, especially those of Arabic or African descent, may encounter some unfriendliness in the Northeast. Though local mayors have tried to brush off this reputation, racism is an unfortunate reality in parts of the Veneto.

Emilia-Romagna

WHERE TO LIVE

Bologna

Bologna's train station is the busiest in Italy, but that's mostly because passengers are passing through on their way to somewhere else. The city can't claim an art gallery on par with those in Florence, and doesn't have the name-brand recognition of Venice or Pisa; Bologna's canals are all underground, and its towers don't seem to lean far enough to draw a crowd. Centuries ago, the city tried to build a cathedral larger than St. Peter's, but those plans were swiftly nixed by the Vatican.

Bologna's appeal is less obvious than that of Rome, Pisa, or Venice, but every bit as urbane. It makes fine machinery and has done so for hundreds of years. Bricks, engines, machines—before Turin started churning out cars at the turn of the 20th century, Bologna was the nation's mechanical capital. Today, the city's Ducati motorcycle factory is just one example of that legacy, and a look around any downtown parking lot shows that the industrial complex is still spitting out its profits.

Marching hand in hand with Bologna's wealth is its reputation for good living—in 2000, the National Statistics Institute considered it the best

place to live in the country—and its appetite for refined cuisine. Only here can you join the Learned
Order of the Tortellini, dedicated to the preserva-
tion of the city's native pasta. Tagliatelle is its
younger brother, typically smothered in a ragu or
sprinkled with the most luxurious of extras: truffles
from the nearby mountains. Sausages are its other
specialty. The term "Bologna" was borrowed by such

> *Only in Bologna can
> you join the Learned
> Order of the Tortellini,
> dedicated to the
> preservation of the
> city's native pasta.*

food giants as Oscar Meyer, but the cold cut in its hometown is no
baloney. Generically called *mortadella,* it is a very respectable meat and not
something to be thrown away on a cheap sandwich.

Bologna is home to Europe's oldest university, founded in 1088. The
University of Bologna and its associated business and medical schools is
just one of several here. Others include the art and literature institute,
DAMS, which figures among the country's most reputable; and the
Bologna campus of SAIS, The Johns Hopkins University's School of Advanced International Studies. For international policy wonks, it represents the pinnacle of studying abroad in Italy.

The university atmosphere adds to a left-leaning environment, but
the cost of living is anything but proletarian. Rents are on par with Milan,
and the demand is steep in such a student-dominated city with a high
turnover rate. A small two-bedroom apartment in the city, for example,
runs about €800 ($1,040) per month (about €200,000/$260,000 to buy it),
and even those can be hard to find. Just outside the city, however, it is a
different story. While the polls show that Bologna itself is one of the
tightest markets for real estate, local agents seem to offer lots of comfortable suburban and country homes at reasonable prices. A nice small
house in the outskirts, if uncharmingly modern, can be had for about
€150,000 ($195,000). For €200,000 ($260,000) and up, you can find a
country farmhouse in decent shape.

Hiking and cycling in the Bologna hills are the best way to keep in shape.
Marco Pantani, the 1999 winner of the Tour de France, was born here and
trained on the steep Apennines, just south of the city. Those who like to take
their sports sitting down can always head out to the Stadio Comunale soccer stadium to see the red and blue take on their Emilan neighbors.

Modena

Modena is what Bologna might look like if it were boiled down to its essen-
tials. It is smaller, but boasts a university and a soccer team, plus an extraordinary level of wealth—specifically, the highest per-capita income in Italy.

Modena's showmanship and culture can be summed up in two last names: Pavarotti and Ferrari. Both the tenor, Luciano, and the race-car pioneer, Enzo, called Modena their home. (For tax reasons, Pavarotti sometimes preferred to name Monte Carlo as his home, a subtle distinction that met with a poor reception at the Finance Ministry.) Ferrari still has its headquarters in the suburb of Maranello, and Pavarotti often does winter concerts at the city's Teatro Comunale.

The food is also world-class. Aside from its tortellini and prosciutto—Emilian staples produced in each of its cities—Modena's best-known product is balsamic vinegar, which carries a DOC label so it's not confused with inferior imitations. Less haughty is its sparkling red Lambrusco wine, present at any simple country picnic along with a *piadina* (roll-up) sandwich.

Deciding between the countryside and the downtown will be difficult. The central square and its 11th-century cathedral make for an idyllic meeting place and cultural venue, often hosting pop and rock concerts. I saw an unforgettable Bob Dylan show there in 2000, his stage sandwiched between the duomo and the medieval clock tower.

Futher afield, the architecture becomes more modern. Modena was bombed considerably in World War II, and much of what was built afterward clearly had a more contemporary look, though perhaps more tasteful and thought-out than the postwar constructions in Milan, for example.

A pleasant house or villa just a few kilometers outside the city can cost anywhere from €150,000 ($195,000) to €300,000 ($390,000). Around Modena, for whatever reason, the rustic houses sell for considerably less than you might expect from such a wealthy city. Attractive brick farmhouses, in need of restructuring but still inhabitable, are on the market for as little as €100,000 ($130,000), reaching €400,000 ($520,000) for a true gem. The average rent in Modena for a two-bedroom apartment is about €650 ($845) per month.

Ferrara

Once upon a time—namely, from the 13th to the 17th centuries—small and unassuming Ferrara was one of the peninsula's most important cultural centers. Its university and wealthy dukes attracted such sought-after minds as Petrarch, Tasso, and Titian. Ferrara was one of the only cities in Emilia with independence from the Florentine nobility in the Middle Ages, and it lays important claims to the development of urban planning and theater.

But in the late 1600s, the Este dynasty fell apart, and Ferrara and its dukes were all but forgotten. It spent the next few centuries as the ugly

© John Moretti

Ferrara

stepbrother of the wealthier neighboring states, and its poorer inhabitants developed a taste for eels from the Po River Delta.

Even these days, Ferrara's enological and gastronomic delights rarely draw a crowd. Much of that has to do with geography. In the powerful triangle that comprises Emilia-Romagna's three major cities, Ferrara occupies the lonely corner. Unlike its twin siblings, it does not share the A-1 autostrada, the country's backbone, nor the parallel railway that handles most of the nation's traffic.

This anonymity can only be a good thing for anyone in search of Italian pleasures without the tourists. Ferrara is a quiet place, clean and livable. Slowly pedaling around on a bicycle seems to be the preferred mode of transportation in this city best known for its Lamborghini cars. It has a network of bike paths that leads from the medieval castle to expansive, leafy parks and stretches eight kilometers north to the banks of the mighty Po. When imagining the downtown, don't assume that the city has lost its grandeur. Its center is dominated by a bona fide castle, with turrets, a moat, and drawbridges From there, the main pedestrian artery leads to one of the most peculiar cathedrals in Italy, crafted of pink marble and flanked by an arcade of merchants.

The moral of this fable is, if you're in search of fairy-tale Europe, where

The World's Oldest Wine Bar

Osteria al Brindisi, located in a brick building next to Ferrara's cathedral, is not just any old wine bar. According to the *Guinness Book of World Records,* it is the oldest one on Earth. That's a hard record to beat. Unlike challengers to the world's largest lollipop (a peppermint-flavored structure in Denmark), al Brindisi's competitors have more than 550 years of history to reckon with.

The first documentation of Ferrara's premier drinking establishment dates back to 1435, and some of the illustrious guests to belly up to its wooden bar include the Renaissance master Titian, sculptor Benvenuto Cellini, and poets Ludovico Arisoto and Torquato Tasso. In those days, it was known as the "Hostaria del Chiuchiolino," taking its name from *ciuc,* a handy term in dialect that means "three sheets to the wind." A few decades later, a fun-loving science student by the name of Copernicus moved into a strategically located apartment in the same building. (Nonetheless, he managed to graduate from Ferrara's university at a still-collegiate 26 years old.)

It should come as no surprise that this corner of Emilia-Romagna has an enological claim to fame. The sandy fields between Ferrara and the Po river are spotted with vines. The *vini delle sabbie* are full-bodied and aromatic when they come from higher ground. When they come from the more frequently flooded land closer to the river, they become smoother and more velvety.

Federico Pellegrini, whose family runs Osteria al Brindisi, can tell you everything you ever wanted to know about the local vineyards. He's been a sommelier for 12 years. "Now I will show you a stupendous wine," he says, a black scarf tied around his neck. With a flourish that would make even Titian himself look artless and sober, he unleashes a stream of red from Mantua into a large, wine-coated glass.

Federico Pellegrini at the world's oldest wine bar

© John Moretti

princesses and knights live among moated castles, Ferrara is the first place you should look—mostly because it won't cost a king's ransom. Real estate here goes for noticeably less than in Bologna: a modest two-bedroom apartment can be purchased for €100,000 ($130,000) or rented for about €550 ($715) per month. Or, for about twice that, you can move your family into a large suburban house. If your budget is healthy and your timing is right, €500,000 ($650,000) will land you a wonderfully restructured villa from the 19th century and a nice plot of land, a miniature fiefdom for the 21st century. Keep in mind that Ferrara lies in a flood plain, not in the hills, so the views can be pedestrian. Stately villas and estates don't appear to be as common here as elsewhere in central Italy—for example, Parma—and if you do find one, it may be difficult to convince the wealthy duchess or farmer to move out.

Parma

Parma's food requires little introduction. Parmesan, prosciutto di Parma, and its cousin, *culatello,* are among the peninsula's most important exports, and are treated as national treasures. Travelers on the Rome–Milan train will find it tempting to jump off at Parma come lunchtime, and in fact many of them do. Those who live here are particularly proud of their gastronomic heritage, but also of their art and music. Giuseppe Verdi, for example, was born just down the road, as was Arturo Toscanini.

The *parmigiani* will tell you that there is no better place in Italy to live. Public transportation is punctual, the streets are immaculate (uncluttered with cars, because many prefer to take their bikes to work), and their community spirit is known nationwide. Prices are also quite reasonable—the average two-bedroom apartment rents for €650 ($845) per month.

Indeed, the close-knit nature of its neighborhoods is one reason why some people are not keen to move to Parma. They say that gossip flies around this city as fast as it does in a small town, and as a foreigner, you may find that people know more about your life than you'd care to share.

Those in search of more privacy may be tempted to find a place in the surrounding countryside. The low-lying hills between Parma and Piacenza are famous for their dozens of medieval castles, revealing the Lombard influences of the Milanese Visconti and Sforza families, who once controlled the city. Gallic flavors are also strong, due to the French connections of Parma's subsequent rulers, the Farnese family. The picturesque burgs themselves attract many tourists today, especially Castell'Arquato and Salsomaggiore Terme. The latter is famous for its natural springs and their allegedly curative waters.

Veneto

WHERE TO LIVE

Verona

One of the selling points of Milan and Turin is that the cities have mountains, sea, and wine just a short trip way. The same can be said about a lot of Italian cities, but none of them can claim to be as centrally located as Verona. It's an ideal spot for those who don't need to work in a major city, but like to have one nearby. It sits halfway between Venice and Milan, about 90 minutes in either direction. Due north are some of the most beautiful mountains in Europe, the Dolomites, and due south is the cultural and culinary haven of Emilia-Romagna. The respective homes of two extraordinary wines are just outside the city: Soave and Franciacorta. And if an hour-and-a-half drive to the Adriatic is too long for you in the summer heat, you can cool off just next door in Lake Garda, a land of both American-style amusement parks and exclusive villas of the European elite.

Then again, you may want to spend all of your time in Verona itself. You will want for little in Shakespeare's setting for *Romeo and Juliet,* even if these

Verona, the fictional home of Romeo and Juliet, and lovers' graffiti

temptations lie outside the city walls. Verona has top-notch culture on its doorstep every year, when opera and concerts come to its coliseum, the second largest in Italy. The food is very good, though not world-renowned, and there are even two top-flight soccer teams in town, Hellas Verona and Chievo (see the sidebar "A Tiny Neighborhood in the Big Leagues"). All in all, not bad for a community of just 250,000.

Those who want to take maximum advantage of small-city living, where you can ride your bicycle to work and walk around the corner to a grocery store, should consider a family apartment in the historic center.

A Tiny Neighborhood in the Big Leagues

Soccer club Chievo-Verona recently moved into new headquarters inside a building it shares with a doctor's office. It has very little in common with other headquarters around the Italian league.

Inter of Milan, for example, occupies Palazzo Durini, built in 1648 and decorated with Pietro Maggi frescoes depicting scenes from Homer. Some 30 people work there under the direction of club owner Massimo Moratti, an oil baron. A.C. Milan sits in a high-rise with red carpeting, championship trophies, and a corporate atmosphere befitting its president, Silvio Berlusconi.

At Chievo's offices, there are five employees and about as many rooms. The only sign of decoration is a single large oil painting. Looking out from the canvas is the club's president, Luca Campedelli, one of two heirs to a holiday-cake manufacturer that sponsors the team. Surrounding him are the players and citizens who helped bring this tiny Verona suburb to the forefront of Italian soccer.

In 2001, Chievo played in Serie A, the premier league, for the first time in the club's 72-year history. These days it tends to finish in fourth or fifth place, just a few points behind the Milan and Turin powerhouses.

It is a dizzying accomplishment for a 33-year-old soccer club president—the youngest in the league—and for a neighborhood team that, until 1986, played on a field donated by the local parish. International attention has turned to this hamlet of 2,800 souls, but Campedelli tries to keep a sense of perspective. "In the end, we're still a soccer team," the president says, sitting by the painting. "We're not the saviors of the world."

They are, at least, the prophets of an unlikely salvation for a few dozen locals at the Bar Pantallona. The same people who spent their own money to upgrade the Bottagisio parish field now gather in this tavern, one of only four in town, to talk of Chievo's exploits against some of the greatest clubs in the world.

"Everyone here has a brother or some other relative who played for Chievo," says Marco Sancassani, who runs both the bar and the fan club. "There is a huge feeling of satisfaction. It's like seeing your father's work finally come to fruition."

Verona can be an elegant city when it wants to be, the sort of place where even a Sunday afternoon walk around the shops calls for a suit and tie, so don't expect rock-bottom real estate prices. Then again, don't expect to pay what you would in Venice or Milan. An average two-bedroom apartment of about 60 square meters near the city center will cost about €150,000 ($195,000), or will rent for about €600 ($780) per month. A three-bedroom place of about 90 square meters, not far from the Arena, should cost about €250,000 ($325,000).

Others might prefer the suburban life, and Verona is surrounded by nice homes on vineyards and olive groves, or else steps from the shore of Lake Garda. A one-family villa with at least 200 square meters will start at €120,000 ($156,000) for a rather ordinary suburban home, while a large architectural wonder with an olive garden and panoramic views will cost closer to €500,000 ($650,000). To live like a country baron or baroness in a historic rustic estate, prepare to spend at least €250,000 ($325,000) for the land and the structure, and possibly just as much to turn it into something livable and attractive.

Padua

Despite its history, few tourists come to Padua except as a launching-off point for Venice. Those who spend the most time here are usually students assigned to programs in the city's 13th-century university, the second-oldest in Europe.

The university testifies to the city's cultural and scientific importance. Padua is a cradle of the arts, exemplified by the Scrovegni chapel and its recently restored frescoes by Giotto. The artist Tasso once studied here, and Galileo was employed as a professor. To this day, the science program often makes headlines in newspapers and academic journals.

Modern-day Padua, population 210,000, is very industrial-looking, and many of its buildings are less than inspiring architecturally. Like Milan, Padua is now a place where people come to study or to find jobs, rather than to tour historic sites and museums. The industrial complex has lured thousands of immigrants, especially from North Africa, adding to the Northeast's racial tension.

Considering the economic health of the place, housing in Padua is reasonably priced. For €80,000 ($104,000), you can find a fully furnished mini-apartment smack downtown. Prices vary, of course, depending on the exact location. Two-bedroom apartments in the city start at about €60,000 ($78,000) for purchase (or about €650/$845 per month for rental) and reach €300,000 ($390,000) for a lovely three-bedroom unit measuring 100 square meters.

If the threat of encountering urban blight doesn't dovetail with your idea of living in Italy, the suburbs might be a better option, as the countryside here is dotted with fortified cities. The most noteworthy towns are found to the southwest, toward Verona: Battaglia Terme, with its 16th-century fortress; Monsèlice, with an 18th-century castle; and Montagnana, a citadel entirely encompassed by a turreted wall. This last town is an excellent compromise between Verona and Padua, with several cheap fixer-uppers for sale.

Padua is a cradle of the arts, exemplified by the Scrovegni chapel and its recently restored frescoes by Giotto. The artist Tasso once studied here, and Galileo was employed as a professor.

Here's one of them: A 150-square-meter house shaded by trees, with a dilapidated vineyard, two floors, and a classic red tile roof that costs just €60,000 ($78,000), but is literally falling apart at the seams. You'll have to build from scratch, but at least you'll have a nice plot of land and the frame of a house to start with. Alternatively, you could land a less charming but more healthy one-family villa in the same area for about €250,000 ($325,000). Not bad, when you consider it's just a 30-minute drive to Venice.

Prosecco and Grappa Country

Though small-city living has its advantages, many Americans who come to Italy aren't looking to socialize much, and tend to settle down in the country. Veneto, more so than Emilia-Romagna, has lots of isolated hills and relaxing vineyards, extending northeast from Verona and Padua toward the border with the Friuli region. This is the land of prosecco, Italy's answer to champagne. The gateway to this hilly region, along the Brenta River and wedged between the Dolomites and the Adriatic, are the small towns of Citadella, Castelfranco Bassano del Grappa, and Marostica.

Like Ferrara, these villages seem cut from the pages of a storybook about knights and princesses. Both Cittadella and Castelfranco are surrounded by moats. Marostica's castle has a giant chessboard where actors in medieval costume play a human-sized version of the game. Bassano del Grappa is the architectural gem of them all, perched around a covered bridge designed by Palladio. Though the area is rustic, it has been discovered by outsiders, and the prices for an old home can reflect this. For a crumbling stone farmhouse near Marostica and Bassano del Grappa, expect to pay about €200,000 ($260,000).

Better deals can be had further north, into wine country. In the Valdobbiadene valley, close to Vittorio Veneto, old farmhouses with stone wine cellars sit in fields, shaded by patches of forest overlooking the

© Monica Larner

Ski lodge in the Dolomites

prosecco vineyards. Here, a 150-square-meter farmhouse, with the walls, roof, and floors in good shape and sitting on five square kilometers of land, sold recently for about €150,000 ($195,000). The facade is loaded with windows and newly fitted with wooden shutters, and the property is bordered by a waterfall.

On the lower end of the price scale is a €70,000 ($91,000) hilltop house of the same dimensions, with solid walls and a decent roof, but sketchy floors. Dozens of others are in the €150,000 ($195,000) to €200,000 ($260,000) range, and massive estates in decent condition, can be had for less than €300,000 ($390,000), small vineyard included.

REAL ESTATE AGENTS: EMILIA-ROMAGNA AND VENETO

Abita Immobiliare
Via Ognissanti 27
35131 Padua
tel. 049/775-459

Agenzia D'affari Radar
Via Marinali Orazio 35
36061 Bassano Del Grappa
tel. 0424/228-711

Ferrara Case
Viale IV Novembre 83/85
44100 Ferrara
tel. 0532/760-330
fax 0532/760-330
www.primacasa.it

Global Studio
Via Garibaldi 57
43100 Parma
tel. 0521/200-380
fax 0521/200-380
www.immobiliareglobal.it

Studio Attici
Viale Carducci 17
40125 Bologna
tel. 051/636-8712
fax 051/303-853
www.studioattici.it

THE NORTHWEST

The Northwest: Piedmont and Liguria

Penned in by the Alps and the Mediterranean on one end and spilling into the Po river plain on the other, Italy's northwestern corner is one of its most diverse. It boasts cobalt-blue seas and snowy peaks, birch and chestnut forests, and misty rolling vineyards, plus a wide swath of foggy rice paddies (Italy is Europe's number-one producer of rice), where locals stir their famous risotto with frogs' legs.

If this is starting to sound a bit like France, it should. Not only do Piedmont and Liguria fit snugly against the border, but much of modern-day Alpes Maritimes and the Haute Savoie once flew the Italian flag as well—or at least the flag of Piedmont's kings, who once controlled Genoa and Sardinia as well. Turin was the capital of this spacious kingdom, and later of all Italy, when Garibaldi and his men unified the country under the Savoys.

The Turinese were then, and continue to be, among the wealthiest and most progressive of their compatriots. The bespectacled liberals were the ones who came up with the idea of a united Italy in the first place, with the blessing of the king. And after their royal family was exiled, another

Piedmont clan soon took their place: the Agnelli family, founders of the Fiat dynasty. Heavy industry drove the local economy throughout the 20th century, though telecommunications and other high-tech industries in and around Turin are changing that now. With high technology, a progressive reputation, and a bounty of sea and snow, Piedmont has a lot in common with Northern California. One big difference is that outsiders haven't flooded in. Why they haven't done so is anyone's guess.

The Ligurian coast has a more international reputation. It would be nice to think that this is because its sun-soaked and wine-drinking citizens regularly set records for longevity, but it's more likely that the wealthy re-sort towns—glitzy San Remo, opulent Portofino, and the newly famous fishing villages of the Cinque Terre—are responsible for attracting home-owner hopefuls. Parts of Liguria are expensive and others are downright elitist, resembling the poshest enclaves of the Cote d'Azur. Much of Liguria, though, is approachable and friendly, especially the family-oriented towns around San Remo and the tucked-away villages on the mountain-ous inland. There is not much land, but Liguria still manages to offer something for everyone who's seeking a little slice of the Italian Riviera.

Piedmont

Turin and Lake Maggiore are two hotspots for tourists, but Piedmont's most prized territory really lies at its heart, starting south of the city and ex-tending southeast toward the mountainous French border. Le Langhe, as the hilly area is known, is dominated by Alba, Asti, and Bra, three small cities each with separate claims to gastronomic fame. Alba is home to the white truffle. The province around Asti produces the *spumante* (sparkling wine) that bears its name. Bra's newfound identity comes in the form of Slow Food, a local nonprofit organization dedicated to the art and science of eating well. The group has attracted tens of thousands of mem-bers and fans around the world. Slow Food's cheese festival, held on odd years in Bra and host to thousands of cheesemakers, is a widely anticipated event, as is the Salone del Gusto, held in the even years and dedicated to organically grown products and local dishes and wines.

The people who come to these sorts of events look forward to a tour of Bra and its environs, which produce some of the country's most prestigious wine. You may already have heard of Piedmont's two most elite growing areas, Barolo and Barbaresco, just around the corner. The hilltop villages recall those in Tuscany, except that there are no camera shops and really no tourist infrastructure to speak of, except the local family-run *agriturismi*

© John Moretti

(rural bed-and-breakfasts) that cater to a mostly Italian-speaking public. In fact, there are few signs at all pointing to Barbaresco, making it difficult for the accidental tourist to find.

WHERE TO LIVE

The trouble for prospective homeowners is that the vineyards themselves are so pristine and priceless that there are very few houses available. Those that do go on the market from time to time are considered too valuable to be used for any other purpose than winemaking. Part of the appeal of Barolo, and one of the reasons it costs more than almost any other wine in Italy, is because the territory where it can be produced is restricted to very few acres. All the space is devoted to growing, and no new construction is allowed. The best place to start looking for a house nearby is in Asti and the area around Nizza Monferrato, also an important growing region.

In the center of Asti, a 130-square-meter home with three bedrooms, surrounded by greenery, sells for about €250,000 ($325,000). Prices decrease from there as you go out from the city, as long as you're not right in the vineyards. About 10 miles out of Asti, you can expect to pay as little as €70,000 ($91,000) for a 150-square-meter house. A vineyard in Nizza Monferrato, though a smallish one, can sell for about €600,000 ($780,000). An antique home there, in good shape, sells for about €120,000 ($156,000).

Lesser-known wine country lies just a few miles to the east, around

A Forgotten Wine is Reborn

For wine amateurs, Oltrepò Pavese is relatively easily defined: It's known as a wine with a decent price tag at the supermarket, a red *spumante* that isn't always the best choice for a dinner, but passes muster at a cocktail party. The area has more sophisticated wines as well, but the fizzy stuff is its trademark.

For the same wine amateurs, the name Oltrepò Tortonese means nothing at all. Although this part of Piedmont near the Lombardy border grows most of the same grapes as its cousin in the province of Pavia, few casual wine customers have ever heard of it.

At the 2002 Salone del Gusto food and wine exhibit in Turin, local producers featured the Timorasso, a naughty white grape from the Oltrepò Tortonese wine family that once covered these hills in abundance, but was only rediscovered in the 1990s. The grape's flaws are many. The fruit is sparse, and picking it is a delicate operation. It's often called "the grape that rolls on the ground." Worse, the plant has several layers of leaves that are notorious for shading the fruit, and so it has to be spread far and wide—eating up lots of valuable land. It has been historically vulnerable to *Botrytis,* a parasitic mold that is harmful to grapes.

But the clay-based soil in southeastern Piedmont is perfect for Timorasso, says vintner Elisa Semino, and its enthusiastic reception by the public has made the resurrection effort worthwhile. Her family vineyard, La Colombera, based in the hillside town of Vho, has grown the grape for five years. It is a small harvest, cultivated on only about an acre of land, resulting in an exclusive label the vineyard calls "Derthona."

Another local producer, Walter Massa, says the renaissance of Timorasso was "a stroke of good luck in my life." Massa is considered the first to start growing the historic grape some 10 years ago, and had what he says was tremendous success with his 2000 vintage of the Costa del Vento label. He has since petitioned authorities for Timorasso to be awarded the DOC label, a decision ultimately made by the European Union. A third producer, Franco Martinetti, sold 2,000 bottles of it that same year, calling the light, pear-scented varietal "Martin."

Wine merchants around Tortona report that customers are now starting to ask for Timorasso by name. Laura Forlino, who owns a wine store in the center of town, says she has sold some 1,200 bottles of it in recent years, whereas in previous seasons, "people didn't even know what it was." Some of the North's most exclusive restaurants are also serving Timorasso: for example, the highbrow Aimo e Nadia in Milan. So are top restaurants around the rest of Europe—at Convivio in London, a bottle of Timorasso sells for the equivalent of about €50 ($65).

Timorasso remains a rarity, however. The Colli Tortonesi area is still better known for its reds. In discussions about Italian wine, it often gets a brief mention as a neighbor to the Alessandria province, boasting a handful of Barbera producers. There are some 30 vintners in the Colli Tortonesi producing a wide range of DOC wines, including Cortese, Dolcetto, and especially Barbera, plus various blends with Pino Nero, Croatina, Riesling, and Cabernet Sauvignon.

Tortona. Up-and-coming vintners produce what they call Oltrepò Tortonesi, a play on the more famous hills just over the border in Lombardy, near Pavia, called Oltrepò Pavese (see the sidebar "A Forgotten Wine is Reborn"). Aside from the wine, Tortona's cuisine draws day-trippers from Milan and Turin. Both cities are about an hour away by car, making Tortona a good option for commuters as well. Houses here cost just a fraction of what they would in Milan or Turin, and are surrounded by misty vines, rather than smoggy streets.

In Tortona, a nice, two-floor walk-up in an older building with a wine cellar and a garden costs about €160,000 ($208,000), or as little as €30,000 ($39,000) if it needs a lot of work. A classic commuter home for young couples—a newly built, two-bedroom house with balconies and a garden—goes for about €120,000 ($156,000) in the small towns around Tortona. For those who prefer something in the countryside, a beautiful new villa, with about 400 square meters of floor space and a stable, surrounded by greenery, was selling recently for €300,000 ($390,000). Period farmhouses with some kind of vineyard attached will cost more.

South of Cuneo, sitting on the peaks of the French border, is the ski area of Limone. To call it a resort would be deceiving. It's a quiet place, far from the crowds that inhabit the rest of Piedmont's periphery—Sestriere, Courmayeur, the Matterhorn—and the prices that reflect their international acclaim. Limone, instead, is Piedmont for the recluse and anyone else looking for peace and scenery, with the option of trotting downhill to Nice or Turin for some excitement. There is even an Alpine train connecting them.

On these mountain slopes, plumes of smoke rise from chimneys on stone houses, the silence interrupted only by the occasional clanging of cowbells. Near the ski lifts and in the tiny villages spread around Limone is an array of housing possibilities, ranging from rustic stone houses to wooden chalets to more modern condominiums.

Compared to houses in the more famous ski resorts of the Alps, some prices here are reasonable enough that you might even consider the property a second home. For example, a simple but cozy and well-built cottage made of fieldstone, with about 70 square meters spread over two floors, can be had for about €50,000 ($65,000). Next up on the price scale are condominiums, which often come fully furnished and are equipped with a communal pool and a large garden. They range in price from €120,000 ($156,000) to €200,000 ($260,000). Finally, individual chalets with terraces overlooking breathtaking panoramas fall into the €200,000 ($260,000) to €250,000 ($325,000) range.

As for rentals, the towns around Alba offer some very inexpensive

© John Moretti

A house in Barolo

places. In Alba itself, you might find a spacious four-bedroom apartment for less than €350 ($455) per month. In Nizza Monferrato, in the heart of wine country, you will likely not pay more than €450 ($585) per month for a nice two-bedroom apartment.

Liguria

Just before Piedmont reaches the sea, Liguria steps in its way. The name is synonymous with the Italian Riviera, a thin, mountainous coastline of fishing villages–turned–tourist attractions that extend from the French border to Tuscany. Vacationers and retirees alike have come here for more than a century to enjoy its seafood, pesto, white wine, and sunshine.

Its capital, Genoa, was once a proud seafaring republic and is now a gritty port city trying to regain its medieval title of "La Superba." While it dusts off itself and its image, tourists head for either side of the region that Genoa cuts in half: To the south is *la Levante* (land of the rising sun), while the north is *la Ponente,* where it sets. Both have famous resorts, but different points of view.

Driving into Italy from Monaco and the French border town of Menton, you know something has changed once you pass into Italy. There is no longer a customs house here— the Schengen agreement wiped them away—but the difference is immediately palpable all the same. The tunnels that cut through the cliff-lined coast get a little grayer, their rocks rougher-hewn. The hillsides are dotted with greenhouses that grow Liguria's famous flowers, and to the west, the sea is tracked by fishing boats hauling in squid. The first visible traces

Vacationers and retirees alike have come to Liguria for more than a century to enjoy its seafood, pesto, white wine, and sunshine.

of civilization show up about 20 minutes from the border: the clifftop town of Imperia, followed by San Remo.

WHERE TO LIVE

Anyone who has seen or read *The Talented Mr. Ripley* has some idea of San Remo's jet-set reputation in decades past. These days, the resort is best known for its annual music festival, where Italian pop stars are made. The festival was started in the Fascist era as a way to build a pan-Italian cultural identity, and that popular spirit pervades to this day. Unlike Portofino and other swanky centers of the Levante, San Remo is unpretentious and hosts hundreds of summer homes for the Milanese middle class. Even its casino has a casual atmosphere when compared to nearby Monte Carlo.

The downtowns of San Remo, and especially Imperia, hold little appeal for homeowners looking for the best of the Riviera. At times, they can be grim. The better real estate lies in the small beach towns on either side of the cities, or in the mountains further inland. In the surrounding villages, you should be able to find a smallish stone home, without much land around it, for less than €100,000 ($130,000). A well-restored, three-bedroom country home in the hills just behind San Remo, with a view of the sea, should sell for between €200,000 ($260,000) and €250,000 ($325,000). These kinds of stone houses often sit on olive groves and almost always have an ample garden where you can grow fresh basil to make pesto. Prices per square meter become much more expensive when you move down to the waterfront. There, villas are generally divided into apartments, as there is little space for new construction on the steep slopes. Expect to hear prices between €300,000 ($390,000) and €500,000 ($650,000) for a nicely furnished family apartment.

Or, you may decide to do what many bargain-hunting Europeans started to do in the early 1990s, and explore the mountain valleys further inland, where local traditions are strongest and the real estate relatively cheap. The hottest spot these days is the group of valleys running from Liguria's highest peak, Monte Saccarello, along route 548 past Badalucco to the coast near San Remo. The tight alleys of Andagna, Triora, and Agaggio are surrounded by oleander and rhododendron, the refinished houses painted pink and ocher, others awaiting final touches of their new owners' choosing. The valley has dozens of characteristic stone homes in need of serious work, but selling for less than €20,000 ($26,000), 12th-century mills for less than €50,000 ($65,000), and fully restored cottages, complete with horse stables, for less than €100,000 ($130,000). These are true mountain hideouts, where small trattorias serve pasta with walnut sauce, and yet the towns also hold festivals dedicated to stockfish—after all, the beach is just 20 minutes away.

Rents are not cheap on the Ligurian seaside, especially in the Levante. Lots of foreign services offer weekly rates for tourists, and the monthly rentals, which are slightly harder to come by, reflect the scarcity. Still, in Rapallo, for example, you can find a large four-bedroom apartment with an expansive terrace overlooking the sea for about €1,000 ($1,300) per month. Renters will have more luck on the Ponente side. San Remo, in particular, has lots of options for short-term rentals, and some great deals—as little as €10 ($13) per square meter. For example, you could find a three-bedroom apartment measuring approximately 80 square meters for about €800 ($1,040) per month.

THE LEVANTE

The Levante is a spectacular place to visit, but good values for homes are few and far between. Portofino is its most elite port of call, a de rigueur stopover for well-equipped yachts and their passengers. Some not-so-famous people have managed to afford homes in the two cities that flank Portofino, Santa Margherita and Rapallo, but there is scant room or tolerance for new construction on the steep rocky coast, and so prices there, too, are very high. South of Rapallo, you'll find the Cinque Terre—five small fishing villages hugging their respective inlets. American guidebooks have given the towns a mythical reputation that eludes most Italians, and so tourists come every year to walk the hilly hiking trails and ponder this pristine scenery.

In my opinion, the nicest two towns in the Levante are at its extremes: Camogli in the north, and Portovenere in the south. The first is a more proletarian Portofino, with the same pastel buildings but more palatable prices. Camogli's finest hour is when the townspeople put on a giant fish fry, preparing the day's catch in pans that are at least 10 feet wide. Portovenere is a little more upscale

With some exceptions, the available property on the coastline consists of apartments in three- or four-family villas, or else in a larger apartment building. In Rapallo, a nice three-bedroom apartment geared towards foreigners sells in the €300,000 ($390,000) range. Alternatively, you might look a little further inland. Just 20 minutes into the hills from Portofino, around Fivizzano, rustic stone houses sell for as little as €50,000 ($65,000), though they would need thorough restructuring.

REAL ESTATE AGENTS: THE NORTHWEST

Gabetti
Via XX Settembre 203
16121 Genoa
tel. 010/530-131
fax 010/587-514
www.gabetti.it

Rinaldo Muratore
Piazza Savona 5
12051 Alba
tel. 0173/333-11
fax 0173/339-35
www.rinaldomuratore.it

Orsini Real Estate
Via Garibaldi 2
16038 Santa Margherita Ligure
tel./fax 0185/288-827
www.orsinirealestate.com

THE CENTRAL REGIONS

The Central Regions:
Tuscany, Umbria, and Le Marche

Well, this is it. The promised land for wealthy foreigners who have always dreamed of owning a house in Italy. It's no mystery why hundreds of North Americans and Northern Europeans have chosen the subtle curves of the Apennines as their new home. Tuscany, Umbria, and Le Marche represent the quintessential Italian retreat, evoking daydreams of cloudless mornings in the garden and homegrown picnic lunches among olive groves. An afternoon outing might include a trip to the thermal spas near Arezzo, wine-tasting in Montepulciano, or a walking tour of some of Florence's finest Renaissance art and architecture. Even the drive between these cities is an experience that other Americans travel thousands of miles to enjoy on vacation.

From Lucca and the Mediterranean beaches of Versilia to the quiet Adriatic solitude of Le Marche, there are countless options for prospective homeowners spread across the breadth of the peninsula. The trick is to find an area that hasn't been "discovered" yet, and determine if there's a good reason why it hasn't. You need to hone in on the regional peculiarities that fit your personality and the housing prices that fit your budget.

Tuscany

Tuscany requires little introduction, as it has become the hottest real estate market for Anglos since the rush to Southern France in the 1980s. The ocher-colored house on the hill with the cypress-lined drive is now faded by camera flashes, and anyone that hasn't been there need only read the deluge of literature expounding on the pleasures of living in this Italian paradise.

The pictures don't lie, and every praising word is true, though it is hard to express in words the unique appeal of Tuscany without coming off as trite, if I haven't already. It is a subtle landscape of olive groves and vineyards, with forests spilling out chestnuts, white truffles, hares, and wild boar, just as they did centuries ago.

Tuscans turn to the Renaissance for their identity. This golden period not only produced the region's beautiful art and architecture, but it also gave the rest of the peninsula Dante, whose Florentine dialect would become the national language. The scent of the era is so strong here, you get the impression that the average Tuscan would prefer to be living in the 15th century. Annual medieval festivals here are highly anticipated events of high pageantry; feudal flags are unfurled, while men in tights and silly hats proclaim the local lore with period music, food, and contests.

Ancient rivalries between the region's major cities endure to this day. Livorno and Pisa still avenge centuries-old grudges on the soccer field and in the grandstands; a Florentine license plate in Arezzo still elicits a snarl. But the feuding doesn't stop at the town line. Within the cities, neighborhoods have a go at each other each year in such anticipated events as the Palio of Siena and the Giostra del Saracino in Arezzo. And then, within the neighborhoods themselves, battles between families and even family members can be dragged out for decades. This region that claims to have united the country linguistically is actually about as fractious as they come.

Rural Tuscany remains a fiefdom of country barons—politically progressive but culturally conservative—and their elected leaders reflect this dichotomy. This is the red belt of Italy, a historically left-leaning community that can claim the first laws in the world outlawing the death penalty. At the same time, local entities make sure that nothing ever

Tuscany

Botticelli graffiti in Florence

changes here aesthetically, demanding that even factories have a characteristic red tile roof. Altering the color of a window shutter can give rise to a protracted battle with the town authorities.

The architectural intactness of the landscape and the aroma of old money have helped lure legions of foreigners—all eager to drive vintage cars on roads winding through sunflower fields to turreted hilltop villas—to Tuscany's real estate agencies. These days, if you stop by an agent's office in Lucca or Siena, be prepared to see a long list of properties selling for well over €1 million ($1.3 million).

WHERE TO LIVE

The High End

The best-known market for foreigners is Chianti, often dubbed "Chiantishire" for the overwhelming number of English homeowners that have moved into the vineyards between Florence and Siena. Since the 1960s, the primary appeal of this region has been its wine—it's been exported to Britain for hundreds of years. In the 1980s, the Dutch, the Germans, and the Swiss arrived, giving the entire region a Northern European accent and bringing the prices of real estate to stratospheric levels. Some

Wholesaling the Tuscan Dream

Don't bother asking in the local tourist office in Cortona where Frances Mayes lives. The American author, whose best-selling *Under the Tuscan Sun* portrays her part-time life there, doesn't seek publicity, and has apparently asked the tourist office to ward off the curious. "It's outside of town, in the hills over there," came the vague response from the functionary at the APT. When asked for more specific directions, I was told, "The house is not on our map, I can't help you."

Ms. Mayes's well-worn formula for success? Buy a gorgeous villa in a spectacularly beautiful location somewhere in Europe, set out to fix it up, and confront the usual predicaments that accompany any housing renovation. Meanwhile, get to know some of the locals and their folklore, imbibe the regional wines, learn at least one ancient art—such as the pruning of olive trees—and write a fabulously successful book about the experience.

As Peter Mayle did in the 1980s with his *A Year in Provence* and its sequels, Ms. Mayes tills the soil of the travel memoir—this time in Tuscany. And she has hit pay dirt: *Under the Tuscan Sun* was on *The New York Times* best-seller list for well over a year. Like Mr. Mayle, she has spawned a merchandising machine with *Under the Tuscan Sun* date books and calendars.

"The town spends a lot of money each year for advertising, but this simple book brings more people to our town than any government initiative," says Marco Molinese, a grocer in Cortona who, like most traders in town, considers Ms. Mayes a friend. "But the locals, they don't know her or the book," he adds. Making further inquiries about the author on a stroll down Via Nazionale, Cortona's main street, I find out that a local bookstore has sold out of her book. Giulio Nocentini, who has run the store for 45 years, says he has read it and thinks it's a suitable primer for Americans visiting the area. "But no Italian would want to read it. We're quite accustomed to having foreigners try to interpret our lives," he says. Mr. Nocentini says the book is selling the Tuscan dream. He has seen a lot more American tourists arrive at his door as a result, in search of that dream or the next closest thing—a glimpse of the author and her house.

—By Paul French,
a Canadian travel writer who
lived in Tuscany for two years

of the more noteworthy neighbors include the rock star Sting, who has a home in the town of Montevarchi.

Chianti's expats have long experimented with making the local wine. More recently, expats in other important growing regions, such as the one between Montalcino and Montepulciano, have begun producing wine. This crescent of vineyards is flatter than the rolling sagebrush of Chianti, but spiked with hilltop medieval towns. Its wealth of monasteries, Renaissance monuments, and thermal springs make it quintessentially Tuscan, and so it should come as no surprise that real estate prices have gone through the roof here, too. The swath of million-dollar properties extends from the outskirts of Pienza, a Renaissance jewel, northeast to Cortona, where Frances Mayes wrote her bestseller, *Under the Tuscan Sun.* If you meet other Americans in Cortona, they're likely to be students in the local language program for foreigners, real estate shoppers, or here to catch a glimpse of Ms. Mayes's home. (See the sidebar "Wholesaling the Tuscan Dream.")

The area between Cortona and Arezzo, called the Valdichiana, is far from undiscovered, but for some reason it has been spared the full colonization of Tuscany's other scenic venues. Its villages are quaint and authentic, braced by medieval walls and towers, but skipping the fanfare for tourists. And while the architecture is nothing special in Chianti, near Arezzo you'll find elaborately finished *palazzi nobili* (noble palaces) with imposing gates and driveways. These are the stomping grounds of many counts and countesses, both bona fide and otherwise.

Arezzo is a particularly well-preserved medieval city, although the Florentines worked hard during the Guelph and Ghibbeline wars to ensure that it would never rise to the prominence of Florence. The beige buildings are so characteristically Tuscan that the filmmaker Roberto Begnini chose Arezzo as the backdrop for *Life is Beautiful.* Locals take much less pride in this silver screen claim to fame than in the city's splendid works by Renaissance painter Piero della Francesca, or even in their renowned antiques industry. Another perk to this area is that it is next to Italy's major north–south highway and a stop on the high-speed Rome–Milan train line.

You may be lucky to turn up something in your price range in one of these exclusive areas, but it's advisable to look a little further afield if you expect to find a bargain. Tuscany still has a few unexplored corners. Broadly speaking, you're likely to discover the best value in the areas east of Chianti and south of Montalcino.

Bargain-Hunting

Driving south of Montalcino along Route 323, you'll arrive in the Val d'Orcia, a more sparsely inhabited area unmarked on many tourist itineraries. The Val d'Orcia produces some wine, but it is more famous for Tuscany's other agricultural products: olive oil, pecorino cheese, honey, and saffron. One of the many high points of life in this rural area is picking chestnuts in the forested hills and bringing them home to prepare flour for bread or even pasta. There is a wealth of hiking trails nearby, especially on Monte Amiata, a modest ski area in the winter. Much of the land is protected, as it is home to such rare species as the European wolf, and this also means that there are relatively few houses. Luckily, the ones for sale aren't very expensive—within the €300,000 ($390,000) range for something in good shape.

The Val d'Orcia produces some wine, but it is more famous for Tuscany's other agricultural products: olive oil, pecorino cheese, honey, and saffron.

The biggest challenge to living here is its remoteness. The largest towns around Monte Amiata have only about 5,000 inhabitants, which means there aren't very many services nearby. Those who plan to settle here should be dedicated to country living. It is a long, albeit scenic, drive to any city.

Further south are the valleys and pastures that make up the Maremma. This is cowboy country, complete with rodeos and a beef-heavy diet. It, too, is remote, well off most guidebook itineraries, and yet full of Etruscan monuments and natural wonders. One of my favorite spots in Italy is here, in Saturnia—thermal springs just off a country road. They are semicircular white pools, formed by the calcium in the volcanically heated water. Romans come up for the weekend to smear themselves with the warm, white mud.

This ancient homeland of the Etruscans extends all the way north to the town of Volterra, known for its mining. This whole corner of Tuscany offers reasonable prices on homes, as long as you steer clear of the Argentario peninsula (the takeoff point for ferries bound for the isle of Elba), which is quickly gaining appeal among foreigners.

There are other hidden niches in Tuscany, which, after all, is a pretty big place. You really never know what might turn up. Maybe someone in Chianti needs cash in a hurry. Who knows? You could even see an entire Tuscan village go up for sale. In 2002, the regional government put a 1.4-square-kilometer medieval burg on the auction block, starting at €300,000 ($390,000). (Don't feel too bad if you missed it—it was described as a real fixer-upper.) Not long before that, all 18 houses in the town of Toiano, near San Gimignano, were placed simultaneously on the market, each priced at about €500 ($650) per square meter. The island of Pianosa was put on the auction block in the fall of 2003, along with its own police station, for €8 million ($10.4 million). If you can't afford an entire Tuscan island, maybe you'd settle for a slice of Tuscan beach? The bidding for one in the town of Portoferraio started at just €5,000 ($6,500).

Rentals

Arezzo is a very stately city with relatively high rents. Downtown, expect to pay €600–800 ($780–1,040) per month for a two-bedroom apartment. But just a few kilometers outside the city, near Cortona, a one-bedroom apartment with a garden can be found for about €350 ($460) per month. Family villas in the area can rent for as little as €650 ($845) per month for something very small in an uninteresting town, to nearly €10,000 ($13,000) per month for the lap of luxury. On average, though, expect to see prices closer to €2,000 ($2,600) per month for family villas in the heart of Tuscany.

Most of the nicer villas in Tuscany are rented out to foreigners on a weekly basis. Websites such as www.tuscandream.com offer a week's stay in gorgeous villas for €2,000–4,000 ($2,600–5,200) per week for a place that sleeps six–eight people. Couples can rent a single-bedroom residence for closer to €500 ($650) per week.

Umbria

If real estate agents blindfolded you, drove you to Umbria, and told you it was Tuscany, you'd have little reason to doubt them when the blindfold came off. Just about everything in Umbria looks, feels, and tastes like Tuscany, at least at first glance. There are fortified hilltop villages with Renaissance frescos, rolling hills, fertile valleys, good local wines, and tasteful stone houses. Even the bread and prosciutto are made without salt, just like in Tuscany. This is a throwback to the days when the popes in Rome denied the central regions their salt to break their independent streak. That was in 1540. Like the Tuscans, the Umbrians don't forget their past.

Aside from the distinct Umbrian accent, the biggest difference between the two regions is in their people's respective characters. While the Tuscans are known for their sarcastic wit and appetite for a good debate, the Umbrians are more inward-looking and gentle people who prefer candid statements and shy from confrontation. After all, the region produced both St. Francis of Assisi and St. Valentine, from Terni, universal symbols of peace and love and all that warm, fuzzy stuff that would be mocked in Machiavelli's Tuscany.

They say that this quiet introspection and humility comes from the region's landlocked hills and the agricultural lifestyle that they breed. Umbria is called the "green heart of Italy," thanks to its position in the very center of the peninsula and its endless shades of green, from the tobacco plants of the Tiber Valley to the grassy hills dotted with olive groves. The painter Pietro Perugino was inspired by this idyllic countryside to produce *The Adoration of the Magi* (1504), considered the precursor of modern

While the Tuscans are known for their sarcastic wit and appetite for a good debate, the Umbrians are a more inward-looking and gentle people who prefer candid statements and shy from confrontation.

landscape painting. It is a lot more lush and fertile than the Middle Eastern shepherds might have remembered it.

WHERE TO LIVE

Running down a list of Umbria's cities, you'll see a lot of familiar names, but they're not necessarily the best places to look for a house. Assisi, for example, is a marvel of a city and a major stop on any religious pilgrimage because of the Basilica of San Francesco, but the ultra peaceful, almost lunar landscape around it is practically uninhabited. Perugia is another stunning hilltop city, renowned for its university for foreigners, but locals grumble that it has become crime-ridden in recent years. Terni, the home of St. Valentine, is not in itself a very lovable city, though the countryside nearby deserves some attention.

From a homeowner's perspective, the number-one place to settle in Umbria has long been Todi, situated halfway between Perugia and Terni. Expat homeowners and those looking to join the club have already pushed the selling price of attractive houses there beyond the half-million-euro mark.

Not far away, however, there are still intriguing stone farmhouses, with four bedrooms and set on a few square kilometers of land, for about €200,000 ($260,000), though you will probably have to invest that same amount to get them into livable shape. Alternatively, there are finished homes of similar dimensions and character for €400,000 ($520,000) to €500,000 ($650,000) if you want to spare yourself the effort. If your heart is set on living very close to Todi, but you are looking to spend about €200,000 ($260,000) or less for something in good shape, you should steer away from rustic farmhouses and look at one-family villas, something that might be called a cottage in the United States.

Further south, along the border with Lazio, is an even better option in the towns between Terni and Orvieto. It's amazing this area isn't more densely populated, the towns of Narni and Amelia in particular. Both are stunning fortified hilltowns, surrounded by olive trees in the low-lying hills west of Terni. They started off life as Etruscan settlements, became important Roman strongholds, and later medieval fortress towns. The flavor of the Middle Ages is everywhere here, especially when Narni holds its annual medieval celebration, La Corsa all'Anello. The municipally owned, underground taverns in each of the town's quarters open their doors to the public, and the pasta and wine flow freely.

Best of all, this seemingly isolated corner of pastoral paradise, teeming with herds of sheep, is just 40 minutes by car from Rome. The prices hardly reflect this. Like anywhere else in Italy, the options range from a €500,000 ($650,000) architectural wonder to a pile of rocks, but there are some real bargains in between. A real estate agent from the Gabetti franchise in Terni told me a story of a Scottish couple who showed up in 2002 looking to spend less than €75,000 ($98,000), and found a nearly inhabitable farmhouse for €30,000 ($39,000). For that price, don't expect anything too fancy, but at least the place will have charm. Houses in this corner of Umbria are often warm and uncomplicated—much like the reputed character of Umbrians themselves. Many are built of rough fieldstones, approached by driveways that are little more than wheel tracks in the grass at the side of a white, limestone pebble road. Inside, the dominant feature will probably be a stone hearth where you can bake bread like the locals, sticking it on a grate over the coals and finishing the crust by covering it with ashes.

In Terni and the outlying towns, such as Narni, rents are low. The monthly rent for a three-bedroom place there, even a massive one, will rarely crest €400 ($520) per month. Rents in Perugia, however, are quite a bit higher. A three-bedroom apartment near the University for Foreigners should run at least €750 ($975) per month.

Le Marche

When American homeowners in Le Marche tell you how they ended up in this mountainous region on the Adriatic, the story often starts out with a dream about Tuscany. A couple plans to buy their dream home near Chianti or Montepulciano. They start clicking through postings on the Internet, and soon come to the conclusion that Tuscany is too expensive for their budget. Then they move on to their fallback, Umbria. Back in the late 1990s, this was a feasible alternative, and English and American newspapers heralded Umbria as the new frontier. But even by the turn of the millennium, much of Umbria had outpriced itself as well.

"Prices in Tuscany can be prohibitive, and Umbria, though a little cheaper, is not miles away," said Mike Braunholt of Britain-based Prestige Properties, one of many foreign realtors active in central Italy. "Le Marche is the third wave." When I spoke to him, his group was listing an unfinished three-bedroom country home in Umbria, sitting on a few acres of olive grove, for about €280,000 ($364,000). At the same time, they were offering a similar three-bedroom house in Le Marche, also in need of renovation, for about €20,000 ($26,000). "Keep in mind," Braunholt said, "that many of these places aren't much more than bundles of rocks." Both houses needed big-ticket items like a new roof and floor, which might add an additional €300,000 ($390,000) to the investment.

Starting an *Agriturismo*

Lori Cintioli and her family used to live in Castelfidardo, a small town in the Le Marche region. Cintioli ran a clothing store, while her husband was a craftsman. Then came the big decision: They sold their apartment and moved to the countryside. "With the money from the apartment's sale and from a bank loan, we bought four and a half hectares [11 acres] of land and an old farmhouse that we started to restore," Cintioli says.

A 1985 law gave farmers the chance to offer accommodation, food, and drink, and to organize activities for tourists. Essentially, it made applying for hotel and restaurant licenses easier. The only conditions were that farming had to remain their main business, and the products served had to be mostly homemade, in order to set up such an *agriturismo*.

That proved to be a sticking point for New York native Nora Kravis, who started renting rooms on her Tuscan farm in 1988. She applied for an agritourism permit in her town of Radda, in the Chianti area, but the authorities turned her down. That was because Kravis was a veterinarian, and she earned more money from that pro-fession than from farming itself. To run an *agriturismo*, farming has to be your major source of income. It took her seven years to get the municipal government to change its mind. After she passed an exam for her license, she started serving local produce and selling the goat milk, cashmere, and related skincare products that she makes on the farm.

Despite the potential obstacles that Italians like the Cintioli family and foreigners like Kravis face, the trend of starting an *agriturismo* is catching on. In 2001, the number of employees working in agriculture saw its first increase since World War II, and there are now more than 10,000 *agriturismi* operating across the country. On an average year, more than two million visitors, 25 percent of whom are foreigners, stay in them.

"When I started my business in 1990, the *agriturismi* of this valley offered accommodation for 50 people only," says Vittorio Cipolla, who manages his own farm resort in Val d'Orcia, Tuscany. "Now there are some 150 *agriturismi* with an average of 10 beds each."

While you can never judge the price of a home by the region alone, it's usually a safe bet to say that a property in Le Marche is going to be cheaper than a comparable one in Tuscany or Umbria. Le Marche is the younger, harder-working brother of the two noble regions, and it bends over backward to market itself as a vacation destination, plastering posters all over Italian airports and train stations, and even on the trains themselves.

It shouldn't be a hard sell. Mountains make up 30 percent of its territory—and real mountains, too, the kind with snow at the top and rocky faces. It has vineyards, some notable art and architecture, and beaches—something you won't find in Umbria. It also happens to be the accordion capital of the world; the town of Castelfidardo is famous for the hand-crafted instruments.

Le Marche takes its name from "borderland," as it was commonly the battleground for the Papal States' expansionist plans. But nature lovers will get more pristine beauty for their money in Le Marche than anywhere else in central Italy. Those restoring old homes can expect less bureaucratic battles. The *marchigiani* are eager to please.

One issue has stifled mass investment by foreigners thus far: Le Marche is not very close to the country's two major international airports, in Rome and Milan. In fact, it is about as distant from them as you can get in Italy. This may become less of a problem in the future. The fast rise of budget carriers in Italy means that the country's smaller airports are gaining European routes, and Le Marche's airport in Ancona has emerged as a front runner for that business—along with Pisa and Bologna, which aren't too far away.

WHERE TO LIVE

For all the snide comments painting the *marchigiani* as backwards sheep farmers, their region has made some impressive contributions to Italy's cultural heritage. The cities of Urbino, Ascoli Piceno, and Jesi aren't on the standard tourist itinerary, though they should be, and they probably will be once travelers start looking to Le Marche to find some of Italy's undiscovered treasures. They are good places to start searching for homes.

Though it won't stun you with its size, the way Brunelleschi's dome in Florence does, Urbino's Palazzo Ducale is considered by many art critics to be the pinnacle of Renaissance architecture. And if that's a surprise, this probably will be as well: The artist Raphael was born here, and a modest local museum holds some of his works. This all may seem unexpected for such an out-of-the-way city, but Urbino is known among Italians as a *città d'arte* and a cultural center, and indeed, its university is respected nationwide. Its students make up half of the population and give the otherwise quiet and somber area a steady nightlife and a decadent edge.

The other cultural hotspot in Le Marche is at the region's southern end, in the province of Ascoli Piceno. Even Urbino fails to gather very much international attention, so you can't be blamed if you've never heard of Ascoli Piceno, though if you lived in Roman times, you certainly would have. Ascoli was an important ally of the Latin tribes, and one of the protagonists of the Social Wars that aimed to overthrow Rome's privileged class. The remains of those days can be seen in the city's gates, its ruined temple, and the Roman amphitheater just outside town, in Ricci.

The city itself can be dirty and noisy, but the countryside around it is peppered with isolated towns and historic real estate at reasonable prices. Fixer-uppers with some land and a lot of charm start as low as €60,000 ($78,000), or €100,000 ($130,000) for something in better shape.

One of the more historically significant towns in the area is Fermo, once a Roman stronghold and later a university town. Its undisturbed beauty and its hilltop position about five miles from the sea give it everything a homeowner could ask for. About €130,000 ($169,000) in Fermo can buy you a historic villa with handsome columns, boasting ornate details but awaiting quite a lot of work, on several acres of forested land.

The disadvantage of this southern corner, and Urbino, too, is that they are both far away from the main city, Ancona. Then again, some people might consider that a blessing. Ancona is a busy port with an interesting walled center, but other than that, it's a pretty dreary-looking place. While *The New York Times* called it a "city of revelations" in a recent travel article, James Joyce put it down as a "filthy hole," and that was before it was bombed during World War II, flooded, and destroyed by an earthquake. It's hard to believe that some of the nicest real estate in Le Marche is less than 10 miles away.

On the hills just inland of the city, the town of Jesi attracts a lot of foreign attention these days, not so much for its elegant theater and churches and 14th-century walls as for the stately homes dotting the countryside around them. A good case study is the stretch of vineyards between Jesi and Osimo that grows a potent white wine, Verdicchio. This varietal was forgotten for many years in Italy, as were many of the vineyards that grew it. The result is a community of rustic houses in need of repair, sitting on lots of cultivated land. Recently, a survey of a dozen of them pegged asking prices at between €60,000 ($78,000) and €120,000 ($156,000) for those most in need of repair. Those that have already been restructured were selling for about twice that amount.

This still seems like a bargain once you take a look inside the refinished properties. A unique farmhouse that recently was selling for about €130,000 ($169,000) boasted 500 square meters on two floors and an annex, and sat on several square kilometers of panoramic vineyards. The ground floor had two large storage rooms and stables fitted with wooden beams. On the exterior were twin stone staircases leading to the second floor, comprising a kitchen, a central fireplace, and six rooms. The catch: You'll need to hook up the water and electricity, as well as rebuild the roof and floors.

REAL ESTATE AGENTS: THE CENTRAL REGIONS

Diamante
Via Firenze 11
06061 Castiglione del Lago, Perugia
tel. 075/951-684
fax 075/965-5399
www.diamanteimmobiliare.com

Gabetti
Via San Filippo 5
05036 Narni Scalo
tel. 0744/737-874
www.gabetti.it

Tuscan Dream
www.tuscandream.com
Offers short-term rentals.

**Tuscan Homes Estate/
Rosanna Marini**
Via Pontevecchio 10
55051 Barga, Lucca
tel. 0583/711-225
fax 0583/724-042
www.tuscanhomes.com

The South:
Naples, Puglia, and Sicily

I f you've never been to Italy before, you might envision a seaside land of spaghetti and mandolins, where families gather at the cemetery on Sunday. You might imagine a lunch with lots of mozzarella, arguments, and gesticulations, until the red wine engenders a spontaneous outburst of Neapolitan song. You've heard about the tradition of women bringing out the coffee as their dark and handsome husbands, named Mario and Salvatore, discuss politics over a game of cards.

In fact, many Americans come to Italy expecting these kinds of stereotypes and instead find something very different. These vacationers never venture south of Rome. The regions of Campania, Sicily, Calabria, Basilicata, and Puglia, collectively called the Mezzogiorno (Midday), represent the Italy of popular imagination, since so many Southerners emigrated overseas and brought their customs with them.

The area is still poorer than the North, and joblessness persists, but many expatriates choose the Mezzogiorno for its soul, which is concentrated on such human affairs as the family.

The region has an ideal climate for a life of leisure. Temperatures rarely reach freezing, the land is dotted with almond and lemon trees, and some of its beaches are the sandiest and most isolated in all of Italy. It offers all of Italy's renowned recreation, but serves it up with a southern twist. For example, other regions may be better known for their skiing, but you can still make turns down Mt. Etna's volcanic cone and some snowy peaks in Calabria. The rest of what made Italy famous—food, wine, and history—the South pulls out in spades.

Most of the *primi piatti* (first courses) and *dolci* (desserts) that inhabit America's Little Italy menus (spaghetti alla marinara, orecchiette, cannoli, granita, pizza, etc.) are Southern creations. Greco di Tufo is a prized wine from Campania, Sicily provides the world with Malvasia and Nero d'Avola grapes and their associated labels, and Puglia is known for its Primitivo. In fact, any enological tour is a good way to discover the South's ancient roots. Italy was *Oenotria* (Land of Wine) to the Greeks—and they weren't referring to Tuscany. The colonies of Magna Graecia comprised everything from Puglia west to Sicily, and its cities were legendary: Syracuse (modern-day Siracusa), in Sicily; Croton (Crotone), the home of Pythagoras, in Calabria; and Neapolis, the "new city," which now seems an odd way to describe Naples.

The South offers everything a tourist could want, but above all, it represents a good real estate investment. There are few foreigners here, even at a time when local governments and the European Union are offering money and low-interest loans to cities to make them more welcoming for tourists. This means that the Mezzogiorno could be pay dirt for pioneers. Old farmhouses are still relatively cheap in Puglia and Sicily, both of which are up-and-coming travel destinations. Naples itself is an attractive place for adventurers because of its undiluted Italian flavor and vibrant atmosphere, all for a cost of living that is relatively low.

Naples

"See Naples and die," they say, a nod to one of the most captivating urban landscapes in Italy. The city is spread out before Mount Vesuvius and embraces an azure bay. If the proverb sounds a little melodramatic, that should be your first hint about the character of this city and its inhabitants. Life is drama in Naples, a city that gave the world the crooner Enrico Caruso, the comedian Toto, and the eternal diva Sophia Loren. Every little triumph and trial evokes an outpouring of emotions, coming hot and fast like an erupting volcano.

The city's tempo is just as chaotic. While the Southern drawl is as drawn out as a typical Neapolitan lunch break, mopeds buzz through the streets at breakneck speeds, and red lights are considered suggestions. Laws are written for someone else as far as the Neapolitans are concerned, and only the smartest people, the logic continues, will find a way to get around them. When new legislation recently went into effect requiring all Italians to buckle up in their cars, someone made a great deal of money selling T-shirts in Naples with a seatbelt printed across the front.

Life is drama in Naples, a city that gave the world the crooner Enrico Caruso, the comedian Toto, and the eternal diva Sophia Loren. Every little triumph and trial evokes an outpouring of emotions, coming hot and fast like an erupting volcano.

The crime rate has improved in the past decade, and Naples is no longer the pit of petty pilfering it once was. The Baroque palaces have been cleaned up for tourists, but make no mistake: Naples is still a gritty town. This unyielding realism is, for some, the city's bane; and for others, its redeeming value. Those who find San Francisco as sterile and unemotional as a Swedish furniture store can seek shelter in unpredictable Naples.

Restaurants here set the standard for a cuisine that is termed "Italian" abroad. Real *mozzarella di bufala* can only be found in Campania, seafood dishes are simple and excellent, and Naples' historic pizzerias serve what is, no discussion allowed, the best pizza in the world. (Warning: Living here can be hazardous to your waistline.)

Again, only adventurous people should consider making downtown Naples their home, but those who do will find reasonable prices for living quarters. For about €200,000 ($290,000), you can find a four-bedroom, 150-square-meter apartment in the city center. Renters can find small places for as low as €400 ($520) per month, while the €700 ($910) per month you would pay for a studio apartment in Rome or Milan can land you a three-bedroom, 100-square-meter apartment in Naples.

THE AMALFI COAST AND THE ISLANDS

Neapolitan music is known around the world, in particular, *"Torna a Sorrento,"* or "Come Back to Sorrento." The song tries to lure a lover back to the Amalfi Coast, a stretch of spectacular coastline south of Naples where the scent of oranges lingers in the air, and medieval villages cling to cliffs that precipitate into turquoise waters. It's hard to imagine a woman packing up and leaving, and it doesn't seem very hard to convince her to come back if she did.

Fountain in the town of Amalfi, Campania

Aside from the obvious attraction of Positano and its moorish domes, the rest of the fractal-like coastline possesses extraordinary beauty in its blue grottoes and smaller towns that once belonged only to fishermen and pirates. Now it is mostly a holiday resort for the wealthy.

The lack of flat, developable land on the cliffs makes real estate expensive, exacerbated by the huge demand for houses from anyone who has ever visited. Furthermore, the disinclination of Neapolitan and Roman families to sell their older homes makes it almost impossible to buy the best ones. There are just a few *Vendesi* (For Sale) signs along the coast. You might be lucky enough to find a three-bedroom home perched on a cliff with a large backyard for €450,000 ($585,000), such as one recently advertised near the town of Amalfi.

It's just as difficult to find real estate on Capri, which families guard jealously (but happily rent out for a week or two). On the island of Ponza, the houses are built into caves, so there is a short supply, and new development is rarely allowed. The one island off of Naples that has a regular turnover of real estate is Ischia, perhaps less attractive than Capri (most of the world is), and certainly more developed than Ponza. Still, it is a hopping summer destination for Neapolitans and Romans, which allows homeowners to ask anywhere from €350,000 ($460,000) to €1 million

($1.3 million) for a single-family villa. One-bedroom apartments start at roughly €100,000 ($130,000).

Renting an apartment on a monthly basis on the Amalfi Coast is difficult—most of the rentals are for tourists who come for a week at a time and pay top euro. In some of the less frequented towns, however, such as Vietri sul Mare (which produces most of the coast's famous ceramics), you can find a two-bedroom apartment for as little as €450 ($585) per month.

Puglia

From the spectacular coastline of the Gargano promontory to the mesmerizing Baroque architecture of the Salento, Puglia possesses a beauty that rivals that of the Amalfi Coast. But aside from that comparison, Puglia, on the other side of the peninsula, may as well be a world apart from the South. Campania is mountainous, Puglia is mostly flat, and the two peoples are just as dissimilar. Neapolitans are compulsive extroverts and wear their emotions on their sleeves, while the Pugliese seem quiet by comparison, as if they were holding back a secret.

The land casts an enigmatic, Eastern charm, and it does hold its share of secrets. Puglia thrives on the inexplicable, as anyone who has seen a rendition of the *tarantella* can tell you. The name comes from the city of Taranto, as does the word tarantula, and folklore dictated that anyone bitten by one of the region's brown spiders (don't worry: the local variety is much smaller than the big furry ones that now carry the name) was supposed to dance out the venom until he or she dropped from exhaustion. Popular festivals reenact the dance to the beat of tambourines.

Perhaps the greatest example of Puglian mysticism is the late Franciscan monk, Padre Pio, recently canonized by Pope John Paul II. Padre Pio's body showed the stigmata, the five bleeding wounds on the palms, feet, and rib cage that Christ is said to have developed when he was crucified. In addition to that unexplained occurrence, Padre Pio was deemed responsible for at least two miracles, and he became a cult figure throughout the Catholic world. His followers believed he could be in two places at one time, and he was known for his ability to cast out demons. More than seven million pilgrims come every year to Padre Pio's shrine in San Giovanni Rotondo (twice the number of visitors to Rome's Colosseum), snatching up pins, mugs, and keychains adorned with the suffering saint's likeness.

Even Puglia's architecture has its own inexplicable miracles. One good example is the Castel del Monte, a puzzling castle built by the Holy

Move Over, Chianti, Here Comes Pugliashire

When Giovanni Veronesi, a paper and pulp business consultant from Milan, went to Puglia on holiday a few years ago with his wife, he was quickly entranced by the Valle d'Itria. Between Bari and Brindisi, this lush inland valley is home to *trulli,* the region's famous cone-shaped buildings, as well as olive groves, vineyards, and the whitewashed hilltop town of Ostuni.

"It's just like Tuscany was 30 years ago," says Mr. Veronesi. He speaks with some experience here, as he is also the owner of a home in Tuscany, though he said he virtually "abandoned" that property. Within six months of his Puglia vacation, he purchased Le Taverne, a 17th-century *masseria* (farmhouse) three kilometers from Ostuni. "It was love at first sight," he says.

He bought the *masseria* from a 90-something-year-old aristocrat who had moved to Rome many years before. Surrounded by 75 acres of knotted olive trees, the stone building with colorful Baroque-era carved trimmings has an ancient olive mill in its vaulted basement and some 20 rooms that Mr. Veronesi and his wife are currently remodeling to convert into an exclusive hotel.

"Our plan is to one day settle down and retire there," he says. Mr. Veronesi is one of many clients who has employed Milan-based architects Ado Franchini and Giovannella Bianchi

Roman Emperor Frederick II, and now featured on the back of Italy's one-cent coins. Frederick was a lover of octagons. Almost every town in northern Puglia has an eight-sided tower, and the Castel del Monte was the granddaddy of them all: an eight-sided building with eight octagonal towers. Frederick based its floor plan on the Golden Ration, coined by his friend, Leonardo Fibonacci, a kindred sprit and a fellow admirer of the Arabic world. The building is perfectly aligned with each of Puglia's other sacred monuments. No one knows why, but it was not likely a coincidence, since Puglia's early surveyors were attentive to these kinds of details. But what is most unusual about the building is that no one can explain its purpose. It was too sparse to be a hunting lodge and too indefensible to be a fortress, so people have stopped guessing and just call it a fine work of art.

Finally, there are Puglia's domed *trulli,* stone houses with cone-shaped roofs and adorned with strange symbols—a crescent, a plain orb, a star, and the like—which may or may not have indicated the profession of the owner. Historians have made guesses about who might have built the *trulli*—even the druids have been mentioned—but no one is quite sure.

di Donnasibilla to make their dream of living under the Puglia sun come true. The husband-and-wife architect team regularly travel to Italy's heel to track down *trulli, masserie,* and other historic buildings with market potential from Foggia to Lecce. They recently unveiled a website (www.sitidoltremare.it) designed to match sellers and buyers and win the ensuing remodeling contracts. What sets them apart from other real estate brokers is that they are the first to focus firmly on a brand of clientele relatively new to Puglia, a region often dismissed as backward and too far off the beaten track.

"The investors attracted by Puglia have an entrepreneurial spirit," says Mr. Franchini. "That's what gives that region such enormous potential." Indeed, real estate prices are 30–50 percent lower than in regions like Lazio and Umbria. In Puglia, some €250,000 ($325,000) can buy a *masseria* with a sizable chunk of surrounding farmland.

More relaxed building regulations are also attracting investors. The forward-thinking town hall of Ostuni allows buyers to add as much as 20 percent in volume to an existing structure. That kind of flexibility is unheard of in conservative zoning further north, where even updating a bathroom involves a tedious wrestle with red tape.

—*By Monica Larner*

WHERE TO LIVE

The Land of the *Trulli*

One of the most picturesque parts of Puglia, and the one that some foreigners have already discovered, is the Valley of Itria. This, in the northern reaches of the Brindisi and Taranto provinces, is the land of the *trulli.* They are concentrated in or near the towns of Martina Franca, Cisternino, Ostuni, Fasano, and Alberobello.

The last is considered the *trullo* capital of Puglia, with more than 1,000 specimens, as well as the oldest ones, most notably the Trullo Sovrano (Supreme Trullo), which was built on two stories. Most of the structures are only one story high, perhaps because the stone domes act as a sort of natural air-conditioning. The conical roofs are still built today using the same sort of field stones, because there is a certain local pride associated with owning a piece of Puglian culture. Newly built *trulli* are, of course, less expensive, and can be had for as little as €20,000 ($26,000). You might pay about the same for one that has fallen apart at the seams. Then there are the real gems. One online agency, dopropertysearch.it, advertises a huge, 14-room estate in an olive grove, featuring a swimming pool with an adjacent *trullo*-style cabana, for about €1.3 million ($1.7 million). These big country estates are called *masserie*. The word comes from *mas,* the Celtic term for house. There are other palaces with nearly that level of luxury at about half the price, which would be a steal anywhere north of Naples. In general, expect to pay about €200,000 ($260,000) for a large, rustic estate, and as little as €60,000 ($78,000) for a villa in an olive grove, though the building will at the very least need some cosmetic work.

It is counterintuitive that Puglia should have so many bargains. Prospective homeowners in Italy tend to look for exactly what this part of the country has to offer: old stone walls surrounding olive groves and their respective ancient mills, just ten minutes by car from the sea. They also look for signs of history, and the scent of the past in the Valley of Itria is overwhelming. It is a kaleidoscope image of whitewashed homes on hilltops, reminiscent of the Greek settlements from which the first inhabitants came; the names Gallipoli and Monopoli belie their ancient Hellenic origin, and the ubiquitous Byzantine cathedrals are reminders that those ties remained close for centuries.

Orecchiette, a southern delight   *Trullo* near Alberobello, Puglia

© John Moretti; © Monica Larner

Bari

Bari is the hub of Puglia, the South's second-largest city, boasting a major airport and an even busier seaport. Today, ferries from Bari carry tourists to Greece and to the Balkans, while immigrants make the opposite journey across the Adriatic and land on Bari's shores. The city serves much the same purpose as it did hundreds of years ago, when it was considered Italy's gateway to and from Byzantium.

Bari still thrives on commerce, some of it illegal—such as smuggled cigarettes and immigrants—and the result is an unfortunate reputation for crime. But, like most reputations soiled by a few teenaged, cocaine-sniffing mobsters, Bari hides a fascinating side that few dare to discover. For example, the modest-looking Basilica of St. Nicholas (known as Santa Claus to the rest of us) holds the relics of the saint from modern-day Turkey and is an oft-cited example of Romanesque architecture.

> *Some of Italy's most pleasant beach resorts are found on the coast between Bari and Brindisi, an ideal place for homeowners to set up shop and unwind.*

For prospective homeowners, Bari is a good place to fly in and out of, do some shopping on Via Sparano, check out the sites near Piazza San Nicola, eat a fantastic dinner of orecchiette and raw sea urchins in fishermen's trattorias by the port, and then make your way south to more tranquil waters. Some of Italy's most pleasant beach resorts are found on the coast between Bari and Brindisi, an ideal place for homeowners to set up shop and unwind. If you're the adventurous type and want to give living in downtown Bari a try, you can rent a three-bedroom apartment for about €650 ($845) per month.

Polignano a Mare and Monopoli are gleaming white coastal towns perched on the blue Adriatic. They were settled by the Greeks before seeing a renaissance under the Byzantine empire, and later the Normans. If your idea of paradise is eating at a restaurant on a rocky beach with blue water seeping into limestone caves, this part of Puglia is Caput Mundi.

And the prices, again, are affordable. In Polignano—which, incidentally, claims to have more ice-cream shops per capita than any other Italian town—you can find a rustic, 100-square-meter, pink-stone *masseria* on an olive grove, with an arcaded veranda, for some €200,000 ($260,000). There are countless such fixer-uppers in this area, some in pastoral surroundings and some not, but all just a short bicycle ride from the sea. Another option in the area, especially for those in search of a simple summer home, would be a similar-sized but more modern villa with the same red-tiled roof, for less than €100,000 ($130,000) and with less work required.

Lecce and the Salento

You'll have to drive to the southernmost tip of the boot to find it, but Lecce stands out as truly one of the most beautiful cities in Southern Italy—even from a plane, you can see its curious cluster of all-white buildings near a blue sea. A center of Southern Baroque, Lecce has a collection of architectural marvels, all built of the aptly named pietra di Lecce, a soft, easily carved stone. Much of it has been eroded by the wind, leaving bizarre impressions on the statues' faces.

Surrounding the city is the Salento, a flat landscape dotted with figs, stone walls, and some very interesting real estate. There are a few *trulli,* pink limestone Baroque homes, and some unusual buildings with almost African architecture and mosaics of Arabic patterns. You'll even find a posh, St. Tropez–like enclave of wealth right here in Puglia, in a little town called Tricase. Its Moorish architecture, with carved windows, and long, tree-lined approaches to princely estates, make it perhaps the most attractive town in the region. Unfortunately, there is no such thing as a free lunch, even in Puglia, and the estate's prices closely reflect their ostentation. Other towns near Italy's southern tip, such as Galatina and Gallipoli, offer decent prices for concrete monsters—about €150,000 ($195,000) or €200,000 ($260,000) for a massive town house—but expect to pay closer to a half-million for a beautiful villa in the Salento countryside. Then again, this isn't exactly Chianti, so who knows what you might come up with after a little bit of hunting? And renting a place is much closer to reasonable—in Lecce, you can rent a nice two-bedroom apartment downtown for about €500 ($650) per month.

Sicily

Most people from Sicily don't necessarily consider themselves Italians. They are first and foremost Sicilians, they'll tell you. They'll even describe themselves as "islanders" before they say they're Italian. The island, which at almost 26,000 square kilometers is the largest in the Mediterranean, has its own soul, its own rhythm, and its own language. Until the highly debated bridge across the Straits of Messina to the mainland is built, Sicily will remain a place unto itself in every respect.

Sicilians have good reason to feel attached to their land. It is like no other place in the country. It holds the only two active volcanoes in Europe, Stromboli and Mt. Etna (though there are several dormant ones in Italy, such as Vesuvius), and is blanketed by lemon and almond trees, olive groves, and vineyards. The local mix of Arabic and Norman cultures gives

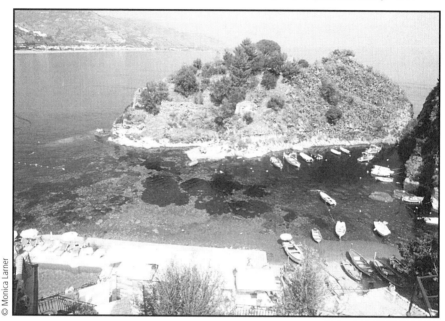

Taormina Beach, Sicily

a unique flavor to the architecture and food, and reflects the diverse ethic background of the Sicilians themselves.

The Greeks were the first to leave their mark on the island. Their traces are found everywhere, from the well-preserved temples of Agrigento, to the amphitheaters of Syracuse and Taormina, to the lonely temple of Segesta. Many of these ruins now provide the backdrop for performing arts, one of the many perks to living in Sicily. The other advantages are more obvious: a fine selection of beaches, nice weather, great wines, top-quality seafood, and more ancient archeological sites than you can shake an olive branch at.

As a foreigner, you may find Sicily a little harder to get used to than other regions. The roads can be rugged, and seemingly simple services like water can be spotty. Although everyone can speak clear Italian if prompted, the dialect is very thick, as in Naples and Puglia.

And, also as in Naples and Puglia, there is organized crime. What separates Sicily from the rest of the South in this category is just how deeply rooted the Mafia is, and yet at the same time how much energy is now devoted to doing something about it. This is not quite the case with the Camorra in Naples or the Sacra Corona Unita in Puglia, where it's still monkey business as usual. The newspapers in Palermo and Catania hit the

Anti-Mafia Olive Oil

Though the political winds of change in Palermo in the late 1990s and a crackdown by investigators in Rome have helped bring Mafia activity under control in Sicily, organized crime and corruption make a tough stain to rub out from the island's culture. The region's roots are some 1,000 years old, and much of the land still belongs to families of the Cosa Nostra. Mafia-owned lands here never bore much fruit, as they were rarely tended or cultivated, but five towns around Palermo are now reaping a long-awaited harvest.

In 1999, 500 acres of agricultural land confiscated from the Cosa Nostra in the towns of Coreleone, Monreale, Piana degli Albanesi, San Cipirrello, and San Giuseppe Jato were awarded to a group of nonprofit organizations, who used the fields for organically grown produce. It was part of a larger plan to seize property that has

so far taken more than €125 million ($163 million) in Mafia holdings and turned them into parks, farms, and public buildings such as schools and police stations.

One of the more famous products to grow out of the mob's old turf is the olive oil created by the Libera association, an anti-Mafia group founded by Turin priest Luigi Ciotti and Rita Borsellino, sister of the Palermo prosecutor Paolo Borsellino, who was assassinated by gangsters in 1992. (The city's airport, Falcone-Borsellino, is named after him and another slain judge, Giovanni Falcone.)

The olive trees sit on an estate that once belonged to Bernardo Provenzano, the Cosa Nostra's presumed *numero uno,* who has been wanted by police for more than three decades. That symbolic provenance has helped Father Ciotti and his youths to sell about 10,000 bottles of their "anti-Mafia" brand oil per year.

subject hard, and many Sicilians now speak openly about the problem, whereas before there was only fearful silence.

In general, Americans need not worry about being the victims of organized crime, especially as it is accompanied by relatively little violence these days. In fact, many Americans come to Sicily precisely to see the land of the mob, to cavort in the town of Corleone on packaged tours aimed at historic Mafia sites. (There's even a Mafia museum there.) One should be cautioned, however, that starting a restaurant or some other retail business could expose you to a real kind of risk that you may never have dealt with back home.

A footnote in some history books, and one that you should be aware of as an American living in Sicily, points out that the United States was partly responsible for putting the Mafia back in power after Fascism by installing allegedly shady figures in seats of power in exchange for their loyalty when the Americans liberated the island during World War II.

This does not mean that Sicilians are anti-American. That historical detail is hugely overshadowed by a strong bond between the island and Sicilian families that emigrated to the United States. For example, one of them, a fisherman named Giuseppe Di Maggio, moved from the small island of Isola delle Femmine outside Palermo to a fishing village near San Francisco, and his son became one of the greatest American ballplayers of all time. Those immigrants are not forgotten in Sicily, and indeed many come back to visit every year. Even Joltin' Joe made an appearance in Isola delle Femmine a few years before he died, and he was welcomed back with great fanfare.

Another reason for the close transatlantic ties is the strong military presence at the Sigonella base, near Catania. If NATO bases in other parts of Europe are sometimes the source of friction, this is rarely the case in Sicily. Overall, Americans in Sicily will feel welcomed by the locals, and those whose ancestors left 100 years before might wonder if a permanent return ticket is in order.

WHERE TO LIVE

Sicily is no stranger to foreign homeowners. Most of them have settled in glitzy Taormina, where nice homes start at €400,000 ($520,000) and skyrocket northward from there. Others have moved to Modica, once Sicily's fourth-largest city, an up-and-coming expat settlement and a beautiful town to visit in the summer, though it is isolated in a valley near Ragusa and, frankly, pretty depressing in the winter.

Then there are pockets of American military families living near the Sigonella base, ouside Catania. Catania is more maligned for crime and urban blight more than any other city in Italy, though it should be pointed out that it has come a long way since its nadir in the 1970s, having cleaned up its black-lava-paved streets and returned culture to its downtown. That may not be enough to lure homeowners, however. Mt. Etna has wiped out the city no fewer than seven times, and potential buyers may feel some trepidation about living in the shadow of an active volcano, especially in residential areas to the north.

While these and other sites—such as the Aeolian islands, the Egadi islands, the Greek temples of Agrigento, the mosaics of Piazza Armerina, and the ruins of Siracusa—are great places to visit, the most appealing choice for homeowners is likely the northwestern corner around Palermo. After all, any two points in Sicily are an afternoon's drive away at the most, and day trips are easy from the northwest corner where the island's two highways meet.

Palermo is Sicily's capital, and its historical significance is hard to exaggerate. In the Middle Ages, when Arabs enriched the island and the Normans made it their southern stronghold, much of the rest of Italy was in

Cefalu's mix of Norman architecture, lively shopping, good seafood dining, and spectacular scenery makes it an excellent choice for anyone looking for a home.

the depths of decay. Yes, the tables have turned on the once great Southern cities, but like Naples, Palermo cleaned up its city center for tourists in the 1990s, pouring light into the dark spaces that once sheltered drug dealers, and these days it is a very livable city for those willing to forgo employment for year-round sunshine.

Since those who choose to live in Sicily—or anywhere in the deep South, for that matter—probably aren't looking for a nine-to-five job, they would get more out of the countryside near Palermo than in the city itself. Some of the nicest spots in rural Sicily lie just to the east of Palermo, near Cefalu, or to the southwest, near Alcamo and Segesta.

Cefalu is a gorgeous beach resort, as well as the home to one of southern Italy's most impressive cathedrals. The mix of Norman architecture, lively shopping, good seafood dining, and spectacular scenery makes it an excellent choice for anyone looking for a home, especially as it is so well-connected to the rest and best of Sicily. The inland highway and the one that practically circumnavigates the island (the part from Cefalu to Messina remains mysteriously unfinished) meet here. There is a daily ferry from Cefalu to the Aeolian Islands in the summer. The place is so inviting that many Italians have vacation homes here and on the islands, and finding one for sale takes just a little bit of work. Expect prices of around €200,000 ($260,000) for a modern villa. For renters, a nice villa just outside town can go for as little as €300 ($390) per month.

Alcamo is Tuscany on a budget. Here you can find vineyards of white Catarratto grapes and a lovely whitewashed town, where modest houses sell for around €150,000 ($195,000). It sits near the northwestern corner of the island, close to the Zingaro natural park, with its seaside hikes. Also nearby are the elegant hilltop town of Erice, the Greek temple of Segesta, the sweet-wine producers of Marsala, and the red-tuna fisherman on the Egadi Islands. You could hardly ask for more within a one-hour radius.

REAL ESTATE AGENTS AND EXPAT CONTACTS: THE SOUTH

Americans Abroad Palermo
Via Vaccarini 1
90143 Palermo
tel. 348/510-4196
Monthly meetings, occasional lunches and dinners.

American Women's Club of Naples
tel. 081/575-0040
Cultural tours, church visits, and professional women's group.

Astro Immobiliare
Via Silvio Pellico 29
73030 Lecce, Puglia
tel./fax 0832/247-138

Casasud
Via S. Allende 14
87075 Trebisacce, Cosenza
tel./fax 0981/500-794
www.casasud.it

Cefalu Immobiliare
Via Mons. Castelli 2
90015 Cefalu, Palermo
tel. 0921/423-375
fax 0921/923-536
www.kefa.it/cefaluimmobiliare

International Women's Club of Bari
Via Petrarca 2
70010 Adelfia (Bari)
tel. 08/045-926-72
Crafts, films, and a recipe collection.

Siti d'Oltremare
Via Leone Pancaldo 9
20129 Milan
tel. 02/295-130-91
fax 02/295-334-45
www.sitidoltremare.it
This site was founded by architects to bring together buyers and sellers in Puglia, and hopefully to win a few renovation bids in the process.

Valore Casa
Via Cardassi 83
70121 Bari, Puglia
tel. 080/555-9956
fax 080/553-9394
www.valorecasa.com

Resources

Contacts

Embassies and Consulates

UNITED STATES

Embassy of Italy
3000 Whitehaven Street NW
Washington, D.C. 20008
tel. 202/612-4400
fax 202/518-2154
www.italyemb.org

Italian Consulate General
100 Boylston Street, Suite 900
Boston, MA 02116
tel. 617/542-0483
fax 617/542-3998
www.italianconsulateboston.org

Italian Consulate General
500 N. Michigan Ave, Suite 1850
Chicago, IL 60611
tel. 312/467-1550
fax 312/467-1335
www.italconschicago.org

Italian Consulate
Buhl Building
535 Griswold, Suite 1840
Detroit, MI 48226
tel. 313/963-8560
fax 313/963-8180
www.italconsdetroit.org

Italian Consulate General
1300 Post Oak Boulevard, Suite 660
Houston, TX 77056
tel. 713/850-7520
fax 713/850-9113

Italian Consulate General
12400 Wilshire Boulevard,
Suite 300
Los Angeles, CA 90025
tel. 310/820-0622
fax 310/820-0727
www.conlang.com

Italian Consulate General
1200 Brickell Avenue, 7th Floor
Miami, FL 33131
tel. 305/374-6322
fax 305/374-7945
www.italconsmiami.com

Italian Vice Consulate
744 Broad Street, Suite 2800
Newark, NJ 07102
tel. 973/643-1448
fax 973/643-3043
www.reference.it/vcnewark

Italian Consulate General
690 Park Avenue
New York, NY 10021
tel. 212/737-9100
fax 212/249-4945
www.italconsulnyc.org

Italian Consulate General
1026 Public Ledger Building
100 South 6th Street
Philadelphia, PA 19106-3470
tel. 215/592-7329
fax 215/592-9808
www.italconphila.org

Italian Consulate General
5222 Balboa Avenue #22
San Diego, CA 92117
tel. 858/277-3395
fax 858/707-0094

Italian Consulate General
2590 Webster Street
San Francisco, CA 94115
tel. 415/292-9210
fax 415/931-7205
www.italcons-sf.org

ITALY

United States Embassy
Lungarno Vespucci 38
50123 Florence
tel. 055/266-951
fax 055/284-088
www.usembassy.it/florence

United States Embassy
Via Principe Amedeo 2/10
20121 Milan
tel. 02/290-011-65
fax. 02/290-351
www.usembassy.it/milan

United States Embassy
Piazza della Repubblica
80122 Naples
tel. 081/583-8111
fax 081/761-1869
www.usembassy.it/naples

United States Embassy
Via Vittorio Veneto 119/A
00187 Rome
tel. 06/467-41
fax 06/488-2672
www.usembassy.it

Making the Move

www.hostetler.net
A family-run website with a very good database of festivals and events happening throughout Italy.

www.informer.it
The definitive reference for those confused by Italian red tape.

www.intoitaly.it
English-language Yellow Pages, containing everything from moving companies to kindergartens.

www.italyemb.org
Website of the Italian embassy in the United States. Contains all the information you need about visas and stay permits.

www.zoomata.it
A very good online magazine with links to just about everything you need to know about living in Italy as a foreigner.

Finance

www.borsaitalia.it
Website of the Italian stock exchange.

www.europa.eu.int/euro
EU website explaining the euro.

www.quantomipagano.it
A handy site (in Italian) that calculates how much you should be getting paid.

Travel and Transportation

www.alitalia.it
The state carrier's website.

www.autostrade.it
The highway company's website, with an English version, very good maps and toll calculators.

www.trenitalia.it
The national railway website, including a timetable and online ticket purchase.

Communications

INTERNET SERVICE PROVIDERS

www.dada.it
www.fastweb.it
www.infinito.it
www.jumpy.it
www.libero.it
www.tin.it
www.tiscali.it

PHONE COMPANIES

www.three.com
www.tin.it
www.vodafone.com
www.wind.it

SHIPPING COMPANIES

The following sampling of Italian shipping companies have English-speaking staff. See the English Yellow Pages website (www.intoitaly.it) for a comprehensive list.

Alpha International
Piazza Francese 3
80133 Naples
info@alpha-international.com
www.alpha-international.com

Bolliger International Movers
Via S. Pertini 51/53
50019 Sesto Fiorentino, Florence

tel. 055/425-1086
fax 055/420-6176
firenze@bolliger.it
www.bolliger.net

D.T.M. Italy
Via Stefanat 42
10078 Veneria Reale, Turin
tel. 011/495-144
fax 011/495-366
info@dtmitaly.it
www.dtmitaly.it

**Interdean Interconex
International Movers**
Via Toledo 265
80132 Naples
tel. 081/401-429
fax 081/411-185
intdeann@tin.it

Italian Moving Network
Via Trinidad 10
00040 Pomezia, Rome
tel. 06/661-818-88
fax 06/661-821-11
italianmovingnetwork@tin.it
www.italianmovingnetwork.com

United Parcel Service (UPS)
Via Fantoli 15/2
20138 Milan
tel. 800/877-877
fax 051/634-2834
www.ups.com

MEDIA (IN ITALIAN)

www.adnkronos.it
A very good news service.

www.ansa.it
The state news agency.

www.corriere.it
Corriere della Sera, the country's leading newspaper.

www.diario.it
One of the more literary magazines in Italy.

www.gazzetta.it
The nation's number-one sports newspaper.

www.ilfoglio.it
This small, conservative paper with an elite readership is controlled by Silvio Berlusconi.

www.ilnuovo.it
An online newspaper with lots of original content.

www.mediaset.it
Berlusconi's private television network.

www.rai.it
The state broadcaster.

www.repubblica.it
La Repubblica, a Rome-based, left-leaning paper with one of the better news websites.

Housing Considerations

www.dopropertysearch.it
An upmarket agency directed at foreigners, with a few very choice pieces of real estate.

www.gabetti.it
A franchise that specializes in higher-end properties.

www.property-abroad.com
A nice selection of real estate from around Italy.

www.tecnocasa.it
Italy's largest real estate franchise.

Prime Living Locations

ROME

www.asroma.its
www.sslazio.it
Websites for the city's two soccer teams, AS Roma and SS Lazio.

www.atac.roma.it
The Roman transportation authority's website, with maps and timetables for subways and buses.

www.multisalapasquino.com
Italian-only website for the Pasquino cinema, which has daily films in English.

www.romaturismo.com
The website for Rome's tourism board.

www.wantedinrome.com
An expat's guide to living in Rome, with English-language classifieds for housing and jobs.

MILAN AND THE LAKES

www.anteospaziocinema.com
Schedule of English-language movies playing in Milan and environs.

www.atm-mi.it
The Milan transportation authority's website, with maps and timetables for subways, trams, and buses.

www.easymilano.it
An expat's guide to living in Milan, with English-language classifieds for housing and jobs.

www.inter.it
www.acmilan.com
Websites for the city's two soccer teams, Inter and AC Milan.

www.milaninfotourist.com
The website of Milan's APT tourism agency.

Glossary

Pronunciation Tips

You will often find yourself spelling out words over the telephone, especially foreign names. In the United States, radio operators use Alpha, Bravo, Charlie, etc. to clarify their ABCs; in Italy, people use mostly city names:

Ancona
Bologna
Como
Domodossola
Empoli
Firenze
Genova
Hotel
Imola
Jolly
Kappa
Livorno
Milano
Napoli
Otranto
Palermo
Quartomiglio
Roma
Savona
Torino
Udine
Venezia
Wagner (or just *doppio vu*)
Xolofono (or, more commonly, "iks")
York (or just *ipsilon*)
Zara

Making the Move

ambasciata: embassy
commune: town; also town hall or city hall
consulato: consulate
libretto di lavoro: employment card (recently eliminated from use)
Ministero del Lavoro: Labor Ministry
Ministero dell'Estero: Foreign Ministry
nulla osta: a document issued by the police headquarters affirming that there is no legal reason to keep you from applying for a stay permit, or from the Labor Ministry for a work permit
permesso di soggiorno: stay permit that comes in several different forms: for work, for family, etc.
questura: police headquarters
visto: a visa, which comes in as many forms as stay permits do

Health

farmacia di turno: late-night pharmacy

ferito: injured

incinta: pregnant

infarto: heart attack

libretto di salute: a bill of health issued by the regional authorities, this may be required for everything from joining a gym to getting a job

mal di testa: headache (*mal di stomaco* is a stomachache, and so on)

policlinico: health clinic, usually private (as opposed to *ospedale,* a regular hospital)

pronto soccorso: first aid, paramedics, and also emergency room

ricetta: prescription

salute: health of an individual

sanità: health, in the public sense

Finance

assegno: a check

azioni: shares

Bancomat: automatic teller machine (ATM)

borsa: stock market

busta paga: a monthly statement of what has been paid to you, and what has been taken out for taxes

codice fiscale: tax identification number

commercialista: accountant

contanti: cash

deposito: deposit

dipendente: employee

in nero: "under the table"

lordo: gross

netto: net

notaio: notary public/paralegal

prilievo: withdrawal

raccomandato: protégé

sindacato: union

tasse: taxes

TFR (trattamento di fine rapporto): severance pay, a buyout package

tredicesimo: literally, "the 13th," as in the thirteenth month—an annual bonus that many workers receive

Communications

abbonamento: a subscription or membership

campo: cell phone, radio, or TV reception; literally, "field"

comporre (or *digitare*)*:* to dial, as in a number

destinatario: addressee

francobollo: a stamp

giornale: newspaper

mensile: a monthly publication

mittente: sender

numero verde: toll-free number

quotidiano: a daily newspaper

raggiungibile: reachable

rete: web or net, as in the Internet or a TV network

ricaricare: to recharge, as in a battery or credit on a cell phone

scheda: a card—usually the little chip behind the cell phone battery that holds your telephone number and address book information, or else the scratch-off card that holds a secret number to boost your credit

settimanale: a weekly publication

sito: website

squillo: a ring, or a call; more formally, *chiamata, telefonata,* or *colpo di telefono*

telefonino: cellular phone (literally, "little phone"; also known as a *cellulare*)

TG: telegiornale, or TV news

utente: user (as in "user name")

Travel and Transportation

autostrada: highway, usually a toll road

binario: train track

biglietteria: ticket counter

bollo: annual registration fee for a car, motorcycle, or moped

centro storico: historic center, or downtown

convalidare: to stamp your ticket; something you must do before getting on a train, bus, tram, or subway

Eurostar: high-speed train (proper name)

finestrino: window (in a car, plane, or train)

galleria: a tunnel

moto: motorcycle (short for *motocicletta*)

motorino: moped

patente: driver's license

pendolino: high-speed, tilting train (literally, "little pendulum")

rallentare: to slow down

ritardo: delay

sciopero: strike

statale: state highway (smaller than an *autostrada,* and usually just two lanes)

superstrada: almost an *autostrada,* but no tolls

supplemento: additional charge for a fast train

uscita: on a highway, an exit; at an airport, a gate

Housing Considerations

affitare: to rent

agriturismo: rural bed-and-breakfast

arredato: furnished

bollete: utility bills (gas, electric, telephone, etc.)

box: garage

bombola: a tank (usually methane or propane, for the home)

camera: room

campanile: bell tower

condomino: homeowner's association, which collectively pays for such things as elevators and garbage removal

gattara: woman who adores cats

geometra: surveyor/deputy architect

inquilino: tenant

mansardo: slanted ceilings

monolocale: one-bedroom apartment (a two-bedroom is a *bilocale,* a three-bedroom is a *trilocale,* and so on)

palazzo: a building

portinaio: doorman or building superintendent

ristrutturato: renovated

soffito: top-floor apartment; not a spacious penthouse, but a small converted attic

sottodichiarazione: underdeclaring the value of a house during a sale for tax purposes (commonplace, but illegal)

spese: normally, this means "shopping"; but in reference to housing, it refers to the utility costs

trulli: stone houses

Suggested Reading

The best way to prepare for any first trip to Italy is to read travel journals, learn the geography, study the language, and, of course, peruse some cookbooks to taste the flavor of the place. Those Americans who already know something about the country, and by now there are many, should start to look behind Italy's facade to get a real understanding of the nation and its people. The following are a few of the better-regarded books in English (or in translation) by journalists, authors, and historians who dig well beneath the surface:

Barzini, Luigi. *The Italians*. Carmichael, CA: Touchstone Books, 1964 (reprint).

Duggan, Christopher. *A Concise History of Italy*. New York, NY: Cambridge University Press, 1994.

Friedman, Alan. *Agnelli: Fiat and the Network of Italian Power*. New York, NY: Penguin, 1989.

Ginsborg, Paul. *A History of Contemporary Italy: Society and Politics 1943–1988*. New York, NY: Penguin, 1990.

Ginsborg, Paul. *Italy and its Discontents: Family, Civil Society, State*. New York, NY: Palgrave Macmillan, 2003.

Jones, Tobias. *The Dark Heart of Italy*. London: Faber & Faber, 2003.

Levi, Carlo. *Christ Stopped at Eboli: The Story of a Year* New York, NY: Farrar, Straus & Giroux, 1947; Noonday Press, 1995 (reprint).

McCarthy, Patrick. *The Crisis of the Italian State: From the Origins of the Cold War to the Fall of Berlusconi & Beyond*. New York, NY: St. Martin's Press, 1995.

Stille, Alexander. *Excellent Cadavers*. New York, NY: Vintage Books, 1996.

Suggested Films

Amarcord, Federico Fellini, 1974

The Bicycle Thief, Vittorio De Sica, 1949

Big Deal on Madonna Street (I Soliti Ignoti), Mario Monicelli, 1960

Caro Diario, Nanni Moretti, 1994

Cento Passi, Marco Tullio Giordana, 2000

Cinema Paradiso, Giuseppe Tornatore, 1990

Death in Venice, Luchino Visconti, 1971 (Based on the 1930 novel by
   Thomas Mann)

Divorce, Italian Style, Pietro Germi, 1962

Il Gattopardo, Luchino Visconti (Based on the 1958 novel by Giuseppe Di
   Lampedusa)

Io Non Ho Paura (I'm Not Afraid), Gabriele Salvatores, 2003

Johnny Stecchino, Roberto Benigni, 1991

La Vita è Bella (Life Is Beautiful), Roberto Benigni, 1997

Mediterraneo, Gabriele Salvatores, 1991

1900 (Novecento), Bernardo Bertolucci, 1976

Pane e Cioccolata, Franco Brusati, 1973

Pane e Tulipani, Silvio Soldini, 2000

A Room with a View, James Ivory, 1986 (Based on the 1908 novel by
   E. M. Forster)

Roma Città Aperta, Roberto Rossellini, 1946

Roman Holiday, William Wyler, 1953

Un Americano a Roma, Steno, 1954

Index

A

Abruzzo: 8, 11, 54
accommodations: 60–61
Agnelli, Gianni: 93
air transportation: 131–133; Le Marche 227; Milan 56; Rome 58
Alaric: 21
Alba: 56–57, 208, 211–212
Alcamo: 244
alternative energy: 137
alternative medicine: 88–89
Alto-Adige: 54
Amalfi Coast and the Islands: 233–235
Amelia: 224
Americans: illegal residency 65–66; in Rome 4–5; social climate 16–17
Ancona: 228
Apennines: 10
architecture: overview 5; history 45; Puglia 235–237; Sicily 244; Tuscany 219
Arezzo: 59, 221
Armani, Giorgio: 180
arts: overview 5; history 44–47; Le Marche 227; Renaissance 25
Ascoli Piceno: 227
Assisi: 60, 224
Asti: 56–57, 208, 209
ATMs: 51, 108
Attila the Hun: 21
Augustus: 20
Aurelius, Marcus: 21
Autostrade: 116

B

banks: 108–111, 114
Bari: 239, 245
Barzini, Luigi: 28–29
Basilicata: 8, 11
bed-and-breakfast, rural (*agriturismo*): 226
bella figura (good impression): 38–41, 43
benefits, employment: 101–102
benessere (well-being): 85

Bergamo: 10, 175, 180, 57–58
Berlusconi, Paolo: 126
Berlusconi, Silvio: 14, 23, 29, 33–35, 79, 94, 103, 111, 126, 128, 185, 201
Bianco, Enzo: 12
Bologna: 57, 164, 194–195
Bra: 208
Brera: 182, 183
Brianza: 185–188, 186
brokerages: 115
bus, traveling by: 135–136
business: behavior 43–44; family 96–97; permits 95; types 97–98
Busto Arsizio: 183

C

Caesar: 20
Calabria: 7, 8, 11
Camogli: 214
Campania: 8, 165
Campari: 116
Capri: 234
cars: cost of ownership 107, 137, 139–140; purchasing 138–140; renting or leasing 140–141; risk of driving 132, 136–137; road rules 138–139; taxes 112
Castelfidardo: 59
Catania: 243
Cavour: 27–28
Cefalu: 244
cell phones: 122–123, 254
Central Region: overview 7–11, 164–165; Le Marche 217–218, 225–228; map 216; real estate agents 229; sample itinerary 58–60; Tuscany 217–223; Umbria 217–218, 223–225
Chianti: 58–59, 219–221
children, moving with: 71–72
Chinatown: 182–183
class acts: 38–41
Clean Hands: 33–35, 181
climate: 52
clothes: costs 107; dressing for the weather 52; in Milan 180

Colli Tortonesi: 210

communications: couriers 126; glossary 254; Internet 121, 124–125, 250; newspapers and magazines 126–127, 254–255; post office 110–111, 125–126; resources 250–251; shipping options 73, 250–251; television 79, 128, 128–129, 254; see also media; telephone service

computers: 52, 73

Constantine: 21

consulates: 248–249

corporation employment: 96

Cortona: 59

cost of living: 6, 106–108

country divisions: 11–13

couriers: 126

courtship: 42–43

credit cards: 51, 108

culture: *bella figura* (good impression) 38–41, 43; business behavior 43–44; classes 38–41; gender roles 41–43; Le Marche 227; see also arts

currency: change to the euro 105–106, 109; for house payments 153; planning your fact-finding trip 51

customs: 50–51

D

Dark Ages: 21–22

di Donnasibilla, Ado Franchini and Giovannella Bianchi: 236–237

dialects: Brianza 186; Florentine 218; the Lakes 189; Milan 181; regional 77–80; Rome 168

diseases: 89–90

domestic help: 72

Ducati: 116–117

"duty of the republic": 15–16

E

education: see schools

email: 121, 124–125

embassies: 248–249

Emilia-Romagna: overview 8, 163–164, 193–194; Bologna 57, 164, 194–195; fall season travel 53–54; Ferrara 57, 164, 196–199; geography 10; Modena 57, 164, 195–196; Osteria al Brindisi 198; Parma 57, 164, 199; real estate agents 205; transportation 194

employment: benefits 101–102; business behavior 43–44; business types 97–98; compensation 95, 107–108; employers 98–99; Fiat 93–94; job security 40–41, 102; landing the job 99–101; Rome 169–170; self-employment 94–97; unemployment rates 107; working *in nero* 102–103; work visas 68, 69

energy: 137

Enel: 117

environmental health factors: 90–91

EUR: 174

euro currency: history 105–106; for house payments 153; ticket prices 109

F

fact-finding trip, planning your: overview 49–50; accommodations 60–61; clothing 52; currency 51; personal items 51–52; public transportation 55; sample itineraries 55–60; timing 53–55

family business: 96–97

family visa: 67–68

Fascism: 28–31, 77

federalism: 12

Fermo: 228

Ferrara: 57, 164, 196–199

Fiat: history 29, 117–118, 164; impact on economy 93–94; location 164

films: 257

finance: banking 108–111; change to the euro 105–106, 109; cost of living 106–108; glossary 254; investing 113–119; resources 250; see also taxes

Florence: 54, 59

food: overview 5; Alba 208; Asti 208; Bologna 195; Bra (Slow Food) 208; costs 106–107; Modena 196; Parma 199

foreigners in Italy: 16–17
foreign invasion: 25–27
Formigoni, Roberto: 12
freelancers: permits 69; visas 68; working *in nero* 103
Friuli Venezia Giulia: 8, 10

G

Garbatella: 175
gender roles: 41–43
Generali: 118
Genoa: 212
geography; see lay of the land
glossary: 253–256
government: country divisions 8–9, 11–13; modern leadership 34–35; politics 13–17
Grappa: 203–204

H

health: alternative treatment 88–89; *benessere* (well-being) 85; diseases 89–90; environmental factors 90–91; glossary 254; homeopathy 88; longevity 39; pharmacies 87–89
health insurance: coverage overseas 50; initial coverage 83–84; no coverage 86–87; proof for permits 69, 86; public vs. private 84–85; self-serve 85–86; superstitions 39
Hemingway, Ernest: 70
Hemingway, John: 70
history: arts 44–47; Clean Hands 33–35; dark ages 21–22; early history 19–25; Fascism 28–31; foreign invasion 25–27; Italy, medieval 22, 24–25; modern history 28–35; reconstruction 31–32; renaissance 25–27; Rome, rise and fall of 19–21; timeline 23; unification 27–28; Years of Lead 32–33
holidays: 53, 101–102
homeopathy: 88
housing: overview 149–150; Bari 239; Brianza 185–188; building and restoring 154–155; common terms 146; considerations 143–144; expenses 155–158; Ferrara 199; glossary 255; Grappa 203–204; Lake Como 190–191; Lecce and the Salento 240; Le Marche 227–228; Liguria 213–215; Milan 182–183; Modena 196; mortgages 153–154; Naples 233, 234–235; Padua 202–203; Parma 199; Piedmont 209, 211–212; prices 6; Prosecco 203–204; Puglia 237–238, 239, 240; purchase contracts 150–153; purchase fees 153–154; rentals 145–149; renting vs. buying 144–145; resources 252; Rome 170–175, 252; Sicily 243–244; Tuscany 219–223; Umbria 224–225; utility bills 155–158; Verona 202; see also rentals
human touch, the: 3–4

I

in nero, working: 102–103
industrial pollution: 91
Internet: email 121, 124–125; house-shopping 150; service providers 250
investments: 113–119
Ischia: 234
Italy, medieval: 22, 24–25
itineraries, sample: 55–60

JK

Jesi: 59, 228
job hunt: 98–103
job security: 40–41, 102
John Paul II, Pope: 132
Jones, Tobias: 33
Juventus: 118

L

Lake Como: 56, 188–191
Lake Maggiore: 56
Lakes, the: overview 163; dialect 189; Lake Como 188–191; Lake Maggiore 56; map 178; resources 252
language: overview 75–77; glossary 253–256; learning 80–81; regional

dialects 77–80; Rome dialects 168; television and 79, 128
lay of the land: overview 7–13; country divisions 11–13; Milan 182; regions 8–9, 11–13; Rome 170
Lazio 8, 11
Le Langhe: 56–57, 208
Le Marche: overview 8, 164–165, 217–218, 225–227; geography 7, 11; housing 225–228
Lecce: 240
lei (you, formal): 78
Levante, the: 214–215
Liguria: overview 8, 164, 207–208, 212–214; geography 7, 10; Levante, the 214–215; longevity of inhabitants 39; real estate agents 215; spring season travel 54
Limone: 211
lira currency: 105–106, 109
Lombardy: 8, 179, 180
Luxottica: 118

M

Macerata: 59
Mafia in Sicily: 242
magazines: 126–127, 254
maps: Central Region 216; Italy 2; Milan and the Lakes 178; Northeast 192; Northwest 206; prime living locations 160; Rome 166; South 230; transportation 130
Maremma: 222
markets. see stock market
maternity leave: 102
Mayes, Frances: 220, 221
Mayle, Peter: 220
media: newspapers and magazines 126–127, 254; resources 251; television 79, 128–129, 254
Mediobanca: 118
Merrill Lynch: 115
Mezzogiorno: 11
Milan: overview 9–10, 163, 179–181; culture 6; dialects 181; fall season travel 53–54; housing 182–183; lay of the land 182; map 178; pollution

problem 91; real estate agents 245; real estate resources 184; resources 252; sample itinerary 56; spring season travel 54; transportation 184–185
Modena: 57, 164, 195–196
Molise: 9
Monte Amiata: 222
Montepulciano: 58–59
Montevecchia: 187
Monteverde: 174
Monza: 175, 185–188
moving: with children 71–72; domestic help 72; glossary 253; illegal residency 65–66; permits 69; personal items 73; with pets 72–73; resources 249; schools 71–72; shipping options 73; visas 66–68
Mussolini, Benito: 29–31, 131

N

Naples: overview 6, 165, 231–233; Amalfi Coast and the Islands 233–235; housing 233, 234–235; real estate agents 245; spring season travel 54
Napoleon: 27–28
Narni: 224, 225
national holidays: 53
Navigli: 182, 183
Nero: 20, 21
newspapers: 126–127, 254
Nizza Monferrato: 209, 212
Northeast: overview 7–11, 163–164; Emilia-Romagna 194–199, 205; map 192; sample itinerary 56–58; Veneto 193–194, 200–205
Northwest: overview 7–11, 164; Liguria 207–208, 212–215; map 206; Piedmont 207–212, 215; real estate agents 215; sample itinerary 56–58
notaio (notary public): 151–152, 153

O

Olgiata: 175
olive oil, anti-Mafia: 242
Oltrepò Pavese: 211
Orvieto: 58, 224

Osteria al Brindisi: 198
Ostiense: 174

P

Padania: 7
Padua: 10, 57–58, 202–203
pajata (calf intestines): 172–173
Palermo: 243–244, 245
Pantheon: 171, 172
Parioli: 173
Parma: 57, 164, 199
people; see culture
permits: business 95; proof of insurance 69, 86
Perugia: 59, 224, 225
pets, moving with: 72–73
pharmacies and prescriptions: 87–89
Piazza Vittorio: 175
Piedmont: overview 9, 164, 207–209; fall season travel 53; geography 8; housing 209, 211–212; real estate agents 215; wine 209, 210–211
politics: overview 13–17; modern 34–35; women and 43; see also government
pollution: 90–91
Ponza: 234
Po River: 7–8
Porta Romana: 182
Porta Venezia: 182
Portofino: 214
Portovenere: 214
post office: 110–111, 125–126
Prati: 172–173
Promos SIM: 115
Prosecco: 203–204
prosecco (sparkling wine): 163, 203
provinces: 8–9, 11–13
public transportation: 55; see also transportation
Puglia: overview 9, 165, 231–232, 235–236; Bari 239; geography 11; housing 237–238, 239, 240; Lecce 240; real estate agents 245; Salento 240; spring season travel 54; *trulli* (stone houses) 237 239

QR

radio: 77–78, 254
Rapallo: 215
RCS: 118–119
reading, suggested: 256
real estate agents: Central Region 229; Emilia-Romagna 205; Lake Como 191; Milan 184; Northwest 215; Rome 176; South 245; Veneto 205
reconstruction: 31–32
recommendations: books 256; films 257
recycling: 90–91
red tape: permits 69, 86, 95; visas 66–68
regions: 8–9, 11–13
Renaissance: 25–27
rentals: overview 145–147; agents and contracts 148–149; Alba 211–212; Amalfi Coast 235; furnishings 73; housing terms 146; Liguria 214; media 251; Milan 182; Monza 186–187; Padua 202; Parma 199; renting vs. buying 144–145; searching for 147–148; Tuscany 222–223; Umbria 225; Verona 202
residency visa: 67, 69
resources: communications 250–251; embassies and consulates 248–249; films 258; finance 250; glossary 253–256; housing 252; making the move 249; media 251; Milan and the Lakes 252; Rome 252; suggested films 258; suggested reading 257; travel and transportation 250
Riviera: 212, 213
Riviera di Levante: 57
Romagna: 10
Rome: overview 162, 167–170; Americans in 4–5; dialects 168; housing 170–175; lay of the land 170; map 166; real estate agents 176; resources 252; rise and fall of 19–21; sample itinerary 58; spring season travel 54; transportation 176–177

S

Salento: 240
San Lorenzo: 175
San Marino: 10
San Remo: 213
San Saba: 175
Sardinia: 7, 9, 10
Saturnia: 222
Schengen agreement: 50, 66, 213
schools: overview 71–72; Bologna 195; public universities 84, 195
seasons, best for travel: 53–55
self-employment: overview 94–97; freelancers 103; permits 69; taxes 111; visas 69
shipping options: 73, 250–251
Sicily: overview 9, 165, 231–232, 240–243; geography 7; housing 243–244
sick leave: 102
Siena: 58–59
Slack, Jefferson: 116–117
Slow Food: 208
smoking: 90–91
soccer: Chievo-Verona 201; games on television 128; Serie A 39, 201; team affiliation 39
social climate: 16–17
South: overview 7–11, 165; map 230; Naples 231–235; Puglia 231–232, 235–240; real estate agents 245; Sicily 231–232, 240–244
sporting goods: 73
stock market: brokerages 115; companies 115–119; investing 113–115; Milan 181
student visa: 67, 69
suggested films: 258
suggested reading: 257

T

taxes: American 112–113; cars 137, 139; garbage 157; hidden costs 107; house purchase 153; Italian 111–112; tax evasion 111; tax police 110; television 129
Telecom Italia: 119

telephone service: cell phones 122–123, 254; land lines 123–124; resources 250
television: communications 128–129; glossary 254; language and 79, 128
Terni: overview 58, 165; buying 224; renting 225
Testaccio: 174
timeline: 23
Timorasso wine: 210
Tiscali: 119
Todi: 58, 164–165, 224
Tortona: 211
train, traveling by: 131–132, 133–135
transportation: air 131–133; Bologna 131, 133–135, 194; bus 135–136; car 136–141; Emilia-Romagna 194; Ferrara 197; glossary 254; map 130; Milan 184–185; public 55; resources 250; Rome 176–177; train 131–132, 133–135; see also cars
Trastevere: 172–173
travelers checks: 51
Trentino-Alto Adige: 9, 10
trulli (stone houses): 237–239
tu (you, informal): 78
Turin: overview 164; pollution 91; sample itinerary 56; winter season travel 54
Tuscany: overview 9, 164–165, 217–219; fall season travel 53; geography 7, 10–11; housing 219–223; real estate agents 229
Twice SIM: 115

U

Umbria: overview 9, 164–165, 217–218, 223–224; geography 7, 10–11; housing 224–225; spring season travel 54
unemployment: 107
unification: 27–28
universities: 84, 195; see also schools
Urbino: 227, 228
utilities: 155–158

V

Val d'Aosta: 6, 8, 9
Val d'Orcia: 221

Valdichiana: 221
Vatican pharmacy 89–90
Veneto: overview 9, 163, 193–194; Grappa 203–204; Padua 202–203; Prosecco 203–204; real estate agents 205; Verona 200–202; winter season travel 54
Venice: overview 10; sample itinerary 57; spring season travel 54
Verdicchio: 228
Verona: overview 10, 163, 200–201; housing 202; sample itinerary 57–58
Veroneso, Giovanni: 236–237
Versace: 96, 97, 180

visas: overview 66–67; family 67–68; residency 67; student 67; work 68
Volterra: 222

WXYZ

weather: 5, 52, 53–55
wine: Colli Tortonesi 210; Oltrepò Pavese 210, 211; Piedmont 209, 210–211; Timorasso 210; Verona 200, world's oldest wine bar 198
work visa: 68, 69
Years of Lead: 32–33

Acknowledgments

I'd like to thank a small group of people who were a great help in putting together these chapters: first, Monica Larner, who turned me on to a book-writing career; and my other coworkers, especially Christopher Emsden, Elisabetta Povoledo, Paul French, Claudio Gatti, Joan Pra Levis, and Luisa Milanese. A big thanks also to my parents, who continue to facilitate this wandering lifestyle, and to Simona Bassano for putting up with it throughout.

U.S.~Metric Conversion

1 inch	=	2.54 centimeters (cm)
1 foot	=	.304 meters (m)
1 yard	=	0.914 meters
1 mile	=	1.6093 kilometers (km)
1 km	=	.6214 miles
1 fathom	=	1.8288 m
1 chain	=	20.1168 m
1 furlong	=	201.168 m
1 acre	=	.4047 hectares
1 sq km	=	100 hectares
1 sq mile	=	2.59 square km
1 ounce	=	28.35 grams
1 pound	=	.4536 kilograms
1 short ton	=	.90718 metric ton
1 short ton	=	2000 pounds
1 long ton	=	1.016 metric tons
1 long ton	=	2240 pounds
1 metric ton	=	1000 kilograms
1 quart	=	.94635 liters
1 US gallon	=	3.7854 liters
1 Imperial gallon	=	4.5459 liters
1 nautical mile	=	1.852 km

To compute Celsius temperatures, subtract 32 from Fahrenheit and divide by 1.8. To go the other way, multiply Celsius by 1.8 and add 32.

Living Abroad in Italy
Avalon Travel Publishing
1400 65th Street, Suite 250
Emeryville, CA 94608, USA
www.travelmatters.com

Editor: Mia Lipman
Series Managers: Mia Lipman, Erin Raber
Copy Editor: Helen Sillett
Designers: Amber Pirker, Justin Marler
Graphics Coordinator: Deb Dutcher
Production Coordinators: Amber Pirker,
    Justin Marler
Map Editors: Naomi Adler Dancis,
    Olivia Solís
Cartographers: Kat Kalamaras, Mike Mor-
    genfeld, Suzanne Service
Indexer: Nancy Kopper

ISBN: 1-56691-634-8
ISSN: 1548-6486

Printing History
1st edition—September 2004
5 4 3 2 1

Text © 2004 by John Moretti.
Maps © 2004 by Avalon Travel
Publishing, Inc.
All rights reserved.

Avalon Travel Publishing
An Imprint of
Avalon Publishing Group, Inc.

AVALON
publishing group incorporated

Keeping Current

Although we strive to produce the most up-to-date book that we possibly can, change is unavoidable. Between the time this book goes to print and the time you read it, the cost of goods and services may have increased, and a handful of the businesses noted in these pages will undoubtedly move, alter their prices, or close their doors forever. Exchange rates fluctuate—sometimes dramatically—on a daily basis. Federal and local legal requirements and restrictions are also subject to change, so be sure to check with the appropriate authorities before making the move. If you see anything in this book that needs updating, clarification, or cor-rection, please drop us a line. Send your comments via email to atpfeedback@ avalonpub.com, or write to the address above.